ONE UP

ONE UP

CREATIVITY, COMPETITION, AND THE GLOBAL BUSINESS OF VIDEO GAMES

JOOST VAN DREUNEN

COLUMBIA UNIVERSITY PRESS   NEW YORK

Columbia University Press
Publishers Since 1893
New York   Chichester, West Sussex
cup.columbia.edu
Copyright © 2020 Columbia University Press

Library of Congress Cataloging-in-Publication Data

Names: Dreunen, Joost van, author.
Title: One up : creativity, competition, and the global business of video
games / by Joost van Dreunen.
Description: 1 Edition. | New York City : Columbia University Press, 2020. |
Includes bibliographical references and index.
Identifiers: LCCN 2020012565 (print) | LCCN 2020012566 (ebook) |
ISBN 9780231197526 (hardback) | ISBN 9780231552219 (ebook)
Subjects: LCSH: Video games industry. | Video games—Economic aspects. |
Creative ability in business. | Competition.
Classification: LCC HD9993.E452 D748 2020 (print) | LCC HD9993.E452
(ebook) | DDC 338.4/77948—dc23
LC record available at https://lccn.loc.gov/2020012565
LC ebook record available at https://lccn.loc.gov/2020012566

Cover design: Noah Arlow
Cover image: Shutterstock

For Max, who always wants to play

We don't know who discovered water, but we know it wasn't the fish.

—Marshall McLuhan

CONTENTS

PREFACE

Studying the business of video games is a fool's errand. After spending the past two decades analyzing this industry from different angles and in different contexts, I've learned as much. For one, few people outside of this entertainment business will take you seriously. Even now, when seemingly every teenager in the world plays *Fortnite* and hordes of people armed with their smartphones scour their hometowns for digital *Pokémon*, many still regard video games as an odd phenomenon. Had I built a career around Shakespearean literature or low-power radio, I reckon, I would have at least been considered intellectually exotic enough to be respected. But studying games? That's just a waste of time.

Worse yet, even people from inside the industry may treat you with disdain. As in many creative industries, the incessant presumption is that artists and designers create all the value. They are the anointed ones. The unfortunate fools who handle the business side of things are an inconvenient compromise necessary to reach a broader audience. Marketers are mercenaries, and the analysts and economists are soulless bean counters who add little magic.

It is perhaps because of this circumstance that the average person's understanding of the business of video games has remained rather limited. Few understand the industry's inner workings at large, including many of the people whose very livelihood depends on it. In my day job as an industry analyst, for example, I deal with financial investors and hedge fund managers. I frequently am dumbfounded by the seemingly inverted relationship between the large amounts of money an investment fund commits to buying shares in publicly traded game companies and the lack of understanding of the business of interactive entertainment. Despite commanding billions in assets and the ability to move markets, insight into this creative industry among most investors tends to be rudimentary at best.

In my role as a teacher at New York University's Game Center and the Stern School of Business, I've repeatedly observed the tendency among aspiring creatives to sacrifice any financial expectations to see their creative vision become reality. All too often, when asked how they would fund their proposed game company, my students answered they'd just eat ramen for six months. This idealized notion of the bohemian creative is a common one. But it is also incredibly naive.

The industry carries part of the blame: many of its professionals abhor conversations about money. They hold to the dogma that "money is evil" and insist that it is merely a by-product of their creative effort rather than a foundational principle of the for-profit activity in which they find themselves involved. Where technical challenges generally are met with enthusiasm, any financial limitations are considered unworthy. In my experience, the mere mention of any of its manifestations (e.g., corporate office, the suits, investors, or quarterly review) immediately provokes a brief ceremony of overt collective disdain during which everyone sides with creativity and distances themselves from the mundanity of money.

In entertainment industries, we often simultaneously encounter an open derision for the business side and an irrational idolization of the creative process. A perfect game will sell itself, the argument goes. Consider, for instance, Eric Barone, the designer behind indie darling *Stardew Valley*, who said, "You can make a bunch of money by creating hype based off just saying stuff, and it works. But it's just not my style. I don't even like hype at all. I don't want any hype. I would much rather create a great game, and I really truly believe that if you create the right game, and it's a really good game, it'll hype itself. It'll market itself."[1] As if by magic, a marketplace will naturally become efficient: players will have no trouble finding content they enjoy, and companies may make some money or whatever, but we'll worry about that later. Because that is how billion-dollar industries function, right?

In the case of *Stardew Valley*, its creator was, of course, correct. Barone's game sold over ten million copies and generated millions in revenues. But this fact conveniently overlooks the fact that *Stardew Valley's* development was largely subsidized by Barone's girlfriend, who despite being in school during most of the process was happy to support him and effectively shielded him from having any financial accountability. Behind every successful independent game designer stands a parent, friend, spouse, or sibling who helped out financially. And having a five-year period to pursue a creative vision is an ideal to many, but a reality to few.

An important omission from the story that the games industry tells is that the mythology of the singular genius is, in fact, a fabrication. Former Apple employee and founder of Electronic Arts Trip Hawkins purposefully established the notion of game designers and computer programmers as celebrities. To Hawkins, composing software was on par with that same effort in music, cinematography, and poetry: a vision that could be leveraged as a shrewd marketing tactic. In an interview in the 1980s, he stated, "Now that each author can do the whole program himself, he is more like a novelist or a rock star. So the microcomputer changes the kind of person involved. They don't really fit well in a corporate environment."[2] This view gave rise to a generation of individual designers who would become the hallmark of what success looks like. This is, of course, a controversial notion: that the myth of the lone, genius creator was just part of a deliberate business strategy. It forces us to consider a broader set of drivers that result in critical acclaim and commercial success. To be sure, talent is a critical component. But it is not the only thing that matters. Or, as famed designer Raph Koster proclaimed to a crowd of several hundred industry professionals and aspiring game makers: "being creative is not necessarily a unique virtue."[3]

To understand how the games industry operates we must look beyond creative singularity and consider the industry's overall structure and aggregate of activity. Creative firms do what they do in tandem with, or in reaction to, the world around them. As philosopher John Dewey put it in a description of art: "Life goes on in an environment; not merely in it but because of it, through interaction with it."[4] We can observe this from an aesthetic point of view. Graphic design, game design, narrative, and kinetic mastery all have something to say. How each ultimately manifests in a game is the result of a myriad of decisions. Similarly, games are seldom born in an economic vacuum and generally are the result of a series of purposeful decisions made by designers and business leaders. These decision-makers have a strong editorial influence on which features do and do not make it into a title's final version. Ostensibly, they base their input on rational economic drivers, such as budget and available resources, but, as we'll see, this isn't necessarily the case. Historically, however, emphasis on the advancement of technological capability has dominated the business narrative about this industry.

In a conversation between Nintendo icons Saturo Iwata and Shigeru Miyamoto on the early design for what ultimately would become *Super Mario*, the two discussed how the decision for Mario to wear overalls and white gloves, to have a moustache, and to don a hat was largely informed by the tension between too few available pixels and the desire to animate the character. Because of the technical limitations, the two designers improvised and arrived at the character most of us know so well today. In their words, because of the lack of pixels, the process of animating the character carried a "sense of inevitability."[5] But that does not explain how Nintendo brought the entire industry back to life in the wake of its collapse in 1983. It also does not explain how an innocuous development studio like Supercell managed to produce not just one but four franchises that each generated several billion dollars. Sony's dominance in the console market is hardly the result of luck. And what should we make of Valve, a company that managed to both produce a series of successful titles and establish the de facto digital distribution platform?

Video games as an artform are influenced equally by business practices and by design decisions and technology. These business practices are poorly understood. I recall sitting in the audience at a conference thirteen years ago overhearing two executives talking about the new iPhone. The conversation went something like this:

"Did you see the graphics on that new iPhone?"

"Yeah, it's on par with what you can get on a Game Boy."

"That's amazing. What do you think people will pay for something like that?"

"Well, if the gameplay is the same and the graphics are the same, I don't see why we can't charge $50 for mobile games, same as we do on console."

This, of course, proved to be spectacularly wrong. To a degree, such an initial assessment was sound: the limitations of hardware have long determined the form factor of game design. But it was not until Apple approved freemium titles two years after its initial introduction that the mobile category started to grow as spectacularly as it did. Instead of becoming a horseless carriage, it was a novel design and an accompanying business model that triggered the prosperity in mobile gaming and redefined the global industry. After two decades, many still look forward through the rearview mirror.

What I propose is to expand our understanding of this industry by taking into account the broader intercourse between game designers, producers, industry analysts, financiers, marketing specialists, and other decision-makers. They earn a living by busying themselves with the creation of interactive entertainment and accordingly shape the industry at large. This is a common line of inquiry elsewhere. We find a similarly intimate connection between business and film. In the early nineteenth century, for example, entrepreneurs behind the blooming film business quickly established that public viewing was more profitable than the "individualized-viewing regime" of peep-show machines. Allowing people to watch together and creating a spectacle around this experience proved to be a far more lucrative revenue model. Initially, business owners converted existing venues, such as music halls and fairgrounds, to meet demand. As the success proved to be sustainable, however, purpose-built cinemas quickly became the norm across all major markets. The size of these buildings and their respective seating capacity was "not determined technologically but rather by an entrepreneur's assessment of the potential demand for film in a particular socio-economic location."[6]

In this same vein, few mysteries remain about the workings of the music industry and how its economics shape the content it produces. A recent work by Princeton economist Alan Krueger explores the degree to which musical artists are subject to economic constraints. Despite the digitization of the music business in recent years, which resulted in a revitalization of its revenue, musicians have largely come to rely on live performances for their bread and butter. Streaming services, in contrast, serve mostly as a marketing vehicle to help popularize a song or an artist. In a product-based industry, concerts served to promote the sales of CDs. In the digital music business, streaming services serve to promote concert attendance. Moreover, as Krueger has observed, "If you listen carefully to songs that feature other singers, you will notice that the star normally appears early in the song, within the first thirty seconds. This is logical because streaming services only pay royalties for music that is streamed for at least thirty seconds. In other words, economic incentives of streaming are directly affecting the way songs are written, composed, and performed."[7] Digitalization of the music industry has shifted its underlying economics which, in turn, changed how artists compose and perform.

Much of the success in the games industry has been the outcome of an effective exchange between a creative vision and an accompanying business model. Limits imposed by noncreatives are merely a design challenge— there is a financial maximum to how long a firm can keep the lights on before all creative effort stops. This limitation is on par with the technical restrictions that originate from material aspects like screen sizes and processing power. These form factors determine a priori what can and cannot be put into a game and historically have intimately shaped creative designs for content and consoles alike. The broader economics of the games business, however, are much less understood. How people think and make decisions in this industry is full of unexamined clichés. Perhaps because of its incredible growth in recent years, a large disparity continues to exist between the games industry's conventional wisdom and an economically grounded approach to how it functions and innovates. This disparity presents us with the opportunity to explore the fascinating oscillation between mental inertia among creatives and executive decision-makers and moments of innovative brilliance.

This book started as a compendium of data and business cases for my students. In the absence of a comprehensive body of work that covered the industry, I figured it would serve them well if I could put together rudimentary information on the industry and identify a handful of remarkable business cases in which companies spectacularly succeeded or failed. In adjacent markets like news, television, radio, film, and music, the effort of studying their respective economics is both common and understood to be of substantial influence on what audiences get from it. Video games do not enjoy the same degree of curiosity. A comprehensive narrative based on the industry's economic underpinnings was missing, and the existing literature on the economics of games tended to be scattered, poorly researched, and wildly specific.

In contrast, however, there is no shortage of books that cover the broad history of the games industry. Among the more notable titles are *Game Over: How Nintendo Conquered the World*; *Super Mario: How Nintendo Conquered America*; *Console Wars: Sega, Nintendo, and the Battle That Defined a Generation*; and *Game On! Video Game History from Pong and Pac-Man to Mario, Minecraft, and More*.[8] Most of this literature is lovingly written, often through a lens of nostalgia, and serves as a way to pay homage to a writer's favorite company, console, or executive. It even presents the occasional nugget of insight on how this industry works (or at least how it used to) and how companies managed to outmaneuver each other. As such, I, too, have dedicated time to review the industry's exciting history. But I have done so within the confines of only a single chapter. More recent years have offered an equal amount of exciting innovation.

A handful of game journalists have written books on the working conditions or accomplishments of specific companies. Consider Schreier's best-seller *Blood, Sweat and Pixels*, which offers a narrated account of the experiences of different developers and how they have navigated the stresses of working in this industry. Similarly, Dean Takahashi, VentureBeat's most popular and prolific writer, produced two books on the development of the Xbox and Xbox 360.[9] The text dovetails with the common technological nostalgia surrounding video games. The MIT Press Platform Studies book series leads this category with its discussion of specific console platforms, such as the Atari 2600.[10] And a few books discuss individual titles, such as David Kushner's books *Masters of Doom*, which covers first-person shooter *Doom*, and *Jacked* on the *Grand Theft Auto* franchise.[11]

Another important text is Casey O'Donnell's *Developer's Dilemma*, which explores the tactical challenges in game development. O'Donnell convincingly shows how technical, conceptual, and social dynamics affect how game makers operate, but ultimately laments the "culture of secrecy" that makes this industry opaque to outsiders.[12] The chronic absence of transparency in business practices ensures that companies repeatedly make the same mistakes, resulting in the growing need for more rigorous information and insight.

Writing by financial analysts has proved far worse. Hal Vogel, an accomplished Wall Street analyst covering the entertainment business, releases regular updates to his 680-page book *Entertainment Industry Economics* (currently in its ninth edition). His section on video games barely covers a dozen pages.[13] And Michael Pachter, the industry's most famous analyst and its *adult terrible*, has unparalleled access to intimate company information and regular face time with senior executives. What ultimately limits financial analysts is the obvious fealty to financial cycles: by and large, their analyses and broader understanding of the industry focus on a handful of publicly traded organizations and their ability to impress shareholders during next quarter's earnings. Consequently, a long-term perspective that captures the implication of digitalization and similar shifts in the economic principles goes missing.

Finally, in academia, we find an abundance of books about interactive entertainment but preciously little on the underlying economics. Take, for instance, an extensive volume, such as *The Routledge Companion to Video Game Studies*.[14] Counting no fewer than sixty chapters, the book covers many aspects relevant to video games, including race, ideology, artificial intelligence, art and aesthetics, sports, death, interactivity, media ecology, and masculinity. But it has exactly zero information on the economic circumstances that affect the design, development, marketing, and publishing of games.

Several accounts have positioned video games within a broader cultural context and have delineated their shortcomings in catering to a broader and more diverse consumer base. Michael Newman's *Atari Age: The Emergence of Video Games in America* chronicles the sociocultural ascension of interactive entertainment.[15] Similarly, Carly Kocurek's *Coin-Operated Americans* examines how video gaming became the seemingly exclusive domain of young men.[16] As we'll see, much of what industry executives believe to be "true" about their consumer base stems from the narratives that were established during the industry's early years.

In addition, several books offer a critical political economic perspective, including *Games of Empire: Global Capitalism and Video Games*; *Global Games: Production, Circulation and Policy in the Networked Era*; and *The Video Game Business*.[17] Take for instance Aphra Kerr's book *Global Games*, which offers a rudimentary assessment of the global games market to illustrate its rise as a cultural industry on par with music and film. It is one of the more comprehensive pieces of literature on the topic. Yet it, too, relies on spotty data and largely excludes how companies create value and innovate. It succeeds in placing games on equal footing with its peers, music and film. It does not discuss, however, how people and companies seek to adapt to new market circumstances and address competitive forces or how that interaction manifests in their creative output. Kerr, in fact, concludes that although "the discourse and promotional rhetoric of the industry focuses on technology, a closer analysis of shifts across segments within the industry and the emergent business models signal that other forms of knowledge (e.g., business and market knowledge, regulatory knowledge, or aesthetic/symbolic knowledge) are as important to the continual growth in this cultural industry."[18]

Video games have flourished as a topic of academic and pop-cultural inquiry. Writers from all corners of intellectual pursuit seemingly agree on the still largely undiscovered relevance of interactive entertainment as an entry point into the contemporary human condition. Consider, for instance, how Clifford Geertz's writing on the meaning of cockfights managed to make obvious the intimate workings of Balinese culture. A common text among game scholars, it establishes the fundamental observation that games are a microcosm of the larger social, cultural, and economic universe in which people go about their daily lives. By providing a careful account of the illegal practice of having roosters fight each other, Geertz managed to uncover what the practice represents to its participants and spectators, how it helps establish social order, and the deeply irrational commitments to this game and its outcome. Similarly, I'd argue, the contemporary phenomenon of video games offers a vantage point from which we may better understand current cultural tensions and our broader historical moment.

Increasingly, literature and research surrounding video games delineates the need for "other forms of knowledge" and the necessity to dispel the industry's persistent "culture of secrecy."[19] It argues that to work in the industry, "both developers and decision makers of video games should understand the *entire* [emphasis added] process of video game development."[20] Yet missing from this growing knowledge base is a rigorous, data-driven, and comprehensive business overview that describes its structural economics and explains how market conditions inform contemporary strategy and, in turn, shape creative output. That is roughly the point at which this book begins.

ACKNOWLEDGMENTS

The village that helped put this together consists of a number of people whom I deeply respect. I am grateful for my circle of industry friends because of their friendship, patience, and generosity in sharing their perspectives with me. They include (in alphabetical order) Jeroen Bouwman, Michael Cheung, Jayson Chi, Brian David-Marshal, Ben Decker, David Edwards, Eugene Evans, Ben Feder, Solomon Foshko, David Grijns, Bill Grosso, Lazlow Jones, Roland Lesterlin, Doug McCracken, Ashley McEnery, Chris Petrovic, Wilson Price, Fabien Rossini, Steven Sadin, Dan Sherman, Kris Soumas, Chelsea Stark, Derek Sutta, Rob Vawter, Matt Wang, and Michael Worosz. Their enthusiasm and energy for this industry has been a continued source of inspiration.

Among my academic peers, I am fortunate to count a list of immensely prolific and clever people. They helped me construct the overarching framework presented here and put my thinking into a broader context. Jesper Juul was one of the reviewers of an early draft of the manuscript and was pivotal in helping me better understand what I was trying to say about casual gaming. Dmitri Williams's 2002 article, "Structure and Competition in the U.S. Home Video Games Industry," served as a starting point for much of the work you see here, and his input later on was equally instrumental and encouraging. I am grateful for the comments from my closest academic peers, David Nieborg and Joost Rietveld. David helped me separate the conversational from the chatty. And Joost helped me hammer out key parts of the underlying methodology. Thanks, brothers.

With regard to the data, Victoria Chen did an enormous amount of work in compiling financial information, for which I am grateful. Similarly, I cannot thank the team at SuperData Research enough. These people suffered through my relentless questions and requests for data over the years. Much of the data presented here are the result of their hard work and integrity. Working with them, for them, and among them has been the most rewarding part of my career thus far.

A special mention goes out to the late Greg Lastowka, a promising legal scholar at Rutgers University whose time came far too soon. It was he who first invited me to speak at his 2010 conference, The Game Behind the Video Game: Business, Regulation, and Society in the Gaming Industry. The paper I presented there started what you are reading today.

Finally, I am grateful to Janelle Benjamin, my wife, for supporting me on this project and always believing in me. You are the love of my life.

ONE UP

Introduction

In late 2015, Bobby Kotick, the CEO of one the world's largest game publishers Activision Blizzard, told a journalist, "We now have 500 million players in 196 countries around the world. In the past, our business was largely concentrated around middle-class consumers who could afford $300 or $400 for a dedicated game console or $1,000 for a PC. Now, with the introduction of high-quality mobile devices, we're looking at everybody being a consumer."[1]

Kotick said this when asked why the maker of popular franchises *Call of Duty* and *World of Warcraft* had acquired the mobile publisher behind *Candy Crush*. To many, the acquisition was odd. By entertainment industry standards, the publisher had just spent a ludicrous amount of money. Activision Blizzard paid $5.9 billion for King Digital, which is more than what Disney paid for Marvel ($4.24 billion) or Lucasfilm ($4.05 billion).[2] Despite several high-profile acquisitions in recent years, transactions of this size centered purely on acquiring content occur infrequently. Yet this purchase indicated a change in the firm's strategy. Having long catered to audiences that play shooter and role-playing games, buying a mobile game maker was a deliberate move to reach a broader demographic. The rationale was based on a different idea about gamers and deviated from the existing stereotypes surrounding this audience. Finally, with a single pen stroke, one of the largest incumbent game makers in the world embraced and acknowledged the shift of the industry to digital. Activision Blizzard built its success largely on the traditional brick-and-mortar business. By moving into mobile, it instantly came to rely for a third of its revenues on a new model it knew little about: digitally distributed free-to-play titles. Why would a top industry firm make such a drastic move by spending so much to enter a territory that it barely knew?

Contemporary interactive entertainment hardly resembles that from the time when the world was infatuated with *Pac-Man* and *Mario Bros.* Over the course of roughly three decades, video games had gradually transitioned from the fringes to become a mainstream form of entertainment. As Kotick pointed out, everyone is a gamer now. For most of its history, however, game makers had targeted a narrowly defined demographic. Aside from the stereotypical gamer who is between eighteen and thirty-four years old, plays shooters until late at night, lives in his parents' basement, and is covered in bits of potato chip, publishers had successfully alienated everyone else. This approach had ensured that the category long remained a sideshow to other amusement markets. Among the broader, socially accepted activities of watching television, going to the movies, reading books, listening to music, and attending sports games and musical performances, video games were the odd one out.

Today, however, this industry caters to a common crowd. In the summer of 2016, for example, thousands of *Pokémon GO* players took to the streets of every major metropolitan area around the world looking for *Pokémon*. News reports of the hordes of people in the streets playing together evidenced in broad daylight exactly how popular and widespread gaming had become. From Washington Square in New York to Shibuya Crossing in Tokyo, droves of players roamed the streets. This scenario presented many with a stark contrast of what they had thought the average gamer audience looked like. If *Pokémon GO* is the most obvious example of how widespread gaming has become, it is by no means the only one. Countless titles now draw audiences that run into the tens of millions of regular players, including *Candy Crush Saga*, *Roblox*, *League of Legends*, and *Fortnite: Battle Royale* (see table Int.1). The audience for interactive entertainment has grown to become an enormous global business. In growing, it also has changed.

As games have grown in popularity, the category has transcended its traditional modes of reaching audiences and emerged as an entirely new cultural and economic phenomenon. In March 2018, a blue-haired

Table Int.1
Top twenty game titles worldwide, 2018

Rank	Title	Parent Company	Monthly Active Users	Platforms
1	*Honor of Kings*	Tencent	207,862,859	Mobile
2	*Candy Crush Saga*	Activision Blizzard	150,216,638	Mobile, PC
3	*Pokémon GO*	Niantic	131,323,177	Mobile
4	*Roblox*	Roblox	120,598,657	Mobile, Console, PC
5	*Fight the Landlord*	Tencent	97,674,969	Mobile
6	*League of Legends*	Tencent/Riot Games	86,350,034	PC
7	*Fortnite: Battle Royale*	Epic Games	70,386,232	Mobile, Console, PC
8	*CrossFire*	Smilegate	61,839,375	Mobile, PC
9	*Homescapes*	Playrix Games	52,498,118	Mobile
10	*Anipop*	Happy Elements	46,891,281	Mobile
11	*Candy Crush Soda Saga*	Activision Blizzard	42,614,901	Mobile, PC
12	*Subway Surfers*	Kiloo	42,420,089	Mobile
13	*Dragon Nest*	Shanda Games	41,912,768	Mobile
14	*Free Fire*	Garena International	38,523,222	Mobile
15	*Mobile Legends: Bang Bang*	Moonton	36,451,241	Mobile
16	*Lords Mobile*	IGG Inc.	33,777,239	Mobile
17	*Dungeon Fighter Online*	Nexon	32,055,004	PC
18	*Clash Royale*	Tencent/Supercell	31,137,339	Mobile
19	*Clash of Clans*	Tencent/Supercell	30,063,797	Mobile
20	*Minecraft*	Microsoft	28,673,361	Mobile, Console, PC

Source: Author's compilation based on data provided by SuperData Research.
Note: Based on aggregated average monthly active user counts for each title across all platforms (non-deduped).

live-streamer on Twitch named Ninja spent several hours playing a multiplayer shooter title called *Fortnite* with musical artist Drake. It resulted in a record number of concurrent viewers on the platform's history and instantly propelled Ninja to become a household name. What followed was a series of appearances on television and social media for Ninja. For publisher Epic Games, it meant that *Fortnite* skyrocketed to become the world's most popular title, generating $4 billion in its first two years and helping the firm raise an additional $1.25 billion in funding. Suddenly, *Fortnite* was everywhere. Not just as a game played by many but also in the form of its odd in-game dances as celebrities and athletes everywhere copied the dance moves in public. A far cry from the 1980s stereotypes, the games industry has come to occupy an entirely new cultural space.

Video games are big business. But that is hardly the most interesting thing about them. What sets this industry apart is that its various value chain participants have managed to thrive in the face of sweeping changes in how amusement is delivered and consumed. Over the past fifteen years, video games have transitioned from the fringes of the entertainment business to become one of the biggest and fastest-growing segments during a period characterized by two developments in particular: the widespread adoption of consumer broadband and the popularization of smartphones.

First, in both industrial and emerging economies, the number of people with access to fast internet has grown explosively in a relatively short period of time. Today, more than one billion people subscribe to a fixed broadband connection that provides download speeds greater than 256 kbit/seconds, and there are almost six billion mobile broadband subscriptions globally.[3] This growth plays an important role in how creative content is produced and consumed. Removing the restrictions historically imposed by physical boundaries, such as geographic limitations, inventory management, and retail distribution, the penetration of high-speed internet connectivity has changed the circumstances in which creative firms now develop content and bring it to market.

Second, the popularization of smartphones has both greatly expanded the total addressable audience and reduced the number of intermediaries between creatives and consumers. The distribution of content through telecommunications infrastructure has profoundly changed how it is produced and consumed. Billions of people walking around with what is effectively a computer in their pocket means content creators can reach a much broader audience. Where previously games were burned onto a disc and distributed by retail channels, internet technology enables end users to directly download and stream content to a myriad of devices. Through platforms like Apple, small creative outfits may access millions of potential customers.

The rapid adoption of smartphones has shifted the existing power distribution on the supply side. Instead of having to go through a specialty retailer like GameStop, a publisher like Activision Blizzard can now deliver its content directly to players using digital downloads. Such an improvement in efficiency and associated margins has benefited both big companies in their pursuit of scale and small game makers who can now reach players directly.

The demand side also has changed. Many people have found that they, too, are gamers. Look on the subway in any major city and you'll see a slew of people playing on their phones. In particular, titles that offer more casual experiences like *Angry Birds*, *Bejeweled*, and *Candy Crush* have managed to reach broad audiences. And with a worldwide consumer market of more than two billion people, it is fair to say that video games currently enjoy a market that is several orders of magnitude larger than it was just a few years ago. Combined, these two technological shifts have resulted in the lowering of entry barriers and provided access to a much larger addressable audience.

Size alone isn't everything, of course. Because of their popularity, video games have emerged as a critical component to the businesses of many of today's largest companies. Indeed, several of the world's largest firms—Apple, Microsoft, Sony, Tencent—rely heavily on interactive entertainment for their success.

Take Apple, for instance. According to its earnings reports it generated approximately $11 billion in 2018 revenues from mobile games. By comparison, its music services and iTunes combined made just over $7 billion (see table Int.2). After a somewhat-lukewarm relationship to the gaming business earlier in his career, founder Steve Jobs gleefully reported during the 2010 Apple event that his company had not "set out to compete with Nintendo or Sony on their PSP, but we are now a significant part of that market."[4] Since then, mobile titles have been a prominent feature in Apple's annual showcase to promote the capabilities and graphics of every new generation of iPhones.

In contrast, Sony, which has long been the dominant market leader, generated $21 billion from device sales, network fees, and platform fees in that same year. With a global install base of ninety-two million PlayStations in 2019, the Japanese console maker holds more than double Microsoft's footprint and almost five times that of Nintendo. According to its financials, Sony relies on its PlayStation division for about 23 percent of its $75 billion in annual income. Its rival Microsoft earned $10 billion in 2018 in interactive entertainment across its PC and console operations that same year, persuading its CEO to acquire more content and invest in new platform and cloud technology to secure the firm's future.

Tencent, a relative newcomer, earned $19 billion in 2018, both from its substantial content inventory that includes well-known subsidiaries Riot Games and Supercell and from licensing fees paid by publishers looking to enter China. Roughly two-thirds of its game-related income

Table Int.2
Gaming revenue generated by leading firms, 2018

Company	Total Revenue (US$, billions)	Gaming Revenue	Share of Total (%)	Mobile	Console	PC
Amazon	141.4	1.6	**1.1**	–	–	+
Facebook	55.8	0.7	**1.3**	+	–	+
Google	136.2	1.9	**1.4**	+	–	+
Apple	260.2	11.0	**4.2**	+	–	+
Microsoft	110.4	10.0	**9.1**	–	+	+
Sony	78.0	21.0	**26.9**	–	+	–
Tencent	45.4	18.6	**41.0**	+	+	+
Total	**827.4**	**64.8**	**7.8**			

Source: Author's compilation based on company reports.

Note: Gaming revenue defined as all revenue generated from interactive entertainment, including publishing entertainment software, selling consoles, microtransaction revenue, platform fees, and ad revenue. Because each of the firms have a different business model, it should be obvious that their revenue models differ, too. As a consequence, these figures are not to be compared against each other, but rather illustrate the exposure each of these companies has to the business of video games. The right side of the table shows the major platform categories in which each of these firms is active.

comes from operating as a local partner to foreign publishers who are prohibited from going directly to Chinese consumers. This has allowed Tencent to achieve a market value that rivals Facebook and makes it the largest game publisher in the world today. It suffered a massive drop in share price value, however, when its government froze the mandatory approval process (to protect consumers, the Chinese government has to approve every title before release and generally is skeptical of the cultural merits of the sector). This freeze meant that Tencent missed out on revenues generated by a popular title like *Fortnite* right as it reached the pinnacle of its success.

Finally, several other tech giants are looking to penetrate interactive entertainment. In late 2019, Google launched its cloud gaming service, Stadia, to capture market share and take on a more significant role as the industry transitions to a new distribution model. Facebook similarly invested in cloud gaming with the acquisition of PlayGiga, after already having invested billions in both virtual reality technology (with the acquisition of Oculus) and content creators like Beat Games. And Amazon has been developing its own gaming division: after establishing its Amazon

Game Studio and acquiring Twitch, it has started to quietly develop its own cloud gaming service under the code name Project Tempo.

Combined, these organizations generate $827 billion in revenue, and video games represent about 8 percent of this total. Interactive entertainment is a vital component to each of their business models and serves as a proxy for their overall performance. Their share prices rise or fall depending on how well they manage to convince investors and consumers alike that their games division is healthy (see table Int.2).

This book reveals how video game companies have adapted to the changing economic foundation of the overall industry. After decades during which games were largely a physical, retail-based business, key economic activities like development, publishing, marketing, distribution, and monetization started to change following digitalization and the popularization of new technologies. This equally challenged and prompted creative firms to formulate innovative strategies and resulted in a drastic change in the industry's overall competitive landscape.

On the basis of an extensive data set combined with detailed case studies, I show that rather than relying solely on creative merit, critical and commercial success in video games is more often than not the result of formulating an innovative business strategy. Set against a background of the broader structural shift from a product-based business to a games-as-a-service model, I discuss how various company types—developers, publishers, retailers, platform holders, and distributors—have solved strategic challenges by formulating novel business models and innovations. I argue that successful companies in interactive entertainment apply the same degree of creativity to strategy as to making video games. The intercourse between the growth of the industry in value, its broadening consumer base, and its digitalization present the key drivers of change that are reshaping its overall market landscape. In this context, I assess how the structure of the industry has shifted, how individual firms have adjusted to these new economic conditions and developed competitive advantages, and how this has affected their creative agenda.

Book Structure

This book is organized in three parts. Each describes a different stage in the evolution of the business of video games. The analysis presented focuses on the practices observed from notable firms and how they capitalized on changes in the industry's underlying economic principles.

Part 1 offers an overview of the traditional business and looks at the challenges of the games-as-a-product model. It starts with a historical perspective to establish how different companies operate, followed by a discussion of how amusement in a broad sense has changed. Chapter 1, "Digitalization of Interactive Entertainment," looks at the remnants of traditional, product-based entertainment publishing and the challenges music, film, and video game companies sought to overcome with varying degrees of success. Chapter 2, "Games Industry Basics," describes in broad strokes how the traditional business has operated for almost three decades and serves as a starting point to better understand the changes that follow. It offers an account of how firms like Nintendo, Naughty Dog, and Electronic Arts successfully tackled business challenges and managed risk.

Next, a key discussion that has emerged as a result of the popularization of downloadable content and digital distribution is the changing role of the brick-and-mortar retailers. To that end, chapter 3, "Empire on the Edge of the Volcano," offers an in-depth account of how GameStop became the world's largest specialty games retailer and how it manages, or at least tries, to reinvent itself. It provides an overview of the retail business in key industrial economies and discusses how core strengths like customer education, promotion, and used game sales are being repurposed to suit the needs of a changing market.

Part 2 categorizes the digital games business into core segments and explains their recent evolution. The underlying business model is games-as-a-service. This part emphasizes how mobile, console, and PC game companies have dealt with strategic challenges as economics shifted. Chapter 4, "Everyone Is a Gamer Now," begins with a discussion of the ascension of video games to a mainstream form of entertainment. The rise of casual titles across mobile platforms and social networks has allowed the gamer demographic to expand both in size and diversity. The chapter explains how the industry has struggled to shift its focus from a traditionally narrow definition of gaming consumers catering to a global, mainstream player base and the implications for both marketing and design.

Chapter 5, "Myth of the Mobile Millionaire," examines the rapid rise of mobile gaming and explains how a company like Supercell managed to produce not one but four titles that generated more than a billion dollars in revenue. It looks specifically at how developers and publishers alike face the increasing costs of development and marketing even as worldwide demand for mobile games continues to grow in size.

Chapter 6, "Greatly Exaggerated Death of the Console," dispels the myth that dedicated gaming hardware is on its way out by outlining the strengths of organizations like Microsoft, Nintendo, and Sony. These companies challenge each other for dominance over the center of the living room and, in the process, incorporate downloadable and streaming content to create a competitive edge.

Chapter 7, "Glorious Return of PC Gaming," examines how PC-based game development has persevered thanks to audience loyalty and the emergence of digital distribution. In addition to discussing the innovative genius that drives the success of an organization like Valve, the chapter explains how Blizzard came to dominate the online role-playing category and how a South Korean firm named Nexon managed to penetrate the U.S. market.

In addition to its various merits, digitalization also presents a series of challenges to game companies. The abundance of available content as a result of digitalization presents a growing challenge for creative firms in connecting with consumers. Part 3 examines more recent innovative developments. It resolves around the emerging business model of games-as-media as the industry looks to both old and new strategies to navigate and monetize the digital marketplace.

Chapter 8, "Epic Quest for Intellectual Property," explores the central role of licensing to the success of conventional titles. It presents an assessment of different companies looking to reduce the financial risk involved in development and publishing by relying on established franchises and brands, as many of these principles are employed by participants in digital games. Examples like *Angry Birds*, *Madden NFL*, and *Pokémon GO* provide key case studies in understanding the role licensing plays as publishers seek to innovate without alienating their existing customer base.

Chapter 9, "Watching Other People Play Video Games, and Why," takes on the topic of live streaming and the popularity of Twitch streamers and YouTubers. The practice of people watching other people play games, providing commentary and input along the way, is a relatively recent phenomenon, but it already has significant implications for the industry at large with regard to marketing and discovery. It further explores the emergence of competitive gaming as it slowly materialized into a global phenomenon over a two-decade period, only to find itself suddenly thrust into the center of mainstream media attention.

This brings us to chapter 10, "Next-Gen Revenue Models," which discusses the viability of new earnings models, including advertising and subscriptions. After several failed attempts to introduce ads into video games, the current size and diversity of its audience suggests there may yet be an opportunity for advertisers to play a significant role in the contemporary games industry. And as new technologies like cloud gaming emerge to disrupt the industry's landscape once more, it explores the question how different financial pressures and operational affordances will govern the overall creative process.

Empirical Procedure

Throughout this work, I have tried to be transparent by relying on accessible data sources and common methodologies. To provide an analysis of the global industry and how it has changed over the years, I relied on a variety of data sources to illustrate the various relevant changes. The appendix provides a detailed explanation of my empirical procedure.

1

Games as a Product

1

Digitalization of Interactive Entertainment

The successes of digital media firms like Netflix and Spotify stand as examples of innovative strategies and a redefinition of existing business models. Netflix's $190 billion market cap value, its clever algorithms, and aggressive content acquisition strategy that more than tripled from $5 billion in 2015 to $15 billion in less than five years is a favorite topic among media analysts and journalists. These experts eagerly monitor how many subscribers the firm adds every quarter and how much it seeks to grow internationally. Similarly, the digital music platform Spotify captured the hearts and minds of industry observers and investors alike. This quirky Swedish startup took on the music industry's incumbents and stayed one step ahead of tech firms with deep pockets, like Apple and Google, in rolling out its digital music service. Its initial public offering was hailed as the future of music consumption and contributed to an increase in consumer spending on music for the first time in fifteen years.

Despite these remarkable stories, we rarely hear about game companies that have embraced the transition to digital. Valve, for instance, launched its digital distribution platform back in 2003. Today, it generates an estimated $5 billion annually, has more than 125 million active accounts, and is home to more than four thousand newly released titles each year. It does not spend billions on content acquisition. By all measures, it is equally, if not more, successful than its counterparts in music and video but has received little attention from people outside the industry. A possible explanation is that unlike Netflix and Spotify, Valve remained private to avoid having to deal with the opinions and input from investors and shareholders (more on this in chapter 7). Moreover, its owner Gabe Newell is a notably private leader and the company actively avoids the spotlight. Subsequently, Valve found that it never had to raise money or impress bankers, allowing it to maintain a low profile.

Even so, the list of game companies that successfully exploited digitization is extensive. Publisher Riot Games earned billions with a free-to-play called *League of Legends*, which at its peak was actively played by almost 100 million people. Apple unified mobile game development and connected millions of developers with billions of consumers with the introduction of the iPhone. Amazon's purchase of Twitch triggered a massive shift in the way games are marketed, enjoyed, and monetized. Facebook introduced a generation of people to casual experiences and added millions of people to the global audience. Western publishers like Activision Blizzard, Electronic Arts, Take-Two Interactive, and Ubisoft all established digital storefronts to connect with their player base directly. And firms like Tencent and NetEase, two tech titans from China, wrote the book on how to leverage massive networks of users to funnel traffic to titles. They also made myriad small investments to keep a pulse on the market and to stress-test potential acquisitions. What does the digitization of gaming tell us about its various industry participants and their approach to innovation and strategy?

For much of the past twenty years, innovation and new approaches to strategy have occurred in interactive entertainment and away from the attention of established categories like film, video, and music. By all accounts, gaming has quietly grown from a derivative product category in the toy aisle to a behemoth industry teeming with creativity and innovation. Despite operating at an unparalleled scale and catering to billions of consumers globally, few industry outsiders anticipated wildly popular phenomena like esports, online multiplayer games, and free-to-play economics. Franchises like *Fortnite*, *Minecraft*, *League of Legends*, *Candy Crush*, and *Pokémon GO* have attracted massive audiences. Games have evolved, in effect, from a sideshow in the carnival to the main act. Or, as Netflix CEO Reed Hastings put it when asked whether rival streaming service HBO was a cause for concern: "We compete with (and lose to) *Fortnite* more than HBO."[1] Video games represent the dark horse in entertainment.

Let's start with the topline figures. If we compare the different markets for in-home entertainment in the United States, we observe that since 1998 consumer spending on digital formats has strongly increased. Combined, demand for digital music, games, and video grew from $881 million in 1998 to $46 billion in 2018. During that same period, physical sales declined from $46 billion to $15 billion, respectively. Digital in-home entertainment accounted for only 2 percent of combined spending in 1998 and grew to 76 percent by 2018.

The music business has struggled for most of the past twenty years and consistently declined. Despite its gradual adoption of digitization and replacing vinyl and cassette tapes with CDs, long-held practices such as selling music bundled as albums eventually lost out to the sale of individual songs. After a period in which the download of singles and full albums compensated for the decline in physical revenue, this, too, lost traction with consumers. Only in the past few years did paid subscriptions for streaming services like Apple Music, Pandora, and Spotify start to contribute meaningfully.

In-home DVD players managed to keep physical video sales relatively strong. By 2004, the market for boxed sales peaked at $28 billion as digital sales oscillated around $1 billion. It was not until 2016 that digital video became the largest category as services like iTunes, Netflix, and Hulu established themselves as popular alternatives.

Finally, video games initially remained the smallest of the three entertainment segments. Even a casual observer of the industry has noticed the fantastic success of mobile gaming. Following the introduction of the iPhone, gaming started to attract more consumer spending across digital channels in 2008, and by 2018, the category accounted for $21 billion compared with music ($7 billion) and video ($18 billion). Notably, consumers have continued to spend money on physical software as well, and games became the largest segment in 2018 with $7 billion, compared with $2 billion for music and $7 billion for video (see figure 1.1).

This difference in performance is remarkable because the games business shares more than a few economic drivers with other entertainment segments. Music and film, but also print publishing, magazines, and cable television, similarly face high and increasing production and marketing costs, strongly seasonal patterns, long development cycles, and hit-driven economics (more on this later). To understand how interactive entertainment has managed to grow so prosperously, we need to take a closer look at two industry eras that roughly coincided with the introduction of disruptive consumer technologies. In the first period from 1984 to 2008, product-based revenue represented the largest source of income for all major

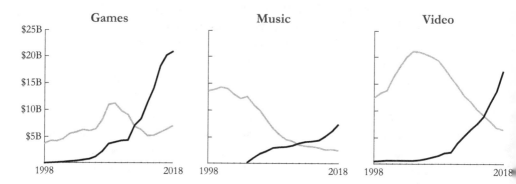

Figure 1.1

In-home entertainment by content category and distribution format (digital, physical), United States, 1998–2018. *Source*: Data from annual reports released by the Motion Picture Association of America, Recording Industry Association of America, public information from NPD, and SuperData Research. *Note*: Revenue in billions U.S. dollars ($). Numbers shown for music do not include live performances. For video, box office sales are excluded.

industry participants. In this model, publishers sold physical discs and cartridges through retailers to consumers who mostly played on consoles. This was the dominant form of monetization for the first three decades, and, as we will see, it followed a model that emulated the toy industry in terms of seasonality and marketing. Because of the persistent increase in development costs, this model ultimately became a strongly hit-driven one, resulting in a comparatively high degree of consolidation among participants, as only a handful of publishers, retailers, and platforms controlled the larger bulk of the market.

The second era, beginning roughly in 2009, followed the widespread adoption of online connectivity and a general digitalization of entertainment. I will refer to this era as games-as-a-service. This value chain is markedly different: consumers download interactive content directly onto their devices (mobile, console, and PC) and are accustomed to paying for additional content and in-game items. A generation of newcomers pioneered business models that offered games for cheap or even free and monetized the games through microtransactions.

Succinctly, games are highly accessible experiences that gradually monetize over time. We can observe this accessibility on a variety of fronts. Many titles are free. But they also are quick and easy to install. And they require low hardware specs. Examples of games that have done well using this model include *League of Legends* and *Fortnite*. Firms seek to build a long-term relationship with their respective player bases and incorporate a variety of different components into their offering to establish a broad community of players, social network effects, and offline marketing efforts like tournaments and events. This model stands almost in opposition to its predecessor because it employs a service model that emulates the software industry, allowing for ongoing iterations of a game. These iterations, in turn, obligate publishers to maintain servers, customer services, and regular marketing and sales efforts. The time it took for games-as-a-service to become popular among consumers also facilitated the entry of several newcomers, which resulted in a global marketplace that was free from constraints like physical boundaries and related logistics that had shaped the industry for decades.

To be sure, the implications of the service model were not immediately obvious to everyone. To most gaming executives, digital sales channels represented an additional source of revenue rather than their primary form of income. For most of its history, the business's core metric centered on the number of units sold. A game's success depended on how many copies it sold, particularly in the first few weeks after launch. If, however, we look at the world through this lens, we would conclude that digitalization has thus far been only a sideshow to the established business. And, understandably, this has long been a perspective shared by retailers, publishers, and investors. Looking at the total number of units sold, we would be correct to conclude that digital remains a modest part of the overall business (see figure 1.2). By delivery format, the CD-ROM first took over from the cartridge and remained dominant even as direct downloadable content continued its rise. By 2018, the volume of titles sold on CD-ROM was still roughly the same as the total number of full game downloads.

Incumbent publishers each have taken their own approach to technological change and have committed different efforts toward understanding the implications of network connectivity and changes in consumer behavior. During the early 2000s, most major publishers were all more or less aware of new categories, such as mobile gaming and online multiplayer games. They made investments according to their expectations of the long-term strategic significance of these emergent technologies.

We can observe this both in the financial resources applied to developing online titles and in the adoption of new terminology in financial

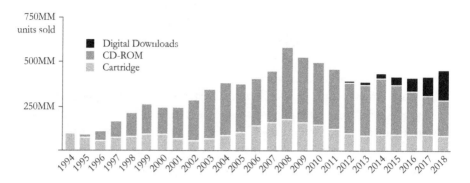

Figure 1.2
Annual software units sold (millions), worldwide, 1994–2018. *Source*: Data from SuperData Research; Michael Pachter, Nick McKay, and Nick Citrin, "Post Hoc Ergo Propter Hoc; Why the Next Generation Will Be as Big as Ever" (Equity Research, Wedbush Securities, February 12, 2014). *Note*: The category "cartridge" includes both console and handheld sales. The category "digital downloads" includes full game downloads but not add-on content.

reporting. In its 2008 annual report, Take-Two announced having signed an agreement with Xbox for the exclusive distribution of downloadable content for *Grand Theft Auto IV*. The word "digital" appears twice in its 2008 annual report and promptly increased in frequency to 28 by 2014. In 2015, however, Take-Two's switch in favor of the term "recurrent consumer spending" indicated a shift in the firm's thinking from applying new technological affordances in the expansion of its existing practices to new ways of doing business. Beyond merely facilitating the ability to download a title, accretive revenue from expansions and microtransactions had become large enough to warrant its own strategic effort. Once consumer spending switched toward digital distribution and the adoption of new devices, the overall competitive value of these new technologies became clear, and all major game makers moved to adopt new innovations and strategies. Rather than selling individual units to consumers and emulating the product model, the service-based approach has facilitated spectacular growth. If we look instead at the value created by revenue model, we get a very different image (see figure 1.3). It becomes clear that over the past decade, digitalization has contributed most of the value.

The games-as-a-service approach presents a different mix of creative affordances and places a variety of constraints on companies. Certainly,

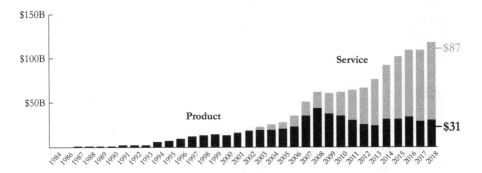

Figure 1.3

Games industry revenue, 1984–2018. *Source*: Data from SuperData Research. *Note*: Product-based revenue is defined as income earned from the sale of physical copies of entertainment software for all available platforms. Service revenue refers to income earned from the sale of full game downloads, microtransactions, subscriptions fees, season passes, virtual currency purchases, and donations. Figures exclude the sale, either via retail or online, of hardware, such as consoles, PCs, accessories, peripherals, merchandise, and internet and telecommunications services.

the ability to reach across natural geographic boundaries allows firms to assemble an audience that is large enough to be financially sustainable. Where in the product model it may have been too costly to reach consumers in different markets, digital gaming facilitates sustainability in niche segments. Another benefit to nonphysical content is the obvious absence of inventory costs. As we will see in chapter 3, it is quite expensive to sell in stores, not in the least because it involves having to ship boxes of software to ensure proper availability. In contrast, online distribution does not incur any of these expenses and thereby avoids one of the most dominant financial risks in traditional publishing. Publishers are in a better position to offer price differentiation. For instance, with access to countries in eastern Europe, they can reach more people. Some of these economies, however, simply cannot carry the same price for content as North America and Western Europe. By having greater control over the value chain, publishers can more accurately price their offering to better facilitate and ultimately generate more revenue from markets that previously were inaccessible.

Perhaps the most important difference resulting from the digitalization of interactive entertainment is the shift away from having to create all of the value for consumers to network effects. Simply stated, in a product-based model, companies compete over production values and the ability to offer a unique experience that stands apart from other available offerings. In the service-based model, many of the most successful titles leverage online multiplayer gameplay to attract an abundance of players who play against each other rather than against a computer-controlled antagonist. Success, then, depends less on production values, although those may very well be equal, and more on emphasizing the creation of positive network effects (see figure 1.4).

In return for inoculating much of the industry against product-related inefficiencies, such as used sales and the cost of unsold inventory, the digital model comes with its own ills. Among them are cloning, piracy, and the cost of localization. In markets that have millions of outfits working on the supply side, the emphasis tends to move away from developing something unique. Instead, competition comes in the form of a surge of quick followers that emulate and copy the mechanics of a popular game to claim a share. A title like *Flappy Bird* was an overnight success released by a single developer from Vietnam, only to be ruthlessly cloned by hundreds of other outfits. Take a look at any mobile app store and you will find a single hit title surrounded by dozens of would-be competitors. Unfortunately, this is a common practice, especially in economies where entry barriers are low and differentiation is expensive. Moreover, because

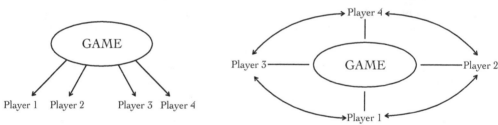

Traditional Game Publishing **Networked Game Publishing**

Figure 1.4

Traditional and networked game publishing. *Source*: Adapted from "Figure 5: Traditional versus Networked Products" from THE CONTENT TRAP: A STRATEGIST'S GUIDE TO DIGITAL CHANGE by Bharat Anand, copyright © 2016 by Bharat Anand. Used by permission of Random House, an imprint and division of Penguin Random House LLC. All rights reserved. *Note*: In the traditional product-based games business, publishers sought to sell as many copies of a single production at the highest possible price. In the service-based business, network effects constitute a large part of the value offering and game makers focus on maintaining an active and engaged player base around their titles.

digital content is easier to distribute and circulate, it is not just the pressure from the supply side: piracy presents another strategic challenge. Especially on PCs, consumers have a tendency to scour the internet and look for cracked versions of popular titles, even if it means they lose the ability to play online. In particular, large blockbuster productions are at risk of losing a disproportionate amount of value to illegally distributed copies. Finally, to fully benefit from the true affordance of digitization and reach a global audience, game makers have to localize their offering. In this context, localization goes well beyond merely translating a game into different languages. It also requires setting up an appropriate server infrastructure to host players and facilitate a smooth playing experience, uninterrupted by latency issues. This goes hand in hand with setting up customer service centers around the world. These aspects are easily neglected but of considerable strategic value for titles like *League of Legends* and *World of Warcraft*.

If we divide organizations that make and publish games into one bucket consisting of conventional legacy publishers and another with digital-only firms, the following image appears. After a long period during which product-based game makers dominated, online-only companies took over by 2014. Having grown from a combined value of around $1 billion in 2005, this group of industry participants generated $67 billion in aggregate revenue by 2018, compared with $47 billion for legacy companies. Incumbents have been slow to adopt digital strategies.

Likewise, newcomers are motivated to raise funding and quickly build strategic differentiators and cater to a global audience (figure 1.5). Firms like Tencent, Valve, Nexon, Niantic, NCSoft, and NetEase, in particular, have managed to claim a significant share of the global market by successfully capitalizing on the momentum provided by digitalization. Incumbents like Sony, Activision Blizzard, Microsoft, Electronic Arts, Bandai NAMCO, and Take-Two continue to perform well, both in their long-established categories and in newly emerged segments, but they have not been able to capture as much market value.

For creative firms, success in the digital era depends on the ability to develop innovative business models. Brilliant content alone is not enough to accomplish critical or commercial success: it also requires identifying and tapping into a talent pool, marketing effectively, securing appropriate funding, partnering with other value chain participants, aggregating and digesting user data and market information, establishing an effective

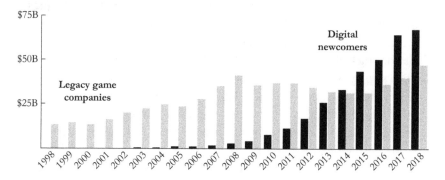

Figure 1.5
Revenue distribution, legacy game companies and digital newcomers, worldwide, 1998–2018. *Source*: Data from company reports. *Note*: Data organized by firms that predate digitalization (legacy game companies) and firms that emerged during or after the introduction of consumer broadband and smartphone (digital newcomers). The latter category generally does not release games via physical channels (retail, e-commerce) and the former have had to adapt to new market conditions. Shaded bars are legacy; black bars are digital newcomers.

distribution network, and making it all sing together. Solving problems around these components effectively is as important as it is to make fun and interesting games.[2]

That is all well and good. But theory does not mean anything if people—specifically, the decision-makers in an organization—either have no knowledge of new circumstances or, worse, regard them with suspicion. Despite the heavy emphasis on technology in most conversations about creative businesses, companies are made up first and foremost of people. Depending on the size of an individual firm, it is the producers, designers, analysts, programmers, marketers, and engineers who work together to realize a particular creative vision. Important in the execution of that vision is how these people—the key decision-makers—see their collective efforts in relation to the larger market. Managers in a game company construct a mental model of how their organization creates, delivers, and captures value. This is known as a cognitive perspective of business model enactment. In the context of business management, mental models consist of at least two beliefs: first is a company's perceived identity and the interpretation of the overall environment in which it operates.[3] Take-Two, for instance, has a habit of postponing the release of its major titles in spite of pressures from its retail relationships and investor community. It proudly dismisses such external pressures for the sake of its artistic output. This delay tends to drive its shareholders mad and would be seen as a detriment if its commercial results were not as spectacular. To Take-Two executives, creative output reigns supreme. Electronic Arts takes a different approach: rather than relying on a massive hit every few years, it focuses on producing fairly predictable, annual results by releasing a new edition in its *Madden NFL* and *FIFA* franchises. Consistency and predictability are the cornerstones of the firm's design strategy. How a creative firm balances its overall output with the interests of its many industry partners gives us a glimpse of how it sees itself and its role within its larger environment.

A second important aspect of these mental models are the causal beliefs of what it takes for a company to successfully compete in its environment. This includes a perceived image of the entirety of the market, a company's specific competitive environment, the characteristics of their organization, the irrationality of consumer behavior and preferences, the nature of investor relations, and technological change. These aspects, in aggregate, invariably inform the type of entertainment experiences a creative firm produces and applies equally to large and small outfits. Small independent studios are not exempt even if they do not overtly pursue a profit motive, because they, too, ultimately operate with a specific organizational structure in which its members rely on available resources to realize their creative vision. Try as they might, they do not live outside of economic rules. Even well-known creatives that prefer to operate in small outfits ultimately surrender to the truth that things cost money. To obtain the necessary funding to produce his critically acclaimed *Fez*, designer Phil Fish eventually relented and committed himself to "weeks of paperwork" to apply for government subsidies.[4] Like him, many others believe adamantly that developing successful interactive content has more to do with intuition and that economic objectives are secondary.

The larger-than-life egos of executives play an important part in the video games business, as they do elsewhere in entertainment. An assessment of financial returns in connection with high-profile leadership styles finds that media businesses are disproportionally prone to cultivating a subjective interpretation of the world around them. Across different businesses, the so-called media mogul injects obfuscation into what otherwise should be rational strategy and decision-making. Instead of deploying rudimentary financial analysis as part of their decision-making, executives and creatives insist that their business is unique and therefore should not be held to the same standards. This has led to tremendous loss of value across companies. The insistence on growth through acquisition, instead of investing in innovation or efficiencies, has caused media firms to lose billions. This, in part, is why making games is such a risky enterprise.[5] At all levels, mental models deeply affect the intercourse between creativity and commerce.

Beyond individual personalities and company culture, the industry as a whole relies on myriad unexamined clichés. Take, for instance, the discussion surrounding the emergence of free-to-play games. Much of the debate around the adoption of this revenue model and how this changes the affordances and constraints made on an organization of creatives has long centered almost exclusively on its exploitative potential. Major publishers like Take-Two and Electronic Arts openly questioned the viability of the free-to-play revenue model, particularly in the context of the console market in which they held dominant positions.[6] According to Take-Two CEO Strauss Zelnick: "Most free-to-play games are not very good."[7] To these executives, the growth in countries like South Korea and China where the free-to-play model dominated was additive to the industry's overall success but unlikely to create a threat in their backyard. Their franchises would be impervious to this development, it seemed. But only a few years later, free-to-play shooter *Fortnite* managed to become the top-grossing title not just on consoles but all platforms. It forced executives to answer a host of questions during earnings calls with regard to the new Battle Royale mode that drove *Fortnite's* success and whether it was going to have a negative effect on the upcoming releases of the new *Call of Duty*, *Red Dead Redemption 2*, and *Battlefield V*. Free-to-play gaming had grown from an oddity into an industry standard and has been eating into the profits of traditional content creators.

It was not just the top-level executives, of course. Many prominent designers also have been fond of vilifying free-to-play. Icons like Richard Garfield, creator of *Magic: The Gathering* and by any measure a traditional designer, have been vocal about how they feel about free-to-play monetization: "Game designers and publishers have stumbled upon some formulae that work only because they abuse segments of their player population. Games can have addictive properties—and these abusive games are created—intentionally or not—to exploit players who are subject to certain addictive behavior."[8]

Despite such criticism from executives and creatives, consumers have adopted this model en masse. As we will see, innovative new business models made video games accessible to more people and greatly expanded the addressable audience. Digital newcomers like Wargaming, King Digital, and Riot Games challenged the perceived merits of, for instance, free-to-play monetization. Their successes serve as examples of the myriad ways in which the industry has changed.

The games industry's digitalization over the past decade has turned its market landscape upside down. Legacy publishers who were used to sitting at the head of the table on account of their massive marketing budgets, suddenly found themselves competing on equal terms with successful newcomers who had steady flows of recurrent, monthly revenue and the backing of venture capital investors with deep pockets. Digital distribution platforms emerged as the dominant point of contact for most online consumers, and retailers started to feel the heat as shopping traffic moved online. Small outfits of only a handful of people now generate millions in annual revenue and regularly find themselves acquired for billions by multinational conglomerates.

With this shift in underlying business models also came a change in the industry's aesthetic principles. Titles like *Fortnite*, *Minecraft*, and *Pokémon GO* and the economics that shape them look nothing like their predecessors. Contemporary interactive entertainment employs features that previously were unavailable. Top-selling titles today offer open-world experiences that allow players to roam freely and explore an increasingly sophisticated and interactive environment. Online connectivity has facilitated multiplayer gameplay across different devices and platforms.

The digitalization of entertainment has dramatically changed the industry landscape, and companies now confront a range of new challenges and opportunities. The move away from its product-based roots to a new digital reality that redefined every aspect of the industry's activity presents an opportunity for us to study how developers, publishers, platform holders, and distributors have managed to both successfully and unsuccessfully navigate the currents in this shifting economic context. The explosive growth of the sector can be attributed to an inherent ability of creative firms to innovate. To understand exactly how they have managed to do so, we first look at the economic fundamentals in interactive entertainment.

2

Games Industry Basics

General knowledge about the business of games amounts to little more than that making games is difficult and unpredictable and that success is mostly singular and virtually impossible to replicate. It is true, of course, that producing a blockbuster title is expensive because it is, in effect, the ultimate differentiated product. It takes several years to complete a game and can involve thousands of people. In addition to the cost of development, marketing and distribution double the overall expense. A title like *Grand Theft Auto V (GTA V)* spent about six years in production and cost its publisher Take-Two Interactive around $260 million, split roughly equally between development and marketing. Budgets for projects with comparable production values run between $50 and $150 million. Game development at this scale is not for the faint of heart. In an interview, Take-Two Chair and CEO Strauss Zelnick described the industry in no uncertain terms: "It's an expensive business, and the risk profile reflects that."[1]

The same is true of the development costs for small independent creatives. In relative terms, the expenses may be much smaller expressed in dollars. But money is not the only way to express cost. Indie designers devote years of their lives and every available resource toward the completion of their creative vision. This approach has delivered some of the most critically acclaimed titles, including *Super Meat Boy, Stardew Valley,*

Shovel Knight, Braid, Fez, and many others. The missed opportunity cost of a stalled career is but one obvious sacrifice. Less obvious may be the strain on personal relationships. Only a precious few smaller projects have yielded massive returns. That is arguably not the point of the exercise for small outfits, but reality does set in when rent is due. At this scale, financial commitments made by these independent creatives do not stand in comparison to those made by big publishers, but they easily can be considered as more expensive.

Strongly hit-driven success is another defining aspect of the games business. A popular title will generate disproportionally more revenue than its immediate peers. According to an analysis of the revenue distribution for several of the classic genres on consoles, the top-ten titles account for more than 90 percent of consumer spending. In 2018, *FIFA 18* was the top-grossing title in the sports category on console with $723 million out of more than $2 billion for the entire top ten, or 28 percent. For the racing category, top sales went to *The Crew 2*, with $114 million (22 percent); for the fighter genre, *Super Smash Bros. Ultimate* dominated with $190 million (57 percent), and among the role-playing games (RPGs), *Monster Hunter World* grossed $264 million (45 percent) in revenue.[2] The number ten game in each of these genres accounted for less than 2 percent of the total. Succinctly put, for every blowout success, dozens of titles fail to deliver on expectations. The winner-takes-most aspect of game publishing means that an organization is either doing really well or dying.

Not even big organizations are exempt from failure. In 2007, THQ reported more than $1 billion in revenue and was one of the top publishers alongside Electronic Arts, Activision Blizzard, Take-Two, and Ubisoft. By 2013, THQ had been delisted and was sold for parts. This example is no exception. Even during the rapid growth and success achieved across the industry, in recent years, regular lay-offs and bankruptcies have occurred among the top-tiered companies, including Lionhead Studios, LucasArts, and Sega.

Seasonality is a third component to the economic dynamic of the industry. Historically, the bulk of annual sales occur in the last two months of the year. On the basis of monthly software sales figures reported by NPD for the period from 2006 to 2018, we can calculate that the months of November and December combined, on average, account for 41 percent of annual sales volume in the United States.[3] Within a brief period, publishers have to make good on their promises to consumers and investors alike, which further exacerbates the industry's "win-or-die" dynamic, as it forces them to compete on marketing expenditure. In the lead-up to the holiday season, they compete over consumer attention. These marketing efforts greatly increase costs and, consequently, a publisher needs to sell more units to cover these expenses and make a profit.

A fourth contributor to the overall risk profile is that a company really has no idea if, after all their effort, their game actually will sell well. Demand uncertainty presents a major problem. Publishers, platform holders, and retailers have to make considerable financial commitments to the promotion and distribution of a blockbuster title well in advance of its release. But it is impossible to know what will drive consumer demand or what the competitive landscape will look like by the time a title finally hits the market. Even then, it may prove to be riddled with bugs as soon as it goes out or receive a cold welcome from reviewers.

Finally, the video games business is a platform-based industry. In simple economic terms, it follows a razor-blade model: hardware is sold at a loss, and only by selling software units (its complementary goods) do platform holders recoup this investment and generate a profit over time. Consequently, it is critical that platform manufacturers quickly achieve a large enough install base to attract content creators. For instance, when Microsoft first launched the Xbox in 2001, it took on a $250 loss per unit to quickly sell as many units as possible to persuade publishers to make games for its newly released console. Only a handful of platform holders are active at once, and any aspiring competitors face high barriers to entry. These barriers also limit content creators in negotiating publishing deals because little wiggle room exists. Firms like Microsoft are able to justify such an investment because of the revenue it will generate from title sales. Moreover, hardware manufacturers historically have released a new platform every five to seven years, which effectively resets the landscape and forces platform holders to rebuild their market share anew.

Collectively, these different aspects result in an economic dynamic that centers on high investment, high risk, and high reward. This dynamic historically has presented a natural barrier to entry for many types of aspiring industry participants and, arguably, has resulted in video games remaining on the sidelines of the broader entertainment landscape (figure 2.1).

Interactive entertainment first emerged as a derivative product group. Analysts regarded video games as a kind of toy, and to skeptics, the category was nothing more than a fad. This skepticism was largely the industry's own fault. Marketers positioned their products as an opportunity to play in the comfort of one's living room and far away from the seediness of the arcade. Large retailers put video games in the toy aisles and emphasized their

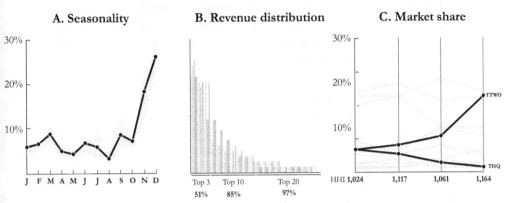

Figure 2.1

Economic foundation of the product-based games industry: strong seasonality, disproportionate revenue distribution, and winner-takes-most market share. *Source*: Data from NPD publicly reported figures; Michael Pachter, "Money for Nothing: How Ancillary Revenues Can Extend the Console Cycle," Wedbush Securities, July 2009. *Note*: Panel A is based on monthly share (%) of annual consumer spending on physical entertainment software from 2006 to 2018 in the United States. Weighted average is highlighted. Panel B is based on title-level revenue distribution from physical entertainment software sales among the top-twenty game publishers in the United States for 2007, 2008, 2012, and 2013. Panel C is the market share held by the top-twenty entertainment software publishers in the United States for 2007, 2008, 2012, and 2013. Highlights show Take-Two Interactive (TTWO) and THQ. Herfindahl-Hirschmann Index (HHI) indicates relative degree of market concentration.

technical capacity and amusement value as key-selling points. To financial analysts like Hal Vogel, the "microelectronic-chip technology [that] enabled game designers to conveniently and inexpensively transform plain television screens into play fields of extraordinary capability."[4]

This emphasis on processing power and the propensity for spectacle mimicked the marketing strategy from the arcades, where better graphics tended to attract consumers. Executives reasoned that audiences cared primarily about being able to play games they had seen in arcades in the comfort of their own home. It ultimately locked the industry and its most successful protagonists like Atari into a mind-set in which hardware enjoyed prominence over software.

At first most organizations dedicated relatively few resources to the development of original software. Early development teams consisted of salaried programmers charged with the task of creating games that worked within the technical confines of a specific hardware configuration. Following the success of Atari's *Pong*—first as an arcade game and later as a home console title—no fewer than seventy-five other companies launched their own version of a similar tennis-style title built into a device. In combination with the momentum behind consumer demand, content was largely a commodity instead of a strategic differentiator.

To compete with a slew of single-game consoles, market leader Atari moved to the manufacturing of programmable devices. Capable of playing multiple titles stored on sold-separately cartridges, this model ultimately became the fundamental business model in product-based publishing. Hardware manufacturers moved away from trying to emulate the high-definition experience of the arcade and instead switched the emphasis to offering a wide inventory of exclusively available titles. In its messaging, Atari emphasized the abundance of titles, claiming "No other company offers you as many video game cartridges as Atari." Other companies, like Fairchild, RCA, National Semiconductor, GE, and Coleco, pursued a similar strategy. Unfortunately, this resulted in a confusing offering of both single- and multi-game devices available at the same time. With a growing number of companies competing over market share by each offering their own hardware and more-or-less undifferentiated content inventory, consumers started to get confused.

Even so, a strong undercurrent in the broader computer industry kept the crowded market afloat. The sudden entry of so many participants was partially the result of a broader exuberance as computers became a defining consumer technology at the time. Apple Computer reached $1 billion in sales and was the first personal computer company to do so. Its rival Microsoft earned a more modest $34 million, had grown to two hundred employees and had started its international expansion by opening offices in Europe. Coleco Industries experienced tremendous financial growth with $510 million in sales and Sun Microsystems, founded earlier that year, earned $8 million in revenue. All of these organizations eventually would rise to importance in addition to a slew of other technology and computer firms founded around the same time, including Autodesk, Compaq, Electronic Arts, Silicon Graphics, Origin Systems (which would later develop the hugely popular title *Ultima*), and LucasArts. The industry benefited from the momentum in the broader computer business.

The inevitable shakeout eventually followed in the late 1970s. Consumers grew tired of the abundance of similar-looking experiences. It forced game makers to shift their focus on exclusive content as a key competitive advantage (see table 2.1). To keep its position, Atari adopted a new

Table 2.1
Worldwide console gaming market, units sold (millions), 1972–1986

Company	Hardware Generation	One					Two							Three		
		72	73	74	75	76	77	78	79	80	81	82	83	84	85	86
Atari	Pong				0.08											
	Atari 2600						0.25	0.55	1.0	2.0	4.0	4.0	1.0	1.0	0.5	0.2
	Atari 5200											0.2	0.7	0.1		
Mattel	Intellivision									0.1	0.6	1.1	3.5	1.0		
	PlayCable										x					
Coleco	Coleco Telstar Arcade						x									
	ColecoVision											0.5	1.2	0.2	0.1	
Magnavox	Odyssey	0.09	0.1	0.1	0.07											
	Odyssey 2							x								
General Electric	PC-50x Family				x											
	Vectrex											0.2	0.1			
Fairchild	Fairchild Channel F					0.1	0.15									
Emerson Radio	Arcadia 2001										0.05					
Entex	Adventure Vision								0.1							
Zircon	Channel F System II						0.05									
RCA	RCA Studio II						0.05									
Bandai	SuperVision 8000								x							
Total units sold		0.09	0.1	0.1	0.14	0.1	0.5	0.6	1.1	2.1	4.7	6.1	6.6	2.3	0.6	0.2
By hardware generation		**0.5**					**21.6**							**3.1**		

Sources: Author's compilation based on company reports, publicly available information. Sales figures collected from www.old-computers.com, last accessed May 2018.

Note: Omitted from this table are handheld devices. Because of the lack of available sales data, the following consoles are excluded: Tele-Spiel (Phillips), Phillips Odyssey (Phillips), CD-i (Phillips), Video 2000 (Interton), VC 4000 (Interton), APF-MP1000 (APF), APF Imagination Machine (APF), Bally Astrocade (Midway), CreatiVision (VTECH), Cassette Vision (EPOCH), Compact Vision TV-Boy (Gakken), and Pyuuta Jr. (Matsushita). x = Missing data values for known hardware releases; Nintendo omitted.

strategy that emphasized content and aggressively marketed its best-sellers *Pac-Man* and *Space Invaders.*

The move to title exclusivity changed the way the industry created content. Game designers, previously considered to be no more than regular employees, became aware of the value they contributed. In an interview, former Atari employee David Crane explains how following a particularly successful year, senior management circulated a memo that disclosed the earnings from its various titles. According to Crane,

> It demonstrated the value of the game designer individually. Video game design in those days was a one-man process with one person doing the creative design, the storyboards, the graphics, the music, the sound effects, every line of programming, and final play testing. So, when I saw a memo that the games for which I was 100 percent responsible had generated over $20 million in revenues, I was one of the people wondering why I was working in complete anonymity for a $20,000 salary.[5]

Not long after, Atari saw several of its top programmers leave the company in search for more recognition and salary. Among these departures was the notable exodus of four of Atari's designers who left to form Activision in 1979. By becoming independent, creatives were able to capture substantially more value for themselves. Within just one year, Activision generated $66 million in earnings selling software to manufacturers, and more than doubled by 1982. By its third year, the newly formed company earned $300 million and grew at an even faster pace than Atari. The overwhelming success of this model eventually forced Atari and other console makers to open their platform up for third-party software. It triggered a growth spurt in development, and within two years, more than one hundred different studios were producing content for Atari's popular console.

Unfortunately, despite the initial boom in content creation, the combination of unfettered optimism in the broader software industry and growing revenue resulted in Atari's executives making bad decisions by overestimating consumer demand. After purchasing the exclusive license for the home console version of *Pac-Man* in 1982, the company ordered twelve million units in the expectation that the game's appeal would expand Atari's existing install base of ten million even further. It proved to be a gross miscalculation when it only managed to sell seven million copies. The disappointing result taught the company a valuable lesson:

low-quality content and poor sales results have a strongly negative influence on the economics of a single title as well as on consumer perception of the overall platform. It presented a sobering realization of the strategic challenge about how to effectively assess the risk involved with investing in content creation and demand uncertainty. Platform holders embraced exclusivity and bid against each other to obtain the rights to publish top titles exclusively. Hoping to outmaneuver the competition by making bigger promises to consumers, they did so without proper quality control and curation. The combination of an increasing lack of demand-side transparency and explosive costs ultimately led to a market correction that decimated the industry in 1983. This self-inflicted injury forced most console manufacturers to exit the market. The sudden malaise in consumer demand made the economics unattractive and gave weight to the idea that video games were a fad.

It was during this historic low point that Nintendo entered the market. In the midst of a humbling decline that had left many speculating that the business would never recover, a Japanese console maker formulated an innovative business model based on several interrelated strategic components and turned the industry around. To move away from what was a market characterized by communized content, Nintendo pursued a highly differentiated offering. It managed to do so by controlling three key variables: the quality of the overall experience on the classic NES console; efficient management of its distribution; and effective, large-scale marketing.

From the start, Nintendo insisted on the highest possible quality standard. In the run-up to the mid-1980s, a glut of competitors both on the hardware and software development side were trying to gain share. In the absence of any standards, consumers predictably had started to pull away. To avoid the oversaturation that had cost Atari so dearly, Nintendo deployed deliberate quality controls across its entire supply chain. Minoru Arakawa, the founder of Nintendo of America and its former president, focused on a single philosophy: quality over quantity. Among Nintendo's executives, a single mantra had emerged that would dictate its broader strategy: "The name of the game is the game."[6]

Nintendo devised several novel features to placate consumers. First, it extended the emphasis on quality to their entire player experience. When an initial batch of consoles went out with a faulty chipset, Nintendo immediately issued a full recall and spent millions to replace the devices. Next, it launched a cheap ad-free magazine called *Nintendo Power* containing tips and tricks for its various titles. Not looking to make any profit from the publication, the magazine was produced and distributed at cost to further keep its player-base engaged. To further that effort, Nintendo also opened a hotline that players could call for any help whenever they had gotten stuck in a level. (I admit having called this line a few times back in the day because my brother and I had gotten stuck somewhere in the *Legend of Zelda*; at ten years old, my English was not quite good enough to avoid misunderstanding. How was I supposed to know that "Grumble, Grumble . . ." meant someone was hungry?) And it started the Nintendo Fun Club: a newsletter that was sent to anyone who submitted a warranty card. In addition to the emphasis on quality gameplay, this multipronged approach to actively engage consumers illustrated a new strategy among game companies.

Nintendo's focus on quality content also meant taking control of the games that it made available for its platform. In dealing with third-party publishers, it dictated a strict licensing program: licensees agreed to pay for manufacturing costs, committed to ordering thirty thousand units at a minimum to circulate for press and marketing purposes, signed a two-year exclusive for each title, paid a 10 to 20 percent royalty fee, and limited themselves to a maximum of five titles per year. To prevent developers from overwhelming audiences with mediocre content, Nintendo imposed limitations that encouraged game makers to submit only their best titles. Naturally, the harsh conditions of such an arrangement did not go over well with everyone. Publishers complained that it limited their ability to make money of what they considered to be their own creation and that Nintendo asked for too much. According to Electronic Art's founder Trip Hawkins, "Most of the people in the industry thought that Nintendo couldn't succeed. Everyone figured it would be a Cabbage Patch doll kind of thing— that it would hold up for another year and then go the way of Atari and Coleco and the other video game systems that had disappeared."[7] But by taking on this strategy Nintendo managed to promote its device and create demand. By pooling resources with publishers, it succeeded in outspending Atari fifty-to-one in marketing.

Next, Nintendo defined a clear approach to its retail relationships. Because many retailers were still licking their financial wounds from the industry's collapse, Nintendo offered to stock stores for free and required them to pay only for the units they had actually sold. With no upfront risk, big chains were willing to try things out in a few locations initially, and nationwide once the strategy had proven itself. Naturally, retailers liked this. Part of this strategy (but much less popular) was Nintendo's insistence on closely controlling inventory and product allocation. With the publishers having signed over control, Nintendo kept more than half of its available inventory inactive rather than flood the market with content once the popularity of its device started to accelerate. It deliberately refused to fulfill retail demand even as retailers begged and pleaded. According to one source, retailers had ordered around one hundred ten million games in 1988, in the expectation of selling around forty-five million units. Nintendo held its ground and shipped only thirty-three million units, much to the chagrin of many of its sellers. But by doing so, it prevented saturation and, as we will read in chapter 3, it avoided a premature decline in average selling prices.

Despite the initial criticism from third-party publishers and its retailers, Nintendo's strategy worked (see table 2.2). Initially prudent, it signed only six licensees who were offered better terms—namely, Namco, Hudson Soft, Taito, Konami, Capcom, and Bandai—and, not unimportant, all of these licensees were Japan-based organizations active in games. By 1988, Nintendo's third-party program counted fifty publishers. Even when it changed the licensing terms in 1989, the head of one its licensees, Namco's Masaya Nakamura, was not happy: "The game industry is still new. I want it to grow soundly. Nintendo is monopolizing the market, which is not good for the future of the industry [and] should consider itself the leader of the video-game industry and accept the responsibility that goes along with it."[8] Nevertheless, Nakamura agreed to the new terms. Other holdouts like Electronic Arts eventually caved, too. According to Hawkins, "All the American publishers avoided the 8-bit Nintendo and had disdain for their model. None of us at that time appreciated how license fees could be used to subsidize hardware pricing and marketing, and thereby help companies like Nintendo build an install base."[9]

In the decades that followed, several firms claimed significant market positions by copying Nintendo's blueprint. A revitalized console business that counted an install base of almost one hundred million units attracted new contenders, each with their own strategy. Sony, for example, leveraged its access to a large distribution network in combination with its size and relevance to the production of compact discs. The CD-ROM, which had managed to boost average revenue in the music industry in which consumers replaced their vinyl record collection and upgraded their audio systems,

Table 2.2
Worldwide console gaming market, units sold (millions), 1984–2018

Company	Hardware Generation	Three				Four						Five				
		84	85	86	87	88	89	90	91	92	93	94	95	96	97	98
Sony	PlayStation											0.3	3.4	6.6	18.2	22.5
	PlayStation 2															
	PS3															
	PS4 (Pro, Slim)															
Nintendo	NES		0.6	3.3	7.7	12.5	15.0	11.5	6.0	3.4	2.2	0.9	0.3	0.1		
	SNES						0.5	1.5	5.0	10.0	11.7	6.1	4.1	2.5	1.1	1.0
	N64												0.5	3.7	7.9	7.9
	GameCube															
	Wii															
	Wii U															
	Switch															
Microsoft	Xbox															
	Xbox 360															
	Xbox One (S, X)															
Sega	Genesis/Megadrive						0.1	1.5	3.0	6.8	6.3	4.8	2.0	1.0	0.3	
	Saturn											0.3	2.1	4.0	1.0	0.6
	Dreamcast														0.4	0.4
Atari	Atari 2600	1	0.5	0.2												
	Atari 5200	0.1														
	7800 System									0.1						
	Jaguar										0.3					
NEC	TurboGrafx-16					1.2	3.7	2.0	1.5	1.0	0.5	0.1				
	PC-FX											0.1				
Mattel	Intellivision	1														
The 3DO Co.	3DO Inter. Multiplayer										0.5	1.0	0.5			
Coleco	ColecoVision	0.2	0.1													
SNK	Neo Geo CD												0.2	0.3	0.1	
Commodore	Amiga CD32										0.1					
Fujitsu	FM Towns Marty												0.0			
	Pippin													0.0		
Amstrad	Amstrad GX4000								0.02							
Pioneer	LaserActive CLD-A100										0.01					
Total units sold		2.3	1.2	3.5	7.7	13.7	19.3	16.5	15.5	21.3	21.6	13.6	13.2	18.1	29.0	32.4
By hardware generation		**14.7**				**107.8**						**106.3**				

Sources: Author's compilation based on company reports, publicly available information. Sales figures collected from www.old-computers.com, last accessed May 2018.

Note: Omitted from this table are handheld devices. Because of the lack of available sales data, the following consoles have been excluded: Tele-Spiel (Phillips), Phillips Odyssey (Phillips), CD-i (Phillips), Video 2000 (Interton), VC 4000 (Interton), APF-MP1000 (APF), APF Imagination Machine (APF), Bally Astrocade (Midway), CreatiVision (VTECH), Cassette Vision (EPOCH), Compact Vision TV-Boy (Gakken), and Pyuuta Jr. (Matsushita).

	Six							Seven							Eight					
99	00	01	02	03	04	05	06	07	08	09	10	11	12	13	14	15	16	17	18
21.1	7.8	9.7	5.9	2.0	1.4	0.4	0.2	0.1	0.1										
	6.4	18.6	24.6	16.9	13.4	14.4	10.5	8.6	5.8	3.3	1.4	0.4							
							1.1	7.1	8.7	10.7	11.6	12.3	10.1	7.2	4.5	3.8	1.0	0.5	
														4.2	13.5	18.0	19.3	19.6	18.0
5.5	3.3	1.6	0.3	0.1															
		1.5	3.8	5.8	4.9	3.1	1.3	0.3											
							2.6	15.2	21.1	17.8	14.8	9.9	4.5	1.8	1.0				
													2.0	2.9	3.2	3.2	1.0	0.3	
																		11.9	17.1
		1.4	4.4	5.5	6.9	3.9	0.6												
							1.0	5.8	6.7	8.7	8.8	11.3	12.0	9.7	5.6	4.7	3.7	1.0	
														3.0	7.8	8.6	8.4	8.2	7.0
3.3	2.9	1.9																	
29.9	20.4	34.6	39.0	30.3	26.6	22.7	22.1	38.0	44.4	40.6	39.1	34.6	26.3	24.7	34.7	37.3	30.7	42.7	42.1
203.5							**245.0**							**212.2**					

now was quickly pushing game cartridges off the market and lowering costs. Moreover, Sony offered better terms to developers than Nintendo, such as requiring smaller production batches, quicker turnaround, and, notably, a lower cost per unit. Combined, this allowed Sony to gain favor from game makers, culminating in the signing of an exclusivity deal with several publishers, including Electronic Arts.

Finally, Microsoft, too, would copy Nintendo's model of heavy subsidies and marketing. For the launch of its Xbox in 2001, the software giant spent $500 million on promotion to quickly establish an install base that was large enough for big publishers to dedicate resources to development for the new device.

Today, console gaming is transitioning into its ninth generation: the PlayStation 5, Xbox Series X are due for release in late 2020 (see table 2.2). A surprise to many, the business for dedicated hardware has proven to be resilient in the face of ongoing digitalization (figure 2.2), and in the first half of 2020, the console business still counts an install base of more than two hundred million units worldwide. Nintendo's two-sided platform strategy and emphasis on controlling content quality, distribution, and marketing became the blueprint for the industry. According to Hawkins, "Nintendo invented the business model that everyone operates now from the platform-side."[10]

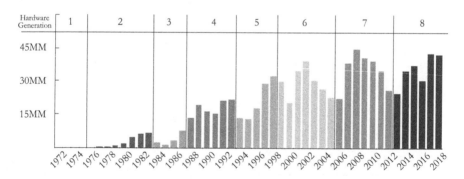

Figure 2.2
Worldwide console gaming market, units sold (millions), 1972–2018. *Source*: Data from company reports; Winnie Forster, "Game Machines 1972–2012," in *The Encyclopedia of Consoles, Handhelds and Home Computers*, edited by Heinrich Lenhardt and Nadine Caplette, 2nd ed. (Utting, Germany: Enati Media, 2011); sales figures collected from www.old-computers.com, accessed May 2018. See also table 2.2.

Content Creators

At the center of the games industry, we find developers, or studios. These are the organizations that make the actual games, and they may be made up of any combination of creatives and technical people, including programmers, artists and animators, game designers, producers, audio professionals, and quality assurance testers. This segment of the overall industry is heterogeneous, flat in structure, and crowded. By some 2017 estimates, around two thousand five hundred studios are active in the United States, which has likely grown in recent years.[11]

A creative endeavor like developing a game incurs a disproportionate share of overall risk, because the effort put into making a game can go to waste in myriad ways. Disagreements among studio managers, cashflow problems, changes in economic conditions, the emergence of a new competitor, shifting priorities among platform holders, consumers adopting a new technology, or just bad luck all compound the risk associated with interactive content development. One common threat for independent studios is to get stuck in project-based earnings cycles. Developers tend to operate as contractors to build a war chest and realize a vision of their own. With limited access to capital or distribution, studios depend on establishing a relationship with one or more publishers to access the consumer market. Creatives compete with each other to win favor from other value chain participants to bring their content to market. This power relationship is similar to artists in the music and film industry—a mostly flat industry structure in which an abundance of creative talent competes over access to resources and contracts. Because it generally is too expensive to develop in-house tools (e.g., physic engines), most studios rely on essentially the same technologies. Consequently, a studio's greatest asset is its talent pool.

Games design is a complicated creative effort and requires a variety of different technical skill sets to come together. Acquiring, cultivating, and retaining top talent is vital to a studio's success. The most important asset to a studio is its people. Technical components like computers, hardware, and infrastructure are available to most any studio. To differentiate and create value, creative outfits emphasize organizational innovation and generally establish a clearly defined strategy for managing their human resources. An indie, for instance, may consist of several close friends feverishly working on a passion project without any regard for broader business practices, such as securing adequate funding, finding proper workspace, setting reasonable working hours, distributing regular paychecks, paying taxes, and ensuring professional development. Large publicly traded companies, in contrast, may enforce a demanding work culture geared toward meeting deadlines to appease shareholders. Finding a balance between creative aspirations and the need to operate within a broader business environment is a challenge at any level. How a company treats its workers, or rather, how it designs its organization, is key to attracting the right people. Ideally, studios create an attractive work environment that encourages collaboration. More commonly, a creative firm establishes a company culture that offers a fair trade between the often-high demands made on developers and the ability to have an impact on the overall creative process.

Game studios compete over talent. More often than not, a studio's personality and reputation can make all the difference. Visiting an established developer tells you as much. Blizzard's European headquarters in Versailles, just southwest of Paris, presents a beautiful atrium with larger-than-life statues of the main protagonists from its games. Here, Sarah Kerrigan, the Queen of Blades from the *StarCraft* series, immediately tells you that you've entered a different type of corporate office. (Its U.S. office in Irvine, California, has an enormous orc statue.) Beyond curb appeal, Blizzard lures new talent with myriad perks, including a fitness center and an on-site nurse. Other studios do the same thing. Russian publisher Wargaming's different offices are each littered with tank-related props and memorabilia. Rockstar Games in New York has a row of old-fashioned arcade cabinets outfitted with its own titles. Wizards of the Coast's office features large, high-definition posters of the artwork found in *Magic: The Gathering* and *Dungeons & Dragons*.

This effort to make their workspace an inviting place is not just about aesthetics. Attracting a variety of skilled creatives is critical to success. A recent study on the diversity and level of experience of different development teams revealed that one of the most important drivers behind a title's success and critical acclaim is the makeup of a studio's talent pool. Seasoned developers, engineers, and producers that have a proven track record and are comfortable working as part of a team produce better results. Contrary to the idea that development should be standardized or uniform, combining a variety of different skill sets and experiences, so-called cognitively heterogeneous groups, proves to be more successful. In a study of no fewer than 139,727 individuals who, throughout their careers over a thirty-year period in the industry, were part of 12,422 production teams, researchers found "teams are most likely to be creatively successful when their cognitively heterogeneous groups have points of intersection."

By bringing together people with different abilities and a willingness to collaborate, the chances of success increase. Critical acclaim originates from cohesive groups of people working together, which, in turn, requires access to a seasoned talent pool. The study's findings stand in opposition to the aforementioned myth of the lone genius. It concludes that "styles and skills become meaningful elements in the production of creativity when they are built, held, and adjusted by groups rather than individuals."[12]

Even so, not all jobs are valued in the same way. Common practices surrounding employment, work-life balance, and the general mobility of this workforce remain largely opaque and poorly understood. Motivated largely by the poor working conditions of creatives, a growing body of literature is bringing greater transparency to the nature of employment in this industry and the associated career prospects.[13] Based on a salary survey, it is clear that despite their visibility and impact on a creative vision, designers are hardly the highest paid people on a project. Producers have much better career prospects (see figure 2.3). This skews the distribution of talent. Many inexperienced people are at the bottom and a limited number of established senior people are on top. This reality forces studios to come up with creative solutions to attract the necessary talent.

A studio like Naughty Dog, for instance, prides itself on extremely high-quality productions like *Uncharted* and *The Last of Us*. Both successful franchises are worth hundreds of millions of dollars. The studio, however, is also known for its hellish crunch time—that is, the final stretch of work before a game's deadline during which developers work more than a hundred hours per week and regularly sleep at the office. In pursuit of

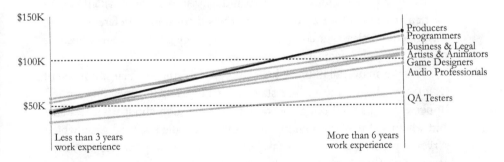

Figure 2.3
Roles and respective salaries at an average game studio. *Source*: Data from Game Developer's Tenth Annual Salary Survey, 2011. *Note*: Average salary in thousands U.S. dollars ($) with less than three and more than six years of work experience.

such high standards, the studio inevitably asks a lot from its people and therefore goes well beyond offering just salary.[14] In the case of Naughty Dog, the company prides itself on an unorthodox development process that excludes producers. By flattening the organizational structure, the studio gives people more input into the final product and a heightened sense of ownership. Instead of having to go through a layer of middle management, programmers can speak directly to lead designers to discuss additions and suggestions. To many of its employees, this trade-off between harsh work hours in the run-up to deliver a release and an increased sense of input on the final vision is a fair one.

Specifically, the ability of a team to come up with an innovative game idea, perform well over the course of the development process, and, finally, deliver on time, is critical. Next, experience with previous projects is often a minimum requirement, and having worked on a particular title or with a specific industry icon can raise one's professional profile substantially. Although approaches vary across different studios, successful development relies on putting together skilled, experienced people with different ideas, amidst a constantly evolving technological environment and changes in consumer demand.

In addition to hiring, a studio ensures that it does not commit to projects that it cannot deliver by using a gated process. On the basis of a specific evaluation, a developer decides to "open the gate" to the next stage to ensure the proper allocation of budget. This process safeguards against demand uncertainty because market conditions may change over the course of a creative process. A developer's full commitment to a project is necessary, of course, but also can be a strategic weakness as a large share of resources will be tied up toward completion. This process greatly reduces a studio's ability to make decisions on current industry information, which can be particularly hurtful for an organization when consumer preferences shift, a competitor releases a comparable offering, key design features become obsolete, or technological changes occur.

Despite an overall intuitive logic, this process still sees a large portion of its finances allocated to a single stage (see table 2.3). After spending around 10 percent of its total budget answering the question about what to make and whether it is worth making, it follows a so-called vertical slice, which serves as proof of concept for stakeholders before pulling the trigger on the remainder of the investment. This name is borrowed from the practice of analyzing each of the necessary components by taking a cross-sectional slice that can involve, for instance, the underlying database, the game's engine, and the user's interface. A vertical slice is often also a point of contention, as a developer might argue that the bulk of the work on playability does not

Table 2.3
Budget allocation in product-based game development

Stage	Objectives	Investment (cumulative %)
High-level game concept	Should we pursue this idea?	2
Concept	Do we pursue it further?	2–5
First playable	Is it worth making?	10
Vertical slice	Do we see this through?	20–25
Alpha	What needs to be done to deliver a beta version and optimize its chances of success?	60–70
Beta	How do we best position the game and optimize its chances of success?	>80

surface in the early stages of playable content. Nonetheless, it is a common part of the overall process in evaluating a title before spending the remaining 80 percent of budget on actually building and completing a game. Navigating these pitfalls pushes a studio to allocate its resources to see its project through to completion. It mitigates risk by establishing a particular talent mix to produce, hopefully, the necessary heterogeneity in effort and results.

Publishers

Publishers generally are responsible for marketing, financial analysis, capital investment, accounting, investor relations, human resources, information technology, operations, and other tasks that fall outside of the creative process. Consequently, this company type focuses its efforts on identifying scalable aspects in their business and cost reduction. Traditionally, development cycles for blockbuster titles are similar in expense and time needed to those for Hollywood film productions and, according to Dmitri Williams, have "elements found in both the prerecorded videocassette and book publishing industries."[15] This commits an organization to a capital-intensive, long-term investment.

Publishers formulate specific strategies to deal with the challenges specific to their role. Electronic Arts, for instance, has managed to obtain licenses to many of the major sports franchises, which has allowed it to reduce demand uncertainty and make annual sales more predictable. Activision Blizzard, in contrast, focuses on a range of different titles across genres. Its broad approach allows it to leverage its intellectual property and release titles across categories, thereby maximizing its addressable audience and spreading risk across a diverse portfolio (see table 2.4). Publishers struggle with de-risking their portfolio, on one hand, and correctly identifying and aggressively investing in a potential breakout hit, on the other.

Further exacerbating a publisher's risk is the constantly growing cost of developing for newer hardware. Partially negating the increase in consumer spending that comes with every new console generation, hardware increases in sophistication and, therefore, in cost. This ultimately amounts to an entry barrier to newcomers and presents a benefit for incumbents.

Large-scale publishing is costly. Game makers are forced into investing a growing amount of capital into their efforts for several reasons. Publishers sign distribution agreements with retailers long before a title is finished. To reserve premium shelf space and gain favor from retail partners—of which there are but a few, as we'll discuss later—publishers incur a lot of expenses, sometimes years before a release. This expense forces them into a hard deadline. Because development at this scale takes years, it is virtually impossible to complete a project exactly as planned. In the final stages of development, a publisher spends a lot of extra money on overtime and hiring additional staff to meet the deadline.

Table 2.4
Titles released by publisher over five years

Title	Franchise	Release Date	Budget	Delay (months)	Metacritic Score	Return on Investment
1	A	2011	130%	12	89	40%
2	New	2012	100%	3	80	20%
3	B	2012	150%	18	80	−30%
4	C	2013	130%	12	86	50%
5	New	2014	130%	12	70	4%
6	C	2015	120%	0	86	—
7	B	2016	120%	12	—	—
8	A	2016	130%	12	—	—

Source: Overview provided by a top-ten worldwide game publisher and anonymized on request.

Note: This table illustrates how publishers rationalize their release schedules and how they might allocate resources. For instance, over the course of five years, this publisher released eight titles in total, only two of which were new intellectual property (titles 2 and 5). All other titles are part of an existing franchise and have a significantly higher Metacritic score (on average 85) than the newly release properties (80 and 70, respectively). Note also that the titles here are on average no less than 10 months late to release and 26% over budget. In fact, only one title's finances were correctly anticipated (title 2), and only one title was released on time (title 6). Finally, title 4 showed the highest return on investment, and the publisher here sought to take advantage of this momentum by quickly releasing a follow-up within two years.

Perhaps the biggest driver of capital risk is the increasing development costs for each new hardware generation in combination with relative price inelasticity. The cost of development and research for a title during the 128-bit generation, for example, was around $750,000. In the following cycle, this had gone up to just under $3 million, and for the hardware generation after that, an average title cost around $20 million to produce.[16] Because the price a consumer is willing to pay at retail for a new release has not increased at the same pace, publishers have had to adjust their strategy and limit the number of titles they release. With fewer shots on goal, the chances of a big win decline. To build a blockbuster franchise, especially in a hit-driven business like gaming, companies necessarily have to invest more money into fewer titles. This investment increases their risk and reduces the time frame within which they can recoup their cost, forcing them to spend even more on marketing to maximize pre-release exposure.

Part of the effort to create buzz around a release, particularly for those that need to sell as many copies as possible in a shortening time frame. As publishers seek to maximize consumer awareness in the lead-up to their title's release date, hoping to reduce demand uncertainty, they are forced into spending a substantial amount of money on marketing. This conundrum is not new or unique to the games business, as the amount of promotional activity continues to be a key indicator for a title's potential success.[17] Publishers may use tactics from parallel entertainment industries. Book publishers, for instance, deliberately put out a large number of copies in an attempt to bolster perceived success.[18] For this reason, it is important to note the difference between "sell-in" and "sell-through," which indicates the actual number of units sold to a channel (e.g., a store) and the number of units sold to consumers, respectively. Eager to create hype around a new release, publishers are keen on issuing press statements that give the impression of having achieved a higher level of success than actually has been achieved. A week after *Call of Duty: Black Ops II* came out, Activision Blizzard issued a press statement that it had "achieved an estimated sell-through of more than $500 million worldwide in the first 24 hours of its release."[19] Such a tactic usually is employed by organizations to assuage the concerns of retail partners and, in the case of publicly traded publisher, to satisfy shareholders with regard to a game's success.

Risk mitigation is quite literally baked into a publisher's organizational structure. Because success relies on a careful configuration of talent management, intellectual property inventory, and capital allocation, large companies establish several layers, as illustrated in figure 2.4. At the creative end, a large studio employs a string of studios and assigns each a specific project. This facilitates a broad base of resources that each work more or less independently and have the ability to develop a specialization. Once one studio has finished, for example, a large blockbuster production, it may hand it off to another studio to develop the release on mobile.

At the next layer are content-specific labels. Much like you'd expect to find in the music industry, labels specialize in particular genres and content types. This specialization is valuable when the label goes to market and seeks to garner attention and feedback from gatekeepers. It does so, for example, by building a brand around its sports capabilities, which improves its ability to establish deeper relationships with distributors, marketers, retailers, and other relevant industry parties. Instead of releasing a single new title every once in a while, a label can offer its industry partners a slate of content. Generally, this is a preferred approach because it allows retailers, to plan their entire inventory a year in advance. And the label is in a better position to negotiate on prices and perks.

Finally, at the corporate level, an organization offers a range of services and a uniform reporting structure. This helps a single senior team of decision-makers determine which projects are on time, over budget, in need of additional resources, and so on. This layer also allows for greater transparency to investors. The core objective of this layer is to identify efficiencies across the entire organization in addition to providing the necessary capital resources and management.

This structure, of course, also poses challenges. Keeping each of these components separate is key but may not always be feasible. The people and

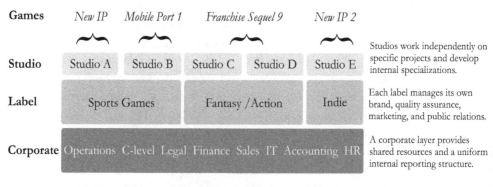

Figure 2.4

Corporate structure of a large publisher. *Source*: Data from notes provided by David Edwards, former Senior Director, Sales Strategy at Take-Two Interactive.

company culture at one layer may be quite different from another. These differences can create friction. Or, as one studio producer told me after the corporate office had moved to another office address: "We were working overtime to get our game done, and the corporate team was having summer Fridays." Despite such challenges, this layered approach is how large publishers seek to offset risk and retain control over their output and ability to leverage economies of scale.

Publishers represent a distinct type of company in the conventional value chain. As the intermediary between creatives and consumers, publishers as we know them today did not emerge until the early 1980s. One firm, in particular, laid the groundwork for product-based publishing: Electronic Arts.

Trip Hawkins was twenty-nine years old when he first founded Amazing Software in 1982. After raising $2 million in funding, college buddy Bing Gordon joined to pursue what they believed to be the future of the interactive entertainment business. The firm would go on to generate billions of dollars in revenue and to define the role of publishers by combining three key components: making game designers into celebrities, establishing a dedicated sales force, and building economies of scale.

At the time, developers were mostly small outfits that tinkered in their garages and dealt directly with console manufacturers. Once a title was completed, designers took it to a platform holder and, hopefully, persuaded them to add the title to the inventory. The crash had not yet hit, games were in demand, and there was plenty of money going around. Hawkins, however, felt that video games were a form of art similar to novels and films, and subsequently, that they deserved to be developed and marketed in the same way. As a teenager, Hawkins had started a company around a football board game but was forced to shut it down as a result of inexperience. In an interview, he laid out the crux of what would later become the foundation of his publishing strategy: "I didn't have enough capital and I had to shut it down. I realized I didn't know enough about business, but this is really exciting, and I want to do it again."[20] To learn more, the aspiring developer joined Apple and eventually became a marketing executive there. Unfortunately, due to a growing frustration in this role, resulting from the fledgling tech firm not fully recognizing the cultural gravitas of games, which "were not a big deal," Hawkins set out to start a company more in line with this vision."[21]

Fundamental in Hawkins's approach was the idea that games needed active promotion and distribution. In an industry that was largely commodified and saturated with indistinguishable titles, quality standards were low, as were consumer expectations. Moreover, software developers were mostly unseen and unknown. Hawkins, however, recognized that audiences would buy from specific creators much in the same way as well-known producers and authors sold movies and books. In his view, celebrity designers were the key to selling a title: "Since a computer game customer isn't pre-sold before he walks into a store the way a record customer is, it puts pressure on brilliant marketing."[22]

To emphasize this approach, Hawkins changed the name of his company from Amazing Software to Electronic Arts, inspired by the Hollywood studio United Artists. He also de-emphasized the software component and instead drew attention to the creativity involved. Software had become a catchall term that did not really allow creative firms to distinguish themselves. Whereas before computer programmers were salaried workers, the shift Hawkins observed was fundamental: "Now that each author can do the whole program himself, he is more like a novelist or a rock star."[23]

In addition to celebrating developers as rock stars, the firm also started to actively sell its titles, and in 1984, Electronic Arts established a dedicated sales force to bypass the incumbent distributors. At the time, these companies marketed interactive entertainment to retail channels but did so as part of a large inventory of different content from different firms. The existing process was perpendicular to the blockbuster strategy as it allowed the publisher no control over the promotion of its titles and forced it to share the spotlight with many others. In response, Electronic Arts made it a priority to sell its titles directly to retailers. By establishing its own sales force, the firm was able to push its upcoming releases at retailers and build excitement.

Adding titles from other creative organizations was the third and next logical step and launched EA Affiliated Labels to identify, curate, and add additional games to its offering. It allowed the company to build long-term relationships with retailers. For a publisher, having efficient distribution relationships was key. Retailers (as I will discuss later) provide a critical function in spreading the word about upcoming titles and helping build excitement around new releases. But they also will do anything to drive traffic to their stores. Having a prolific publisher ensure that their shelves were full of new titles meant they always had something exciting to announce. Notably, Electronic Arts even helped organize celebrity appearances to drive traffic to stores and quickly won a lot of favor and could count on preferential treatment (and better rates!) as it negotiated sales orders.

Since then, many other publishers have adapted a similar model. Games have come to adopt a development cycle that is similar to that of Hollywood films and that commits creative firms to a capital-intensive, long-term investment. To offset this obvious capital risk, publishers tend to rely on a portfolio of titles that provides a regular release schedule to maintain a constant stream of income and mitigates risk by allowing them to analyze the relative success of each individual title and to greenlight, or not, potential sequels. A typical publisher portfolio looks like those shown in table 2.4. Many titles go over budget and run into delays, but not all of them provide the same financial return. A publisher generally will try to increase the predictability of its portfolio's performance by investing in new intellectual property and expanding its existing portfolio. For Electronic Arts, an obvious example is the success it has had with sports games and releasing a new edition of its *FIFA* and *Madden NFL* games every year.

Inevitable in such a capital-intensive model is the need for scale. By the early 1990s, it was shipping around one hundred titles annually, and Electronic Arts started to acquire competitors and look for efficiencies in its organization. Over the course of several years, the firm acquired a slew of firms, including Distinctive Software in 1991, which was known for its titles *Test Drive* and *FIFA International Soccer*; ORIGIN Systems in 1992, known for *Ultima*; Bullfrog Productions in 1995, creator of *Theme Park*; Maxis in 1997 for its now well-known franchises *SimCity* and *The Sims*; Tiburon Entertainment in 1998 for *NCAA Football* and *Madden NFL*; Westwood Studios in 1998 for *Command & Conquer*; and finally DreamWorks Interactive in 2000 for *Medal of Honor*.

The result of this blockbuster approach by Electronic Arts changed the industry in multiple aspects. First, and most important, it firmly cemented North America as the dominant market. Since the crash, Japanese organizations had both manufactured the consoles (Nintendo, Sega, Sony) and made the games (Bandai, Capcom, Konami, Namco, Square Enix). With the emergence of the blockbuster publishers like Electronic Arts and its Activision Blizzard, THQ, Take-Two, and (to a degree) Ubisoft, North America had become an equal to Japan.

Second, it redistributed market power across the value chain. As we discussed earlier, throughout the 1980s, Nintendo pursued a strategy of vertical integration as a central strategic component. To maximize the sales of its hardware, Nintendo ensured that at the release of every new console, a new *Mario* and a *Zelda* title would drive demand. Through its ownership of first-party studios, Nintendo controlled the lion's share of the market, which forced creative firms to agree to its terms. To get out from under the monopoly held by Nintendo, Electronic Arts backed Sega. By creating demand for their own games, Electronic Arts and other third-party publishers gained leverage and ultimately forced platform holders to collaborate.

Among the legacy firms (see table 2.5), in 1998, first-party content accounted for a little over eight billion dollars, or about 62 percent of total

Table 2.5

Legacy publisher earnings based on worldwide publishing revenue, 1998–2018

	1998	1999	2000	2001	2002	2003	2004	2005	2006
Sony	6,187	6,376	6,158	5,817	6,487	6,887	7,046	6,237	6,772
Activision Blizzard								780	1,108
Activision	432	584	597	748	904	910	1,365	1,484	1,389
Vivendi				1,789	2,137	1,125	848	809	927
Microsoft	179	219	238	537	1,085	1,251	1,292	1,568	2,164
Electronic Arts	1,148	1,403	1,309	1,562	2,489	2,822	3,173	2,864	3,119
Nintendo	1,744	1,876	1,376	1,766	1,928	2,413	2,118	1,896	2,992
Take-Two Interactive	211	358	403	574	923	998	1,255	964	1,050
Square Enix	195	196	347	194	178	448	812	695	1,500
Eidos	338	323	259	148	87	252	166	169	170
Ubisoft						752	852	815	1,010
Bandai Namco					432	501	604	640	896	916
Konami	397	642	717	778	1,073	1,282	1,250	1,093	1,185
Capcom	336	340	310	439	509	564	546	605	602
Sega Sammy					338	95	1,584	1,139	1,127
Disney			240	385		366	392	332	342
AT&T									
WB Games									
Koei Tecmo	93	94	84	75	91	102	127	104	98
Majesco						58	127	51	60
THQ Inc.	217	304	347	379	481	585	708	830	1,003
Midway Games	407	391	249	116	192	93	162	150	166
Acclaim Ent.	339	427	160	207	251	bankrupt			
Total Legacy revenue	13,030	14,275	13,173	16,378	20,192	22,096	24,843	23,555	27,581
C1	47%	45%	47%	36%	32%	31%	28%	26%	25%
C4	74%	72%	73%	67%	65%	61%	56%	53%	55%
C10	91%	90%	90%	88%	89%	86%	84%	81%	81%
HHI	2,594	2,355	2,493	1,689	1,516	1,429	1,249	1,140	1,084
No. of firms > 1%	15	15	15	15	14	16	16	17	16

Source: Author's compilations based on company reports.

Note: Legacy refers to companies whose primary business activity initially centered on a product-based publishing model, often in combination with an almost-exclusive focus on console game publishing. Numbers shown are revenues in millions of U.S. dollars ($) from games publishing activities only and include both revenue from physical and digital channels (e.g., mobile, downloadable PC, and console, microtransactions). Numbers shown exclude revenues from other divisions, such as amusement machine sales, animation, motion pictures, and comic books, as reported in company earnings. Total Legacy Revenue is total revenue from all

2007	2008	2009	2010	2011	2012	2013	2014	2015	2016	2017	2018
8,047	8,999	7,545	9,016	8,414	7,682	7,224	6,792	5,103	6,468	8,373	10,191
1,349	3,026	4,279	4,447	4,755	4,856	4,583	4,408	4,664	6,608	7,017	7,500
2,608	Activision Blizzard										
1,108	Activision Blizzard										
2,759	2,519	2,464	2,455	3,646	3,620	3,195	3,889	4,104	4,228	4,165	5,518
3,150	4,480	3,535	3,478	3,865	3,956	3,575	4,515	4,396	4,845	5,150	4,950
6,172	9,184	7,017	5,749	4,361	3,228	2,017	2,109	2,135	1,833	1,921	4,382
945	1,446	982	1,287	860	1,063	2,455	978	1,083	1,414	1,780	2,668
1,382	1,508	1,801	1,911	1,596	1,560	1,404	1,431	1,679	2,266	2,265	2,357
172	218	Square Enix									
1,509	1,517	1,254	1,344	1,356	1,548	1,568	1,611	1,402	1,647	1,954	2,289
1,037	1,215	1,057	1,182	1,396	1,392	1,200	1,145	1,209	1,277	1,413	1,572
1,298	1,702	1,433	1,599	1,717	1,338	1,055	908	1,005	1,138	1,047	1,090
687	868	1,017	1,080	1,004	1,208	919	624	612	688	778	769
1,041	1,174	1,089	1,262	1,294	841	995	861	808	792	836	745
366	764	724	769	861	741	782	938	885	862	754	726
											343
	37	100	200	300	464	297	132	706	210	372	AT&T
108	131	286	371	386	432	368	365	315	340	330	336
55	78	91	95	143	90	46	16	4	bankrupt		
1,016	847	872	739	771	bankrupt						
157	bankrupt										
34,894	**40,829**	**35,653**	**37,104**	**36,895**	**34,180**	**31,950**	**31,011**	**30,355**	**34,884**	**38,462**	**45,750**
23%	22%	21%	24%	23%	22%	23%	22%	17%	19%	19%	22%
58%	63%	63%	61%	58%	58%	58%	63%	60%	60%	63%	62%
84%	87%	88%	88%	88%	88%	88%	89%	88%	88%	91%	93%
1,157	1,301	1,224	1,216	1,138	1,135	1,119	1,176	1,013	1,121	1,162	1,156
16	15	14	14	15	15	14	14	17	15	15	15

legacy firms in the entire available data set for this project and not just the companies shown in this table. The measures C1, C4, and C10 indicate the total market share held by the top-one, -four, and -ten firms, respectively, throughout the twenty-year period. HHI calculated for group total only to illustrate relative distribution of market power among legacy firms.

consumer spending. By 2018, revenue earned from the publishing activities controlled by manufacturers was down to 44 percent. This redistribution of market power allowed the industry to grow as revenue generated by third-party game makers from that period increased roughly tenfold over the course of the 1990s. In this expanding ecosystem, a broader group of companies held creative control and allowed dedicated publishers to creative value. By elevating the making of games to an art and treating designers as creative talent instead of engineers, Electronic Arts changed the way the industry produced games forever.

Whether we talk about Nintendo's unique platform strategy that revitalized the market, the different approaches studios take to hire talent, or the formulation of blockbuster releases as first deployed by Electronic Arts, the interactive entertainment industry knows a rich history of business model innovation. Success, in other words, requires formulating a creative business strategy in addition to making great games. As the market for entertainment began to shift, this innate ability of prioritizing strategy and content creation equally would prove to be immeasurably valuable. Before delving deeper into the changes brought about by digitalization, let's first check in with gaming retail.

3

Empire on the Edge of the Volcano

As the final component of the traditional product-based business, we find retailers—that is, the brick-and-mortar stores that sell boxed games, console hardware, and accessories. Most notably in industrial economies, retailers historically have played an important role in marketing and distribution. As consumers have started to embrace the practice of downloading content directly onto their devices, however, the role of physical stores has started to change. None more so than the specialty retail chain GameStop.

The predicament of a retailer having to adapt to an increasingly digital environment is not unique to games. Several high-profile bankruptcies can be found in the parallel universes of the music and toy industries. For years, music retailer Tower Records was a hugely popular destination. Started in an empty warehouse in San Francisco, the store's unique approach consisted of offering a huge selection at low prices, hiring cool and hip youngsters as its staff, and successfully associating itself with up and coming artists. It provided the store with a distinct aura that had an irresistible appeal to music fans. Tower Record's initial success cemented a company culture in which the shared enjoyment of music played a more prominent role than generating revenue. Even as vinyl gave way to the music CD, Tower Records adapted to the new market circumstances. But, eventually, its empire came undone once consumers moved onto digital distribution services. First illegally, in the form of Napster, and later legally, in the form of digital distributors like iTunes, audiences became accustomed to buying individual songs rather than entire albums. Known as unbundling, these online services allowed consumers to purchase individual songs rather than an entire album and proved devastating for music retailing. Unable to formulate a strategy to negate the effects of digitalization, Tower Records saw its income decline as music publishers relented and adopted new ways to reach listeners over the internet. After more than four decades of success, Tower Records filed for bankruptcy in 2006.

Toy store chain Toys "R" Us suffered a comparable fate. The economics of the toy industry are similar. Success in this industry, too, is hit driven and capital intensive. Firms like Hasbro and Mattel generally spend several years between the initial work of designing a new toy, conducting research and initial testing, and then marketing the toy before finally bringing it to market. These firms also rely heavily on existing intellectual property and are tied to a strongly seasonal sales cycle. All of this predictably adds up to an industry that is heavily consolidated and relies on economies of scale. How close retail businesses are to bankruptcy is best illustrated by the unexpected popularity of fidget spinners in the summer of 2017. Incumbent toy makers and their retail partners were caught off guard as a seemingly innocuous toy grew into the must-have item of the season. The combination of fidget spinners being cheap to produce, requiring no license to make or sell, and benefiting from unprecedented free promotion from a generation of teens and tweens that took to social media, resulted in the conventional toy retailers failing to capitalize on the success. For Toys "R" Us, this set the stage for several of its majority shareholders to pull the plug and force the firm to file for bankruptcy.

In both the music and toy business, a digital competitor emerged for every physical store. The rise of online video services like Netflix, with its offering of an unlimited buffet of television shows and movies, contributed to the decline and ultimate bankruptcy of Blockbuster. And the rise of e-commerce and online shopping brought smaller consumer electronic chains like RadioShack to their knees. Collectively, this has created a commonly shared narrative of physical retail declining as digital distribution and its associated earnings models have continued to rise in popularity. Across categories, entertainment retail has suffered noticeably as consumers have moved to digital distribution. Where other specialty retailers have been forced to close their doors, however, GameStop has continued to play an important role in the way games are marketed and sold. Even so, online alternatives have grown significantly in popularity. This continued growth raises the question how GameStop has managed to hold out for as long as it has compared with its cousins elsewhere. To answer this question, we first look at how GameStop managed to become the dominant games retailer.

GameStop is a retail chain with 5,500 stores across fourteen countries that specializes in interactive entertainment and generates $8 billion in annual revenue. Founded in 1984, the same year the market for video games collapsed, two Harvard Business School graduates opened a software retail store that would later, after a series of acquisitions, bankruptcies, and spin-offs, become GameStop.

During its first fifteen years, the company went through a string of acquisitions and reorganizations. At the same time the industry spent most of the late 1980s and early 1990s recovering. Total income grew to around $500 million in 1995, but then it flatlined for a few years. This brought bookseller Barnes & Noble's (B&N) to acquire it for $215 million in 1999 and subsequently merge it with regional retailer, Funco. Unfortunately, B&N saw itself forced to offload some of its secondary assets in response to the dotcom burst and determined that the synergies it had expected between games and its other categories were insufficient. In 2004, it spun off GameStop.

Even as the supply side struggled, demand had fully recovered. Further fueled by Microsoft's push behind the Xbox 360 in 2005 and the launch of the Nintendo Wii in 2006, GameStop doubled its revenue to $3 billion within just two years following its divestiture. With fat pockets and its newfound independence, management started expanding its retail footprint. It acquired its most prominent rival Electronics Boutique, in addition to buying Rhino Video Games from Blockbuster and a French games retailer called Micromania. It expanded its total number of locations from 1,038 to 5,264 in just six years, and by 2012, the retailer had managed to increase the average earnings per store by more than 37 percent compared with when it still was a B&N subsidiary.[1]

The popularity of video games had not escaped other retailers. Walmart, Target, and Best Buy all emerged as rivals for the growing category. Between 1999 and 2013, Walmart's share of physical games sales grew from 17 percent to 25 percent, Target's share grew from 6 percent to 15 percent, and Best Buy held steady at around 13 percent for the period.[2] As top retailers grew their economies of scale by aggressively competing on price and distribution, smaller market participants began to struggle. Movie Gallery, and its subsidiaries Hollywood and GameCrazy, which had been the number-two specialty retailer following the GameStop–Electronics Boutique merger, exited the business. Accelerating consolidation also eroded the overall strength of toy and tech retailers like Blockbuster, KB Toys, CompUSA, and Circuit City. Remarkably, Toys "R" Us continued the sale of both hardware and software, including M-rated content, and remained a viable retailer for brands like Nintendo, Warner Bros., and Lego, until it filed for bankruptcy in 2018. Finally, online retailer Amazon entered the business around 2007, and by 2013, held a 7 percent share. In a few years' time, physical retail had transitioned from a relatively unconcentrated market structure with a Herfindahl–Hirschman index (HHI) of 936 in 1999 to moderate concentration with an HHI of 1,932 by 2013 (see figure 3.1).

To compete with these massive retailers, GameStop formulated a strategy that others could not follow. It developed a clever business model around a deep specialization for consumers that rests on several strategic components. Knowing all too well that its younger customers depend on a parent or adult to drive them to a shopping center, GameStop first ensured that multiple storefronts were located within proximity to their average consumers. Often, several GameStops are located inside a single shopping center. Sheer ubiquity is a key differentiator. To a degree, this was a by-product of its acquisition spree as its footprint overlapped largely with Electronics Boutique. Having a pervasive presence removed any physical constraints and enabled potential customers to easily find a local store.

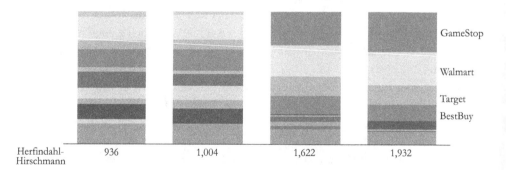

| Herfindahl-Hirschmann | 936 | 1,004 | 1,622 | 1,932 |

Figure 3.1
Games retail market structure based on U.S. share of console and PC software sales, 1999, 2002, 2007, 2013. *Source*: Data from Michael Pachter, Nick McKay, and Nick Citrin, "Post Hoc Ergo Propter Hoc: Why the Next Generation Will Be as Big as Ever" (Equity Research, Wedbush Securities, February 12, 2014).

The retailer's emphasis on accessibility goes further. If you've ever been to a GameStop store you probably have noticed that it has a ramp. This has less to do with being wheelchair accessible and more with parents pushing strollers. Because they generally control the purse strings, GameStop redesigned its storefronts to accommodate this demographic and to allow for a convenient entry as parents made their way into what was otherwise a store that appealed to young boys. For that same reason, aisles are wide enough to easily navigate a stroller and put parents at ease.[3]

GameStop's store-clerk training program is a second strategic innovation. Employees train extensively so that they can answer any questions customers might have about titles, accessories, or hardware and can make recommendations. This creates value in several ways. For one, it provides transparency. Most people own only one console, which means they have to make a decision on what to buy. Because hardware manufacturers compete on exclusive titles, advising customers in the store goes a long way toward market efficiency and customer loyalty as they contemplate purchases. This approach counts doubly so for people who are making purchases for others. (I recall my mother persistently referring to any and every type of gaming device as a Nintendo. This invariably triggered a gentle panic right before a birthday or holiday causing my brother and me to fear our parents would come home with the latest release for the wrong console and thus our having to wait until stores reopened to exchange it. But I digress.) In this regard, GameStop differs dramatically from a Walmart or Target in that the latter generally has no one available in the store to make recommendations or provide any such advice.

Its expert sales force is another important source of leverage with publishers and platform holders. Clerks play a critical role in consumer education and marketing, which allows GameStop to instruct its staff to push one device over another. It gives the retailer bargaining power during negotiations with Sony, Microsoft, and Nintendo as well as with the major game makers as they all compete over unit sales. Its thousands of stores function as a single marketing channel catering to shoppers who are looking for games and is valuable for publishers. By this positioning, GameStop has been able to price the various components of its marketing reach (e.g., in-store, online, in-ad, store clerks) and to generate additional revenue.

GameStop's aggressive loyalty program is a third part of its strategy with different components. GameStop offers a card program that gives you discounts on purchases for $10 a year. It also allows you to reserve titles on sale and serves as a marketing channel. This approach reduces demand uncertainty across its stores and establishes more accurate inventory

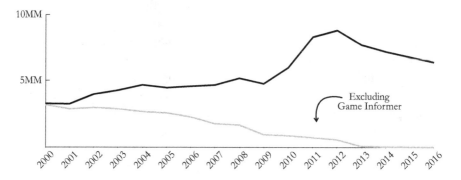

Figure 3.2
Gaming magazines, annual circulation (millions), United States and United Kingdom, 2000–2016. *Source*: Data from Alliance for Audited Media, RetroMags. *Note*: Total circulation both with and excluding GameStop's *Game Informer* magazine.

management. GameStop also distributes a monthly magazine called *Game Informer* that features articles about and reviews of the latest titles. It is free for members of its paid loyalty program. This is an important component: GameStop has subsidized the magazine's circulation for the better part of the past two decades, resulting in *Game Informer* becoming the fourth-largest consumer magazine in the United States. Understandably, circulation for print magazines has declined because consumers now have more ways to learn about new titles. The ascension of gaming video content services like Twitch have come to play an integral part of these novel marketing channels and provide a new way for consumers to determine where to spend their money and time (see chapter 9). Figure 3.2 shows that GameStop is single-handedly responsible for the lion's share of overall gaming magazine circulation.

Establishing a strong relationship with its customer base is a natural approach for a specialty retailer. But GameStop's most pronounced innovation and strongest strategic differentiator is its buy-sell-trade program. Unlike its peers, GameStop offers customers the ability to re-sell any titles they previously purchased in exchange for in-store credit. This option reduces consumer risk and increases in-store traffic.[4] It also has become a tremendous revenue driver. Given that a retailer will fetch roughly 20 percent of the purchase price of a new release (see table 3.1), the economics of used sales break down as follows. At the initial transaction, a consumer pays $60, of which the retailer keeps $12 and the publisher receives $24. The moment a customer comes back to re-sell the game, GameStop pays them,

Table 3.1

Traditional value chain participants and revenue share from a $60 game

	Example	Role	Share	Value
Developer	Rockstar Studios	Design, writing, programming	20%	$12
Publisher	Take-Two Interactive	Capital, legal, marketing	40%	$24
Platform	Microsoft, Sony, Nintendo	Hardware manufacturing	15%	$9
Distributor	GT Interactive, Koch Media	Transport, storage	5%	$3
Retailer	GameStop, Best Buy, Walmart	Sales channel, marketing	20%	$12

Source: Author's compilation.

Note: Numbers are averages and vary depending on arrangements made among the different types of value chain participants. A platform holder, for instance, may offer lower licensing fees to a publisher in exchange for temporary exclusivity of a specific title. Similarly, a retailer may offer a price discount on hardware to draw foot traffic to its stores in exchange for more prominent in-store display for hardware manufacturers.

for instance, $25 in store credit. As the next person now buys the same title a second time, the retailer sells it for a reduced price of $55. This allows to both offer a better price than other stores (which are still selling brand new copies) and, more important, keep 100 percent of the selling price. Add to this that a popular game is sold and re-sold on average five times over, and you get the earnings structure shown in table 3.2.

To distinguish itself from competition, GameStop had to develop three distinct sales capabilities. First, selling used titles requires keeping two sets of accounting books. Specifically, one for new games, including their price and cost, and one for used inventory, including their price and cost. To do this at scale quickly becomes a complex task especially across thousands of storefronts, and consequently, requires a dedicated staff that tracks and sets prices for the entire available catalogue of titles. For nonspecialty retailers it is inefficient to establish a separate accounting structure specifically for re-selling games because it would amount to only a small fraction of the total number of products they sell in their stores.

Second, controlling inventory of preowned titles is different from regular inventory. Trade-in values constantly diminish, and it is difficult to control the in-take volume of used games. Anticipating the balance between demand and supply is complex enough even when you have control over the number of units you allocate to each store. This is doubly so when you do not, as in the case of secondhand sales. It is difficult to know with certainty

Table 3.2
Used game sales revenue for a $60 title

Sale/Trade-In	GameStop	Publisher	Consumer
New sale	+12	+24	−60
First trade-in	−25	+0	+25
First re-sale	+55	+0	−55
Second	−20	+0	+20
	+50	+0	−50
Third	−15	+0	+15
	+45	+0	−45
Fourth	−10	+0	+10
	+40	+0	−40
Fifth	−5	+0	+5
	+35	+0	−35
Net	**162**	**+24**	**−210**

Source: Author's compilation.

Note: This model assumes that an average blockbuster title starts at $60 and is sold and re-sold up to five times. Every time GameStop sells a title again to a different consumer, it optimizes between offering the lowest possible value for the seller and highest possible price for the next buyer.

which titles consumers will be looking to sell back and which titles will create demand. This process requires a dedicated inventory system.

Third, to best facilitate thousands of used-game sales, the transaction must be made as easy as possible for both the store clerk and the person looking to trade. As one executive explained it to me, "Transactions must be simple, seamless and meaningless on both sides of the counter." Clerks must be able to quickly navigate this process across thousands of titles for lots of different hardware platforms, and customers must be offered complete transparency with regard to the process and the credit they receive in return. This is a practice that works only with a dedicated effort. To that end, to ensure that it has a healthy inventory of secondhand games available, GameStop offers a higher in-store credit value than payout price on a title to incentivize customers to spend their money at the store rather than elsewhere. Because no retailers have been willing to invest to this extent, GameStop's used sales logistics benefit from positive network effects: the more people resell games, the greater its inventory and ability to manage this inventory effectively. GameStop's used sales program strengthens its existing efforts to establish customer loyalty. The firm realized that in addition to catering to players, targeting parents with their trade-in program was equally important as heads of household. A former GameStop executive explained this me, "Parents often noticed the stacks of unplayed games littering the house while vacuuming, and we used that realization to offer them an incentive to trade those unused games for in-store credit."

Competitors like Walmart and Best Buy have tried to replicate the success by launching their own trade-in programs.[5] But after pioneering the practice and making it synonymous with its name, GameStop was established as the most popular destination for trade-ins. This approach has proven to be immensely beneficial, providing the retailer with a large inventory of competitively priced titles that drive traffic to its stores. Moreover, after six transactions, it earns around $160 in net earnings from one and the same copy compared with but $24 for the publisher. These earnings offset the growing pressure on margins, which have declined from 30 to 20 percent over the past decade. Consequently, trade-in revenue accounts for a quarter of annual earnings.

Unsurprisingly, GameStop is aggressive with this practice: used games often are available within just days of the release of a new title, and the retailer has no reservations about placing used copies side-by-side with new ones. It does not need much explanation that publishers are less thrilled as they face an ongoing increase in costs. The advances in technological sophistication of dedicated gaming hardware has forced average selling prices to go up. According to Raph Koster, a well-known designer who looked at the rising costs of development for more than 250 different titles over a period of thirty years: "Costs on average go up around 10 times every ten years."[6] Even if we assume some discrepancy based on incomplete data, expenses for creative firms rise much faster than their ability to charge money from customers. According to Koster's findings, the cost of console development was sixteen times higher in 2016 compared with 2000, yet the average selling price increased by factor of only 0.7, from $29 to $44 (see figure 3.3). GameStop's re-seller program further exacerbates this trend because it offers a cheaper alternative for customers. Putting trade-in copies front and center in its stores shortens the length of time during which titles can command their full price. The practice negatively affects a publisher's ability to recoup its initial investment and make a profit. It invariably forces game makers to increase their marketing spend to persuade as many people as possible to buy a release immediately at launch. This further depresses margins by driving up costs and increases overall risk as multiple competitors seek to drive momentum for their titles simultaneously. Consequently, publishers need to sell more copies just to break even and make a profit. Over time, the threshold of what it means to have a successful title has gone up and many millions copies need to be sold before it can be considered a hit and a commercial success.[7]

With this shorter earnings window, the interests of game makers and the retailer are clearly at odds. Of course, GameStop has no interest in completely souring its relationship with publishers. To placate them, it also offers a preorder program that allows customers to reserve an upcoming title before launch to secure their copy. The practice mitigates capital risk because it reduces demand uncertainty and a more efficient rollout. Often, both publisher and retailer will mention the success of a preorder program in their earnings calls to indicate the immanent success. Preorders generate additional income as game makers purchase shelf space in the trade-in section to persuade customers to use their in-store credit for new games. Publishers fill shelves with empty boxes of their upcoming games to promote sales even further.

GameStop is a good example of an organization that has managed to outperform its peers by innovating its business model. Despite heavy competition from large retailers throughout North America and Europe, it cemented its position as the largest and most important retail relationship for publishers. In addition to acquiring many other chains to expand its

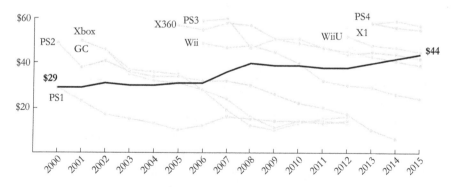

Figure 3.3
U.S. selling price for console games by platform, 2000–2015. *Source*: Data from Wedbush Securities. *Note*: Excludes handhelds. Weighted average selling price highlighted.

footprint over the years, GameStop also developed an ingenious strategy that combines expert staff, a heavily subsidized loyalty program, and an aggressive trade-in program. But no strategy is flawless: the popularization of online shopping and digital downloads over the past decade presents a new challenge.

Today, GameStop sits at the center of a debate on how digitalization is changing the retail entertainment market. The bankruptcies of comparable chains like Blockbuster, Toys "R" Us, and Tower Records suggests that GameStop's empire may soon, too, start to crumble. In 2019, it lost more than half of its share price after it failed to find a buyer and started to stumble as the industry initiated its transition to a new generation of console hardware and cloud gaming began to emerge. It now faces three predominant threats to its business model. Considering GameStop's relatively low percentage of sales volume through its online store, the meteoric rise of Amazon should be of particular concern. This growing popularity of online retail is a first threat. With even greater scale and a formidable distribution system, the online retailer has managed to chip away at GameStop and other brick-and-mortar businesses. Despite GameStop's investment in optimizing its back-end logistics, it is no match for Amazon's scale. Moreover, retailers always fight over margins, or, as Amazon's CEO Jeff Bezos is fond of saying, "Your margin is my opportunity." Considering that GameStop historically tends to sacrifice its margin on new game sales to draw traffic to its stores, it has little wiggle room left to compete, especially if consumers are willing to delay their gratification and wait an extra day or two to receive their order. By and large, the expectation among industry observers is that GameStop is destined for decline purely because internet-based businesses are more efficient, especially when they are called Amazon.

Second, digital sales gradually have become more important to publishers than physical sales. Organizations like Electronic Arts, Activision Blizzard, and Take-Two Interactive have long made up GameStop's most valuable industry relations. Their businesses have shifted away from physical unit sales at retail and toward direct downloads and microtransactions. According to their earnings reports, combined digital revenue for these three firms increased from 23 percent in early 2014 to 77 percent by mid-2019. As physical retail erodes as a relevant sales channel, it weakens GameStop's ability to charge more for desirable store placement and to capture an equal share of overall marketing budgets.

On the demand side, this transition is most obvious. People increasingly have started to buy console titles through digital channels. In 2012, U.S.

consumers spent around $615 million annually on full-game downloads on console; by 2018, this had increased more than sixfold to $4 billion.[8] Annual spending on physical games has remained largely flat at around $7 billion from 2012 to 2018. In addition, the proportion of consumer spending on full-game downloads during the critical holiday months November and December grew from 4 percent of total monthly sales in 2012 to 39 percent in 2018.

The move by consumers toward online sales channels presents a third threat because it prevents GameStop from claiming an equal share of overall revenue and forces it to confront many more competitors. Across mobile, console, and PC, organizations like Apple, Facebook, Valve, and Alphabet have all managed to become shopping platforms on which audiences download games directly and enjoy an almost infinite selection of available titles. By 2013, even the largest publishers had figured out the appeal and potential of distributing content online, as evidenced by Electronic Arts' COO Peter Moore, who disclosed during his firm's first-quarter 2014 earnings report that "Apple was EA's biggest retail partner measured by sales" for the first time that year. Despite the overall growth of the industry, GameStop's share has not grown with it (figure 3.4).

Collectively, these industry developments have confronted GameStop with the strategic challenge of having to adapt to an increasingly digital marketplace. In this case, too, existing practices appear to come before business rationale. Historically, if you sat in on GameStop's earnings calls,

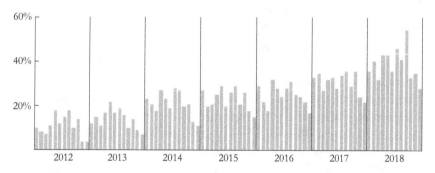

Figure 3.4
Digital share of U.S. monthly sales, 2012–2018. *Source*: Data from NPD and SuperData Research. *Note*: Consumer spending on full-game downloads as a percentage of combined revenue generated by digital and physical game sales. Data exclude any additional digital add-ons and microtransactions.

its executives seemed to be largely tone-deaf to the changes in the world around them. In 2006, its CEO stated in a shareholder letter, "We don't see digital downloading as a threat to our business; in fact, we see it as an incremental factor in making video gaming even more compelling. Publishers are currently experimenting with micro transactions generally paid for with 'points,' often from point cards that we sell in our stores."[9] The concept of selling points cards for use online in a retail store as a way to capture the momentum of digitalization in interactive entertainment is hardly a credible strategy. If that were true, Tower Records could have survived by selling iTunes cards in its stores. It also reduces the totality of what is truly a revolution in video games to a modest payment issue—as if to say that for GameStop to benefit from this fundamental change it needed only to better facilitate the transaction between gamers and game makers. This is not, of course, the case. Publishers draw tremendous value from being able to collect and analyze user data that they otherwise could not, allowing them to use that data to inform their creative agendas and portfolios. Moreover, the sale of point cards, which contain a code that users enter in-game to add funds to their accounts, can be managed entirely online and does not require the actual sale of a physical card. Nevertheless, GameStop stubbornly announced by 2016 that its digital sales totaled almost $1 billion. Even if we accept its shoddy definition of these sales, this revenue amounts to roughly 11 percent of the total, excluding hardware, which puts it well below the share of online sales compared with that for its key publisher relations (44 percent) and at only one-fifth of digital consumer spending (60 percent).

In facing the shift toward digital distribution, GameStop will have to change its approach and adjust to a new landscape. To do so, it has employed several different tactics. Consistent with the approach that historically has worked so well, GameStop has continued its cadence of regular acquisitions. Unlike its efforts before 2008, however, the company has moved its attention to online firms and has made several purchases, including a majority ownership share in a browser-based studio in Ireland called Jolt Gaming; Kongregate, a social network–based platform focused on role-playing games; digital distribution platform Impulse and its parent company Stardock; and Spawn Labs, an online streaming service. Combined these acquisitions follow a predictable strategy for a product-focused retailer looking to expand its online distribution options.

By 2012, GameStop became seemingly satisfied with its ability to distribute games online. Instead of building this out, it acquired several smaller retail chains that offered products and services in parallel with GameStop's core business of selling interactive entertainment. These included Simply Mac, a retail chain certified to sell new and refurbished Apple products; Spring Mobile, an AT&T wireless retailer; ThinkGeek, a retailer focused on computer enthusiasts; and another 507 AT&T Mobility Stores. GameStop also entered into a partnership with Cricket Wireless. In an August 2016 press release, company CEO Paul Raines stated that the acquisitions were part of the firm's "diversification efforts" as it tried to reinvent itself and become a "technology brands business."[10]

This decision makes sense. The typical gamer audience tends to buy accessories and peripherals in their stores. Broadening the range of available products promises to increase the average earnings per customer and prevent revenue from going to its main rivals. Initially, the diversification-through-acquisition approach appeared to pay off as the company observed a spike in sales during the peak of the *Pokémon GO* craze in the summer of 2016. Many of its customers spent their days roaming around looking for *Pokémon* which, unsurprisingly, drained their batteries. With its ubiquitous presence, GameStop managed to sell out all of its battery packs and, as a newly minted licensed AT&T reseller, benefited from an increase in demand for data plans. In a televised interview on CNBC, Raines stated, "We surveyed our stores, 462 of them were either *Pokémon GO* stops, or *PokéGyms*, and our sales in those stores are up 100 percent this weekend alone" and observed "over 100 percent growth in our Pokémon collectibles."[11]

Finally, GameStop has explored a vertical integration by establishing a publishing division under the name GameTrust. Together with Insomniac Games, a studio well known in the industry for its *Ratchet & Clank* franchise, the retailer announced its first title *Song of the Deep*. In August 2016, the company disclosed having sold 120,000 copies, roughly 80 percent through its physical stores (figure 3.5).

None of these initiatives have resulted in their desired outcome of turning GameStop's dwindling business around. The move into adjacent product categories did not bring the results it expected, and key parts of its digital strategy started to come undone when AT&T changed its agreement structure with licensed retailers. Foot traffic started to decrease. It has been forced to close stores to reduce its retail footprint and lower its monthly financial commitments. After its acquisition spree, GameStop faces a lot of debt, and shareholders have begun to abandon the retail chain after it ceased to pay dividends. It also tragically lost its CEO to illness, and despite months of effort, was unable to find a buyer to provide it with a financial lifeline.

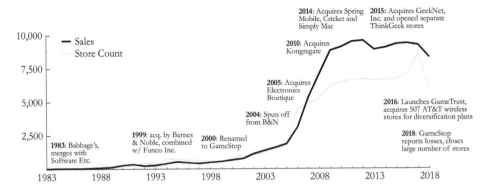

Figure 3.5
GameStop's annual sales compared with number of physical retail outlets, 1983–2018. *Source*: Data from company records. *Note*: Revenue in millions U.S. dollars ($). Selected company events shown.

Today, GameStop's survival is far from certain. After successfully out-maneuvering its competition for years, GameStop's days finally seem numbered as a result of the industry's digitalization. GameStop's case shows that despite having a history of developing key innovations for its business model around scale and employing an effective differentiation in the face of a shifting landscape, change has remained the only constant. At the start of 2020, the firm continued its decline despite strong sales of Nintendo's Switch and the upcoming launches of Sony's PlayStation 5 and Microsoft's Xbox Series X. Will the launch of the next console generation help turn the company's fortunes around, or will it finally be game over for GameStop?

2

Games as a Service

4

Everyone Is a Gamer Now

I was surprised by how wired we were to a particular target audience of 18- [to] 34-year-old guys. It was a challenge to change the rule book of designing games for fraternity brothers.

—CHIP LANGE, GENERAL MANAGER OF ELECTRONIC ARTS' CASUAL LABEL[1]

Video games have become a mainstream form of entertainment thanks to two notable and equally important changes. First, executives and developers have come to the recent realization that playing is a universal human activity. After ignoring about half of the addressable market for decades, game makers discovered that they had been stuck in an outdated mind-set that focused on a narrowly defined consumer segment. Second, digitization removed traditional geographic barriers and facilitated access to a global consumer market. The combination of these two changes has triggered the emergence of a new generation of content creators.

The 2006 launch of the Nintendo Wii changed a lot of people's minds about gaming. It showed Nintendo's critics that the company was not to be underestimated. After the Nintendo Entertainment System's initial success in the mid-1980s, every following generation of its hardware had sold fewer units. This decline in sales led many to believe that its efforts ultimately were going downward, and its share price had followed. Worse, Nintendo's prominence in the industry had suggested that gaming as a whole was in decline. The success of the Wii dispelled many of these concerns, however, and Nintendo regained favor from investors. It also forced both the world at large and much of the industry to reconsider what it meant to be a gamer. The Wii's success made it evident that everyone—and not just a subset of consumers—liked to play video games. After two decades during which publishers and platforms insisted on mitigating risk by producing content almost exclusively for a homogeneous market of young males, Nintendo went the other direction. It designed the Wii console around accessible games, like tennis and bowling, and introduced an innovative controller that made it easy for anyone to play.

It was a spectacular success. The Wii sold well more than one hundred million units, making it the second-best-selling device in the industry's history after the PlayStation 2. This success stupefied both critics and fans alike. The Wii made visible the consumer's ravenous appetite for video games. An entire industry that designed and published games for general audiences began to crop up around the world. The emergence of the "casual" category that included games that offered more accessible gameplay, were cheaper, and were more readily available through digital distribution provided strong momentum. This change forced a fundamental shift in the minds of executives and analysts. Seeing the popularity of interactive entertainment that lacked the high-end graphics, sophisticated narrative, or intricate online multiplayer gameplay, it became clear that well-designed, yet comparatively simple games resonated with an enormous audience. According to Jesper Juul, the emergence of this casual category was "something of a revolution—a cultural reinvention of what a video game can be, a reimagining of who can be a video game player."[2]

For years the industry had been systematically ignoring an enormous part of its addressable market. Initially, video games had catered to the whole family as they moved from the arcades into the living room. In the late 1970s and early 1980s, Atari and its peers spent a fortune on television commercials showing three generations playing together. Over time, however, the core content strategy among publishers came to oscillate largely among titles that offered action, sports, speed, and spectacle. As hardware capability and processing power became the central driver behind the design and marketing of interactive entertainment, the industry started to narrow its output. The ever-increasing price tag for an average game and the growing complexity in gameplay ultimately meant that only 18- to 34-year-old males regarded themselves as gamers. And, as a result, so did everyone else. The main barrier to the broader popularization of video games was, as Juul put it, not "computer technology, but game design."[3] Decision-makers and designers stubbornly focused their efforts on attracting only a single audience segment. Unable to see beyond the boundaries of their existing strategies, it was clear as day (to them) that simply no other consumer base existed. Consequently, a large portion of the industry interpreted the popularization of the smartphone as an opportunity to "drop its reliance on traditional demographics." In reality, however, game makers hadn't bothered to look.[4]

On the basis of audience data collected and published by the Entertainment Software Association, an organization that busies itself with the interests of game companies in North America, the demographic makeup of the gamer population had remained largely the same over the course of a decade and a half. The gender distribution among gamers also had remained stable: throughout the entire period, the consumer market was between 60 percent male players and 40 percent female players, and half of all players were between 18 and 49 years old.

Eventually, a few executives began to take notice. The success of relatively unknown and small game makers had started to add up. Newcomers started to make real money on Facebook: Zynga grew to more than $1 billion in revenue in just four years. Meanwhile, legacy firms dragged their feet. According to a manager at Electronic Arts: "I was surprised by how wired we were to a particular target audience of 18- [to] 34-year-old guys. It was a challenge to change the rule book of designing games for fraternity brothers."[5] Rekindling the idea of gamers as mainstream consumers, however, had vast implications in the way interactive entertainment would be developed and monetized. Ultimately, this led to the emergence of an entirely new industry segment (figure 4.1).

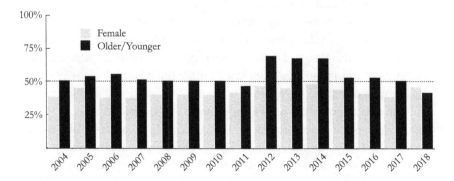

Figure 4.1

Total gamers in the U.S. consumer market outside of the traditional target audience, 2004–2018. *Source*: Data from annual industry report, Entertainment Software Association. *Note*: Older/Younger refers to the percentage of people that fall outside of the traditional 18–34 year old target audience.

Table 4.1
Global games market revenue by country of origin, 1998–2018

	1998	1999	2000	2001	2002	2003	2004	2005	2006	2007
United States	3,740	4,428	3,922	4,993	6,914	7,614	8,967	9,468	10,662	12,764
China		1	2	3	44	98	250	489	682	986
Japan	8,951	9,524	8,991	9,500	11,105	12,395	14,122	12,693	15,251	19,906
Europe	338	323	260	1,942	2,228	2,133	1,870	1,629	1,942	2,670
South Korea	1	7	46	97	155	190	280	340	407	424

Source: Author's compilation.
Note: For brevity's sake, Europe here refers to the aggregate revenue generated by companies based in Austria, Belgium, Cyprus, Czech Republic, Denmark, Finland, France, Germany, Iceland, Ireland, Israel, Italy, Lithuania, Norway, Poland, Russia, Serbia, Sweden, Switzerland, Turkey, and the United Kingdom. Revenue in millions U.S. dollars ($).

In tandem with this moment of clarity, the industry's digitization resulted in its globalization. The combination of audiences coming online, and the popularization of the smartphone dramatically changed the makeup of the supply-side markets (see table 4.1). After decades of supremacy, Japanese game makers eventually had to share control over the worldwide market. Their particular brand of vertically integrated organizations, which combined consoles with content segments and relied heavily on strong third-party relationships, allowed Japanese organizations like Sony, Sega, Nintendo, Konami, Capcom, and Square Enix to claim 87 percent of the global consumer spending for years. A slow decline in global market power had started around 2001 with the introduction of the Xbox. It benefited Western publishers and started to "undermine the exclusive advantages of cultural proximity" that Japanese game makers had enjoyed until then.[6] In 2008, just after the introduction of the iPhone, the combined income of Japanese firms totaled around $25 billion globally, the equivalent of 57 percent of its total at the time. And even then, rather than getting out-innovated, the success of newcomers like Mixi, DeNA, and GungHo (known for its *Puzzle & Dragons*), capitalized on new social and mobile platforms and further boosted the Japanese industry's growth from $7 billion in 1997 to $29 billion in 2018. Its share of the global market has dropped to 25 percent.

Digitalization and globalization, by and large, benefited China. From a virtually nonexistent industry in the late-1990s, it became a juggernaut.

2008	2009	2010	2011	2012	2013	2014	2015	2016	2017	2018
13,543	13,485	14,353	17,011	17,827	18,483	20,030	23,348	25,432	27,725	32,843
1,719	2,196	4,509	5,275	6,896	9,116	11,672	17,548	23,752	33,178	31,453
25,062	21,599	22,626	21,743	20,612	20,692	20,549	20,095	22,906	25,126	29,003
2,862	1,438	1,642	1,884	3,056	6,162	7,966	8,435	7,360	8,851	10,483
383	1,120	1,747	2,735	3,189	3,896	3,926	5,389	6,220	8,504	8,820

In combination with economic policies and cultural preferences, Chinese game makers thrived. The Chinese government had long regarded gaming consoles with suspicion (see chapter 6), and most people traditionally played at Internet cafes rather than at home. In contrast, the Chinese government's protectionist policies ensured that relative newcomers like Tencent and NetEase were able to build up large domestic audiences without having to compete with foreign rivals from the United States and Japan. Moreover, for Western publishers to be allowed to sell their games to Chinese consumers, they are required to partner with a local organization. As a result, Tencent generated $19 billion in game-related revenue in 2018, and NetEase has grown into a $6 billion company. It is easy to interpret the success in China as a market opportunity. As in the case of the Xbox launch there, it has been quite difficult for non-Chinese firms to penetrate this market. It is culturally different from the traditional geographies like North America, Europe, and Japan.[7] Consequently, Western content firms historically have needed to overcome both distribution challenges, including regulation, and a cultural gap. Domestic firms have disproportionally benefited from the growth of the Chinese market. Today, China knows a string of smaller firms that generate anywhere between $100 million and $600 million annually that did not exist before 2016.

Next, digitalization also facilitated the rise and success of game makers from other parts of the world. Countries that previously were invisible burst onto the global stage: South Korea rose to become the fourth-largest industry in the world. Like China, its domestic business benefited from government policies. Rather than protecting its borders, however, regulation encouraged the development of an economy around information technology, which resulted in broadband speeds much faster than anywhere else. This stimulated the domestic consumer demand that allowed publishers like Nexon, NCSoft, and Netmarble to thrive. It was not without its detriments: following the rapid growth, fluctuations in the availability of capital, high concentration, and market saturation all have contributed to the same high-risk, high-reward economics familiar in Western territories.[8] Collectively, South Korean companies grew from obscurity to a combined $9 billion in revenue by 2018.

Finally, in the Western Hemisphere, their well-known IP and access to a high-spending consumer market meant U.S. firms generated $13 billion in 2007 revenue and accounted for 34 percent of worldwide earnings. The combination of controlling many of the most valuable franchises and having a strong existing relationship with consumers and industry partners allowed U.S. game makers to grow to $33 billion by 2018. In Europe, it was the Nordic countries that made an indelible mark. At the top, Finland managed to develop a $3 billion business. Similarly, Russia, Sweden, Poland, and Turkey almost literally "came online" by each cultivating their own publicly traded publishing industries valued between $500 million and $1 billion.[9]

Despite the historical relevance of, for instance, the United Kingdom's industry, the absence of related industries combined with a lack of access to investment capital had resulted in only a handful of firms that managed to go public.[10] According to a recent study, different value chain participants in the United Kingdom deployed different strategies.[11] Publishers have operated as generalists to "occupy as much resource space as possible," thereby boxing out competitors by raising entry barriers. Its supply side has nevertheless remained privately held or governed by foreign entities. Even Edinburg-based studio DMA Design, which developed the *Grand Theft Auto* franchise, had been acquired by Take-Two Interactive for just $11 million in 1999. Conversely, developers have operated as specialists, in pursuit of product innovation by leveraging new technologies and network resources. In this regard, digitalization has afforded companies greater creative and economic independence by providing access to a global market, resulting in a growth spurt in the United Kingdom and throughout Europe.

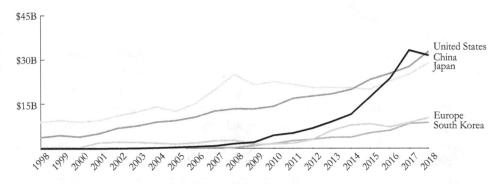

Figure 4.2
Global games market revenue by company country of origin, 1998–2018. *Source*: Data from company reports. *Note*: International mergers (e.g., Tencent's acquisition of Supercell, Activision Blizzard's acquisition of King Digital) have been ignored in allocation revenue by game company country of origin. Categories Europe and ROW (rest of world) are aggregates. Revenue in billions U.S. dollars ($).

In aggregate, the European industry grew from a few hundred million annually to $10 billion in 2018.

Over the course of barely a decade, the video games business evolved from a predominantly Japanese–American affair into a global industry (figure 4.2). This, in combination with many of its executives losing their blinders to what they regarded to be their core audience, resulted in a massive growth spurt and a shift in the industry's underlying economics.

Accessing a Global Market

Digitization also changed the economic geography of the games industry. In Japan, for instance, companies had emerged alongside parallel creative industries like animation. Moreover, the Japanese have long regarded interactive entertainment as a relevant cultural expression. This view differs from the United Kingdom where most of the industry emerged from under-capitalized amateurs—so-called bedroom coders—who largely depended on foreign entities to provide project-based work. As a result, UK-based firms historically have struggled to establish themselves independently and most have remained privately held. Despite the importance of its consumer market, digitization further exacerbated the ability of foreign companies to capture value in the United Kingdom.

As a culture industry, interactive entertainment is most relevant for consumers who live in relative cultural proximity. The popularity of specific game types tends to be skewed geographically: *Madden NFL* does well in the United States for the same reason that *FIFA* is popular in the United Kingdom. An important benefit of digitalization, however, is globalization: in the absence of traditional geographical boundaries, game makers can, presumably, distribute to a global audience. The rise of mobile gaming in particular has changed the structural makeup of the worldwide games industry. Aggregating countries into specific regions—Asia, Europe, North America—allows us to calculate the percentage of their total revenue derived from these individual markets.[12] The data in table 4.2 reveal who is making money and where. Asian game makers earned about 78 percent of total earnings from Asian territories in 2018. North American firms made 56 percent of total earnings in their own region. And European companies are more or less evenly split between North America and Europe: 45 percent and 42 percent, respectively.

In real dollar terms, in 2018, the Asian games business generated $45 billion in earnings from the Asian consumer market, compared with $12 billion for North America and $4 billion for Europe. Following the popularization of the smartphone, North American firms turned their eyes toward Asia and increased their exposure to countries there, on average, from 6 percent in 1998 to 14 percent by 2018. Their European counterparts saw an increase from 4 percent in 2004 to 13 percent in 2018.

Asia, in contrast, greatly reduced its reliance on foreign markets. After Japanese behemoths like Sony and Nintendo had long relied for about half of total sales on Western markets, their focus became notably more myopic: Asia's reliance on its own region grew from 47 percent to 78 percent between 1998 and 2018. In real dollar terms, that's from $3 billion to a whopping $44 billion. This was, of course, largely the result of the success in China, which experienced a massive growth spurt. This growth, however, was combined with a tight regulatory policy that prevented foreign firms that produced cultural goods from easily entering the market. As we now know, this policy backfired in 2018 when China's regulatory approach underwent a broad set of changes that caused a backlog for major firms: between 2017 and 2018, Asian game makers experienced a decline of approximately 5 percent (figure 4.3).

Table 4.2

Revenue generated by major game companies in home markets, 1998–2018

	1998	1999	2000	2001	2002	2003	2004	2005	2006	2007	2008	2009	2010	2011	2012	2013	2014	2015	2016	2017	2018
Asia																					
Total revenue	5,728	6,138	6,283	7,604	9,127	10,078	10,376	12,001	13,591	14,784	16,722	15,849	20,328	22,629	22,457	25,152	34,649	39,193	47,740	58,069	57,058
From Asia	2,688	2,951	2,816	4,186	4,974	5,515	5,926	7,693	8,922	8,997	10,262	10,308	14,198	17,527	18,134	21,111	26,738	31,375	38,214	46,891	44,604
Share	47%	48%	45%	55%	54%	55%	57%	64%	66%	61%	61%	65%	70%	77%	81%	84%	77%	80%	80%	81%	78%
North America																					
Total revenue	1,846	2,413	2,429	2,793	4,385	5,314	5,879	6,578	6,149	9,057	10,815	10,463	10,494	11,997	12,627	12,302	13,939	15,654	18,829	21,290	20,337
From North America	981	1,302	1,490	2,005	3,204	3,758	4,005	4,683	4,453	5,668	6,379	6,372	6,539	7,913	7,346	7,253	7,899	9,170	10,846	11,952	11,486
Share	53%	54%	61%	72%	73%	71%	68%	71%	72%	63%	59%	61%	62%	60%	58%	59%	57%	59%	58%	56%	56%
Europe																					
Total revenue							630	666	673	877	1,225	1,456	1,288	1,671	2,469	3,783	4,526	5,713	6,256	7,156	8,817
From the European Union							311	360	336	434	632	822	683	737	1,131	1,539	1,805	2,371	2,607	2,836	3,702
Share							49%	54%	50%	50%	52%	56%	53%	44%	46%	41%	40%	41%	42%	40%	42%

Source: Author's compilation based on company reports.

Note: Revenue in millions U.S. dollars ($).

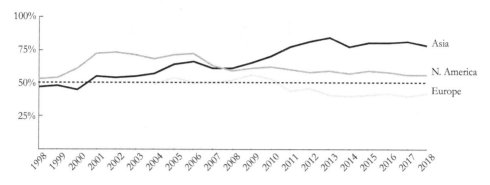

Figure 4.3
Percentage of total revenue generated by major game companies in their markets for
Asia, North America, and Europe, 1998–2018. *Source*: Data from company reports.

Social Games

An important milestone in the transition of gaming from the fringes of the
entertainment business to its center was the emergence of casual games.
As audiences gradually came online, the demand for browser-based and
downloadable titles grew. With the scale and structure of the industry
now changing, new business models became viable. To many, this was a
shock to the system. The juxtaposition between hardcore players, on one
hand, and this rapidly emerging yet massive audience of people playing
relatively simpler-seeming games, on the other, generated an industry-
wide debate.[13] Following a period during which especially small outfits
managed to find audiences online on their own or through partnerships
with portals like Yahoo! and AOL, it was in particular the popularization
of Facebook that shifted the economic emphasis among many publishers.
Relying on a mix of advertising dollars in the form of banner ads and
the sale of virtual currency, a new breed of industry participants started
to design content that offered experiences that were easy to learn but
difficult to master. Like newspapers and television shows, social games
served as a mechanism to keep people in front of ads longer. This model
led developers to think differently about design, which now served as a
vehicle to capture people's attention and to discourage them from leaving
a site.

Among the various industry participants that emerged around this
time, one company stood out above the rest: Zynga. Founded by Mark

Pincus, a serial technology entrepreneur who earlier had made his fortune with the sale of a business software firm, Zynga launched its first title, *Texas Hold 'Em Poker*, on Facebook in 2007. Developed to work within the confines of the Facebook canvas, social games offer a relatively casual interactive experience. Often centered on accessible mechanics, such as gem-swapping or match-three, what differentiates this category from the broader casual category is their emphasis on having players ping their friends in exchange for a (modest) in-game benefit. The objective in this type of game is to acquire as many players as possible for a specific title and to retain them for as long as possible. The additional tactic to build a player base by asking people to recruit a friend strengthens the overall network effects.

To appeal to advertisers, Facebook needed a way to keep people on its website longer. It found its answer in social games. Because Zynga was the largest social game company, Facebook offered it heavily discounted traffic, and the two organizations entered into a five-year relationship to expand the use of Facebook Credits across Zynga's catalog. Between 2008 and 2012, Zynga's annual revenue grew from $19 million to well over $1 billion, accounting for roughly one-fifth of all of the platform's income at its peak. The company continued its growth and dominance, which culminated in its initial public offering in 2011.

Revenue largely depended on free-to-play monetization firms like Zynga, Playdom, and King Digital, which all competed to attract the largest possible audience. With fewer than 5 percent of players converting to spending, these organizations required millions of players to play their games. Therefore, most social publishers had ambitious taglines, aiming to "connect the world through games" (Zynga), "to enrich lives through games and experiences that people love to play and share" (GameHouse), "to make fun and simple games for everyone" (King Digital Entertainment), or, simply, to "unite the world in play" (Spilgames). An obvious tension exists between the lofty mission statements of bringing interactive experiences to the masses and the fact that so many social publishers offered experiences that emulated a never-ending click hole that squarely benefited the interests of digital marketing. Even so, the platform's popularity had allowed an entire industry segment to emerge that focused squarely on creating simple, accessible titles.

This success, however, invited competition (see table 4.3). Many of the game makers that previously had been out on their own on the internet saw Zynga's success and quickly joined the semi-walled garden. They enjoyed

Table 4.3
Top 10 casual game companies on PC and mobile, 2008–2018

	2008	2009	2010	2011	2012	2013	2014	2015	2016	2017	2018
Activision Blizzard									1,674	2,081	2,175
King Digital			58	64	164	1,884	2,102	1,999	Activision Blizzard		
Playrix									209	537	871
Zynga	19	121	597	1,140	1,280	873	690	765	741	861	907
IGG Inc.				9	35	46	157	130	161	312	524
Caesars Entertainment					268	241	294	416	477	626	497
Glu Mobile	90	79	64	74	108	106	223	250	201	287	375
Rovio			8	92	186	212	193	126	177	276	279
Playdemic									0.04	144	257
Playtika						41	99	133	150	133	198
Aristocrat									136	148	197
All others	256	366	837	1,365	984	1,858	1,511	1,499	812	924	1,176
Casual revenue	**346**	**445**	**912**	**1,546**	**2,205**	**4,111**	**4,461**	**5,114**	**5,014**	**6,857**	**7,399**
C1	26%	18%	7%	6%	28%	32%	35%	32%	33%	30%	29%
C4				12%	54%	49%	53%	53%	57%	60%	59%
C10							66%	69%	78%	84%	83%
HHI	672	318	51	59	1,054	1,140	1,407	1,213	1,403	1,326	1,305
No. of firms >1%	1	1	3	4	5	7	8	10	12	12	11

Source: Company reports

Note: Based on 2018 revenue in millions U.S. dollars ($) for companies that exclusively focus on the casual games market, including social network–based and mobile games (e.g., Glu Mobile, Rovio, Zynga), or the relevant subsidiaries for larger conglomerates where available (e.g., Activision Blizzard's subsidiary King Digital). Firms like DeNA (Japan) and Mixi (Japan) are excluded from this because they operate primarily as social network platforms.

at least some degree of structure in their ecosystem, with Facebook taking on the responsibility of a platform owner to optimize the user experience. Moreover, Facebook was understandably weary of its reliance on a single content provider and started to create some distance.

With its prominence in decline, Zynga rallied and prepared a sequel to *FarmVille*. Up to this point, it had earned it around $85 million, and it needed to come up with something new. In September 2012 it released *FarmVille 2*, which skyrocketed. Within two months, the game counted fifty-six million monthly active users, as Facebook users eagerly jumped over to the new title. At its peak in early 2014, it generated $18 million a month in revenue.

Next, Zynga turned to mobile. In early May 2014, the firm released a long-awaited mobile version of the *FarmVille* franchise called *FarmVille Country Escape*. Although total earnings and monthly active users did not amount to the same numbers as it saw on Facebook, Zynga effectively offset its reliance on the platform by drawing multiple revenue streams (figure 4.4).

Consumer adoption of the casual game category fueled the growth of a host of small newcomers. The enthusiasm for the novel smart-phone devices meant that little need existed for marketing. Consumers were eager to play anything: their tastes were largely indiscriminate, and investing in high production values and branding, which characterized the traditional games publishing business, was of relatively little use. An important part of this initial success also had to do with the low price point. Costs for paid titles on the iPhone varied from $20 on the high end, for a title like PlayFirst's *Diner Dash*, to around $0.99 on the low end. Most titles were free, which resulted in the commoditization of casual titles. Cheap to make, easily copied by competitors, and likely to bring a return on investment in an eager marketplace, the industry became subject to a gold rush.

New challenges emerged for the would-be game moguls. After the costs of development were low initially, the quickly crowding market soon demanded greater expenditure. To reach a global audience, for instance, casual titles had to be localized in a range of different languages. Translation and tailoring payment options quickly increased the costs of casual game development. At the same time, data presented a new competitive edge. Because it was now possible to track the behavior of millions of players, firms needed to start tracking everything to optimize gameplay. Removing key obstacles in a level, for instance, meant longer engagement and higher lifetime spending. In turn, this meant that development teams now needed

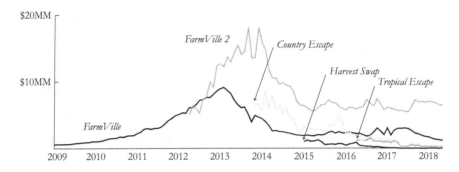

Figure 4.4
Monthly revenue for *FarmVille* franchise (Zynga), 2009–2018. *Source*: Data from SuperData Research and company reports. *Note*: Revenue in millions U.S. dollars ($) for mobile and social platforms.

to hire data analysts to effectively track and interpret the reams of available data. Marketing costs quickly started to increase. To differentiate their titles from copycats, the bigger publishers like King Digital started to invest in user acquisition and advertising.

By all accounts, the casual games category started to evolve and a consortium of dedicated publishers, each with their own operational advantages and design budgets, emerged. What had started as an add-on to Facebook's strategy and a complementary to Apple's iPhone ambitions had grown into a separate market segment. After ignoring a large contingent of consumers for years, the other half of the industry's addressable audience had become a key growth area.

We find another example of the meteoric rise in mainstream gaming in *League of Legends*. As the best-known multiplayer online battle arena (MOBA) title, *League of Legends* successfully evolved from a modification created for the *Warcraft* franchise into one of the most successful titles of all time. Its publisher, Riot Games, formulated an initial strategy with three components: *League of Legends* was to be a lightweight download, offer robust tutorials, and be free-to-play. Although existing titles still required consumers to download several gigabytes, reducing the file size of the initial installer program was an important first step. This meant that the addressable audience for *League of Legends* would be as widespread as possible as potentially anyone with a PC could play. It was an important reversal in the strategic approach PC games had taken. For a long time, PC titles depended on content delivery networks to facilitate and make as painless as possible the process of a new user downloading a game and starting to play. Nexon's *MapleStory*, for instance, still required a seven-hundred-megabyte download that could take on average between fifteen and twenty minutes. During that time, a lot of prospective players would abandon the download and move onto something else. Riot learned from that example that its download requirement needed to be minimal.

Next, like *World of Warcraft* had done before, *League of Legends* invested quite a bit of time in helping people get started. This investment was the second component to its strategy: helping new players find their way around when they just started playing. The strategy proved important, because newbies that made no financial commitment would be likely to leave the game if it proved too difficult to figure out how to play, and an inevitable disadvantage would emerge between experienced and new players over time.

Last, offering the game for free was a critical component to ensure wide appeal. In part this was consistent with its overall approach to be universally accessible. But not unimportantly, by doing so Riot hoped to quickly build a large player base. Monetization would avoid making the experience pay-to-win, thereby giving people who spend money an advantage over those that do not. Instead, it would merely charge for aesthetic items. After playing for a while and developing an affinity or preference for a particular character, players would want to have a slightly different avatar. Riot had learned from Nexon and Tencent that people were more willing to spend money on items and features that facilitated personalized expression rather than functionality. It was a relatively novel approach at the time and not unique to games. Tencent (which would later acquire Riot) had made its fortune by giving social networking services away for free and charging for vanity items, such as particularly desirable usernames and customizable content, none of which altered the experience. From its inception, Riot planned to do the same thing. According to its investor deck, it proposed a revenue model that consisted of selling "collectible digital content," including playable characters, custom avatars, and accessories ranging in price from $0.29 to $12.99. Notably, Riot initially also planned to monetize in other ways. It proposed selling annually released expansion packs for $29.95, establishing a premium subscription service that provided access to exclusive servers and content, and advertising.

Combined, this three-pronged approach was evidence of its long-term focus and emphasis on the player experience instead of driving revenue. Later on, it also added an active tournament circuit and a variety of other ways to interact with other fans of the game. At its peak in late 2016, *League of Legends* had more than 100 million monthly active users and generated $3 billion annually.

Of course, its success drew other game makers. To insulate itself against competition, it doubled down on the strategy to reach as many people with its games as possible. Even with the smaller download size, *League of Legends* still suffered from latency issues. Disappointed in the inefficiencies of third-party internet networks, Riot decided to "build its own internet."[14] This certainly was an ambitious strategy. After it rolled out its data centers across the United States, the results were quite spectacular and it increased its percentage of players with a ping of eighty milliseconds or less from 50 percent to 80 percent overnight. In so doing, it accelerated the overall network effects as people had a better experience and found it more enjoyable to play. For instance, after initially hosting its Brazilian players from servers in Miami, it invested in the infrastructure in the country. Reducing latency had a positive effect on the size of its player base because the experience improved and was comparatively better. Moreover, by incurring a large capital investment, Riot was essentially creating an analog moat. In a market in which you abstain from monetizing audiences until much later into their life cycle, the threat of going to another service or game is always present. By having a better connection, Riot discouraged competitors from doing the same. In a digital world, it successfully identified an analog competitive advantage.

Cross-Platform Gaming

Another outcome of gaming becoming mainstream is the push toward cross-platform play. The ability to play against others irrespective of the device they use greatly expands the value of a title. And given the heavy emphasis on multiplayer game design, it would seem obvious to institutionalize this capability. The console segment, however, has long been fragmented into three entirely separate walled gardens. Microsoft and Sony remain rivals that each invest billions in the development of their own proprietary platform and services. Therefore, collaborating on a shared multiplayer service would not make immediate sense to them. But with games becoming mainstream, it nevertheless creates an awkward situation for consumers and is akin to different telecom providers allowing people to talk only to others within their network and not outside of it. As video games have grown into a juggernaut industry, the walls have come down.

Console gaming has historically catered to markets in which most people by and large owned only a single console. To incentivize these so-called 'single-home consumers' to choose their device over that of a competitor, platform holders invested in first-party content. Atari did this in the 1970s and Nintendo in the 1980s. If a rival has more and especially more desirable content, the value of their platform for the consumer increases accordingly. Consequently, the console market has shaped itself to this principle, especially during the period when physical sales were the primary revenue model. Cross-platform play as an outcome of digitization challenges the long-term industry dynamic.

For content creators, having a presence across not just all three consoles but all platform types—mobile, console, and PC—is a more powerful position than being in only one or two of them. There are obvious benefits to game makers in pursuing such a strategy. For one, it allows companies to cross-promote. As marketing expenses inevitably increase, leveraging one platform to push consumers of your game onto another platform is an effective way to build an audience. After 2009, Facebook, for instance, eventually became a key channel for game makers to funnel traffic to the mobile version of their titles. Instead of focusing on playing on Facebook, it became a departure point from which people would install the smartphone version. A firm like Zynga managed to offset its declining revenue from social networking–based titles by bringing players over to its mobile version.

Next, a cross-platform strategy affords game makers the ability to gradually roll out their title and improve it along the way. Most firms today would be remiss to publish for only a single platform given that mobile, console, and PC each cater to audiences of millions. A staggered release across different devices allows companies, for instance, to allocate development or marketing resources with lower financial risk. For instance, when Activision Blizzard released *Hearthstone: Heroes of Warcraft*, it did so gradually. First announced in March 2013, the game went into an invite-only closed beta in August and accumulated a million players. A worldwide open beta followed in January 2014. A few months later *Hearthstone: Heroes of Warcraft* officially was released for Windows and MacOS operating systems. A version for the iPad followed in April, and one for Windows touchscreen devices in August. By December, it had an official Android tablet version, and, finally, by April 2015, Activision Blizzard released versions for iPhone and Android smartphones. This approach allows a publisher to assess which mechanical features work, how the in-game economy behaves, and where the infrastructural weaknesses are that may jeopardize a seamless global multiplayer experience. It also allows for a growing momentum in marketing and better overall risk mitigation.

But most important, a platform-agnostic approach allows games to benefit from strong network effects. As we'll see in the discussion of *World of Warcraft* and how it managed to become a cultural phenomenon, making online role-playing more accessible to mainstream audiences was key to its success. It meant that its servers were always filled with plenty of other players to join on a quest. Similarly, the growing emphasis on online play among shooter games has created a dependence on attracting enough players to keep its momentum. As you are eliminated from a round, you may watch how the fate of your teammates unfolds. To that end, these conventional 5v5 style shooters only need a handful of active players. The more recent phenomenon of *Battle Royale*–style titles, however, are much more demanding. In this case, one hundred individuals play against each other until one last survivor wins. Players are dropped on a large map that gradually decreases and thereby forces them to confront each other. Because it involves so many more people, an average round can last around fifteen minutes compared with just two minutes in *CS:GO*. To prevent people from leaving after they've been eliminated, a game's servers need lots of players to quickly start another round elsewhere. Cross-platform interoperability, then, is not a luxury but rather a necessity for specific genres.

One title that remarkably managed to convince every major platform holder—including Steam, Tencent, Sony, Apple, and Nintendo—to open up for cross-platform play is *Fortnite*. Epic Games first released the game as a proprietary in-house developed title to showcase the performance capabilities of the game engine that it licenses to other developers. Originally designed as a multiplayer title in which a group of players builds structures and levels up weapons to work together against an onslaught of zombies, the game's *Battle Royale* mode gained traction so quickly that Epic abandoned the original design. At the time, a military shooter called *PlayerUnknown's Battleground* (*PUBG*) had popularized the Hunger Games–style gameplay in which one hundred people play against each other until the final winner remains. Epic jumped on the bandwagon and released its own version with one important difference: where *PUBG* was a premium PC game that cost $30, *Fortnite* was a free-to-play title.

It allowed more people to try the game and see what the fuss was all about, without any of the financial risk.

Next, similar to *World of Warcraft*, which had managed to claim a massive market share in a crowded online role-playing segment by launching with a friendly colorful aesthetic and accessible gameplay, *Fortnite*'s look and feel deviated from the classic military-style shooter. Instead of trying to approximate realism by including real-life weapons and excluding any fantasy elements like *PUBG*, Epic offered a more cartoony, tongue-in-cheek type of experience that resonated with a general audience. It also made it easier for live-streamers on Twitch to start playing the game and plug into the goofy fun. A steady release schedule of updates and upgrades ensured that the game did not go stale.

Another component to its success was its cross-platform gameplay. Previously, most titles had been siloed and were playable only on PC or console or mobile. The few exceptions, like *World of Tanks*, lacked mainstream appeal. After initially releasing on PC globally, Epic's minority owner Tencent helped facilitate the game's launch in China on smartphones. To stay ahead of *PUBG*, which was quickly spreading as the go-to *Battle Royale* title throughout Asia, *Fortnite* not only launched on a myriad of platforms but also ensured that the entire player base could play against each other rather than remain sectioned off in their respective walled gardens. This effort reached its zenith when Sony conceded as the last manufacturer. After *Fortnite* had been ported to the Switch and Xbox One, Sony eventually agreed to facilitate cross-platform gameplay. This agreement amounted to the largest possible addressable audience for Epic, and further fueled its hype train as the news media fell into a frenzy about *Fortnite*'s spectacular growth. The combination of piggybacking off an up-and-coming gameplay innovation by integrating a free-to-play revenue model, offering a friendly colorful aesthetic, and facilitating cross-platform gameplay allowed *Fortnite* to quickly capture market share and become a mainstream favorite. Despite its earlier release, *PUBG* struggled. Although most coverage of *Fortnite*'s stellar growth during 2017 and 2018 emphasized its revenue (figure 4.5), having successfully facilitated cross-platform play is arguably Epic's most pronounced accomplishment.

If cross-play broke down walls between platforms, the players themselves still maintained plenty of separation. Despite the industry becoming more inclusive of a broader consumer group, the makeup of the development community remained largely homogeneous. In a 2016 report by the International Game Developer Association (IGDA) on workplace diversity,

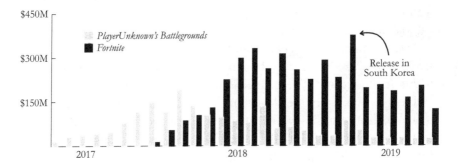

Figure 4.5
Monthly worldwide revenue for *Fortnite* and *PlayerUnknown's Battlegrounds* since launch, all platforms. *Source*: Data from SuperData Research. *Note*: Revenue in millions U.S. dollars ($).

it found that "demographic data reinforce our understanding of video game development workers as predominately young, white, male, heterosexual and without dependents."[15] It is a terrifying thought to consider that, given gaming's growing cultural relevance and role as a form of expression, the greater part of this industry remains operated by a singular demographic. If the *New York Times*'s editorial team was largely white, male, heterosexually oriented, and without dependents, it would be out of business. This raises the inevitable question of whether such a creative community is capable of bringing a broader range of narratives to the medium.[16]

For a long time, companies had a perfect consumer in the more-or-less homogeneous gamer audience: as production costs increased over time, having a clearly defined group of people in mind provided a useful shorthand to mitigate demand uncertainty. Combined with the winner-take-all dynamics of a hit-driven business, publishers got in the habit of sticking to formulas that offered a high degree of revenue predictability, such as serialization and licensing. Selling to an eager consumer group that may be homogeneous but high spending can sustain an industry for a long time and, more important, cement the idea that video games are mostly for eighteen- to thirty-four-year-old males.

The accelerated collapse of the gamer identity over the past two decades triggered a resistance among this audience as they saw others trespass on their carefully constructed sense of self. It was akin to people who frequent concerts and live performances not wanting to share music with radio listeners. And so, when games became an activity enjoyed by a more diverse player base, introducing a broader examination of the dominant values it circulated, it unleashed a fierce discussion. Suddenly, the purveyors of the gamer community and its culture found themselves challenged by people who did not resemble them. According to MIT sociologist T. L. Taylor: "the general rise of gaming into popular culture is eroding the geek gamer stereotype. . . . Being a gamer has offered a convenient shorthand identifying a specific orientation to play and technology, helping people make connections to each other."[17]

The popularization of smartphones had generated an enormous audience of people playing titles like *Angry Birds* and *Candy Crush*. Much more accessible than its console counterparts and de-emphasizing the need to identify as a gamer, mobile and social games brought back a simpler sense of enjoyment. These casual games did not lack complexity or depth but had removed the boundaries that had long prevented a broader consumer group from playing. So much so, in fact, that the term "gamer" lost its ability to identify a clearly defined consumer group and ascended to the same rank as terms like "reader" or "viewer." As one industry observer phrased it: "Gamers are over."[18]

A final consideration in this context is regulation. The 1980s and 1990s had a rich history of government officials looking to impose rules on the video games industry because of the alleged connection between antisocial behavior and violent games.[19] Arguably, much of the debate around video game regulation remained limited because the industry lacked cultural capital and catered to a specific audience. By actively self-regulating, publishers and platforms managed to avoid draconian rules, and the anxiety about video games gradually subsided even if its stereotypes persisted. With interactive entertainment becoming mainstream and appealing to a global audience, governments everywhere have started to take a new look at regulations. Several governments have begun to form regulatory frameworks that affect the industry both directly and indirectly.

The most obvious regulation is the increased scrutiny on monetization. Here, in particular, Electronic Arts did not do the industry any favors when it implemented loot boxes in the late-2017 beta release of *Star Wars Battlefront 2*. Succinctly, in addition to charging for the game, it also featured a progression system to upgrade characters and avatars for online play. One of the main pillars of advancement are loot boxes: a gameplay component in which players earn a random bundle of items, materials, and characters for use in the game. These loot boxes can be won by playing or by purchasing with real-world money and can be used to unlock new play styles and upgrades. According to early beta-reviewers, Electronic Arts placed a disproportionally strong emphasis on spending real money to advance.[20] The firm immediately turned off in-game spending, but to many, the damage was done. Fans berated the publisher. Disney, worried about the upcoming release of its *Star Wars* movie, called Electronic Arts to the mat. The incident fueled the widely held theory that by incorporating randomized results, video games (especially those that catered to younger audiences) were a steppingstone toward gambling. As a result, countries like the United Kingdom, Sweden, and Belgium began investigating predatory monetization practices.

Another area at which games and governments intersect is around the practice of data collection—in particular, digital titles rely on the collection and analysis of player data. For many firms, this is a competitive advantage. Crunching the numbers helps inform a publisher's creative agenda and optimizes the rollout strategy and timing of marketing. It tells companies which items and avatars are most popular and fetch the highest price. Nevertheless, data collection also touches on privacy and the boundaries around what can and cannot be gathered. At a broader level, large technology firms like Facebook and Google have come under scrutiny. They face a growing amount of criticism about the way they handle user data and privacy, suggesting that it is only a matter of time before industries that have a prominent technology component (e.g., video games) face similar questioning and legislative challenges. In particular, the General Data Protection Regulation (GDPR), a regulation in EU law on data protection and privacy for all individual citizens of the European Union and the European Economic Area, has resulted in broader scrutiny of who owns data and how that information is handled. Following the implementation of the GDPR in May 2018, game makers now have to be upfront about the data they collect and have to ask for permission. The regulation adds a few more steps for an average user to go through between installing a game and starting to play. In particular, for free-to-play titles, this creates additional hurdles by possibly lowering the total number of people that it can add to its player base and, more generally, by increasing costs. Depending on the type of information a company collects as part of its game mechanics—anonymized user data in online multiplayer or geographic location data like *Pokémon GO*—firms are obligated to ask for consent and keep a closer eye on whether they operate within the rule of law.

A concern for consumers is also what drives one of the industry's largest markets: China. Its government has proven to be both a benefactor and the worst enemy for the largest companies in the world. After observing the rising popularity of video games—a category that is regarded with great suspicion—China promptly announced a reorganization of its approval process and the formation of the State Administration of Press and Publication. Chinese gamers spend around $30 billion annually, which makes it a highly desirable market for both foreign and domestic publishers. Its rapid growth resulted in a growing concern around violent content, gaming addiction, and myopia, and it is the committee's job to ensure that "games abide by the social values that China holds dear."[21] The reorganization came with an eight-month hiatus during which very few titles were approved for release. This meant that many game makers, including several of China's biggest firms, could not capitalize on the success of games like *PUBG* and *Fortnite*. Tencent suddenly suffered from the market protectionism upheld by the Chinese government from which it initially had benefited so greatly.

Globally, the industry's success has attracted the attention of governments everywhere. How a game monetizes, how and what data it collects on its players, and what type of content are deemed appropriate for specific audiences are all important and necessary questions to ask. In particular for a cultural industry that has grown so much in relevance, regulation is only to be expected. Simultaneously, the legal framework within which the games industry has come to operate is the fruit of its own success and a new form factor to any creative design agenda.

Only after ignoring roughly half of the addressable audience did game makers then spend more than a decade trying to reconfigure their strategic approach and appeal to common consumers. In the interim, a host of new developers managed to claim their share by offering accessible titles that targeted audiences who were equally committed to their playtime as the more typical demographic. Moreover, these newcomers accomplished key revenue model innovations that enabled them to generate earnings from a diverse but much more price-sensitive consumer.

The industry's landscape has changed in a variety of ways. Firms that focused on providing content to a much larger, more diverse player base instead of a homogeneous slice of gamers found success and rose to the top. It also resulted in a wider acceptance of interactive entertainment by society at large and revitalized dialogue about what video games are and how to define their role in terms of socialization, cultural relevance, and digital literacy. Previously, the alleged causality between violence and games dominated the social dialogue. The success of *Pokémon GO* and *Fortnite*, however, has taken this generally ill-informed debate and pushed it to the center of social life. This provides an exciting prospect for both designers and players alike. Next, the rise of the casual gamer underscores the price creative firms pay if they fail to recognize and capitalize on an opportunity. Their inability to abandon existing ideas about who a gamer is and determine how to put together a team of developers ultimately has contributed to incumbents losing share to newcomers.

The ascendance of games to a common form of leisure activity comes with the obligation to abandon the practices that kept it from the mainstream in the first place. By forcing itself to become more inclusive, the industry serves a broader range of ideas and hopefully frees itself from the mental constraints of antiquated strategies.

5

Myth of the Mobile Millionaire

Each generation thinks they invented sex; each generation is totally mistaken.

—ROBERT A. HEINLEIN

Today, mobile gaming accounts for roughly half of the worldwide video game market. The ten-year period of rapid growth that followed the introduction of the Apple iPhone in 2007 resulted in the emergence of an entirely new segment. Initially, low entry barriers allowed for a host of new organizations to enter the market and claim a share as incumbent publishers dragged their feet. To many, the explosive popularity of mobile games proved irresistible. A string of small firms finding enormous success and visibility resulted in initial exuberance that set unrealistically high expectations. Unknown developers like Rovio and Supercell rivaled established publishers in earnings and became synonymous with the excitement and popularity of the smartphone. Since then, the landscape has changed substantially: consumer spending on mobile games grew to $45 billion by 2018, and behemoths like Tencent, NetEase, and Activision dominated the market. Yet much of the enthusiasm from its earlier stages persists today. This is the myth of the mobile millionaire: the idea that ten years after it took off, the mobile category remains an accessible marketplace in which anyone with a good idea can become a successful smartphone-based game developer. But does this myth that the mobile games market remained open and accessible as it started to mature hold true?

It is hard to dismiss the exuberance. Early on, mobile gaming proved an exciting new segment for creative firms as a result of several interacting developments. As a consumer electronics firm, Apple's main objective behind lowering the entry barriers for creative firms was to sell as many of its devices as possible. In the Apple universe, content serves as a complementary asset that increases the use value of its various gadgets and computers. This is the opposite strategy to that followed by most console manufacturers, which sell hardware at a loss to subsidize the sale of content. The abundant availability of apps, short for applications, greatly increases the use value of the device beyond making phone calls, text messaging, and checking email. Once Apple figured this out, it made sure that the barriers to entry were as low as possible. Any developer could purchase the necessary license to publish in the App Store for just $100, which stood in contrast to the publishing requirements in the console space. Compared with the PC market, Apple further removed obstacles for creatives by handling distribution, promotion, and payments in exchange for a 30 percent cut of sales. This resulted in a rapidly growing developer community and available inventory. By 2016, Apple reported no fewer than two million apps across all categories and stated that it expected that number to more than double in the years to come. According to its 2018 annual report, Apple generated $13 billion from its App Store, or more than twice the amount it generated with its music and video services combined.

Additionally, this thriving marketplace lacked apex predators. The large publishers that dominated the PC and console segments initially were absent from the mobile space. Naturally risk-averse, incumbents hesitated to invest in what they considered to be an immature platform. Their experiences with mobile gaming before the arrival of the smartphone had left them only mildly excited about this category's potential. Before 2007, mobile development had been cumbersome. Governed by large telecom firms that did not feel they were responsible for content, providing games for their devices was an afterthought. Technical capabilities of handsets were limited and the overall experiences the industry offered stood in no comparison to what consumers were accustomed to finding on PC and console. Worse yet, for a studio to release a title on a telecom provider's network, it had to support every single type of handset. That meant having to port a single title to well over four hundred devices, each with their own technical specifications (e.g., screen size, processing power), every single year. Because telecom service providers did not see the potential and refused to make this market more efficient, mobile games before 2007 remained a small, low-margin business and a niche category.

Consequently, publishers like Activision Blizzard, Capcom, Electronic Arts, and Konami deliberately dragged their feet on the quickly emerging opportunity. For some, this made strategic sense. Activision Blizzard's preferred strategy was to wait before a category or genre had developed sufficiently before entering it in a big way. For others, it meant having to invest in a relatively small and consolidated market segment. Because Electronic Arts had acquired Jamdat in 2005 for $680 million, it controlled the pre–smartphone mobile games market. Even as smartphones became more popular and affordable, the demand for mobile amusement did not grow so quickly as to become critical for incumbents. Initially, Apple's App Store offered mostly premium titles, which, it would turn out, were much less financially profitable than the free-to-play titles that emerged in 2010. This presented a natural opportunity to newcomers.

The slow pace of the legacy firms and the initial emphasis on premium titles drove relatively little growth: between 2007 and 2010, mobile gaming grew to about $2 billion in annual revenue, split roughly equally between legacy publishers and newcomers. The emphasis changed in 2009, when Apple adopted a new content policy to include "freemium" titles that did not require an upfront purchase in the App Store. The model did not make much sense to incumbent game makers, especially in North America and Europe, but it made perfect sense to a broad contingent of smaller outfits that had been developing titles to run in browsers. Within a year, total revenue earned by newcomers more than doubled even as revenue remained the same for incumbents. Creative organizations like King Digital and Rovio, which had been relatively small and active in highly competitive markets, recognized the opportunity. Simultaneously, a growing number of smaller firms entered the market and a growing number of consumers bought iPhones. Demand grew incredibly fast, from 11 million units in 2008 to 218 million ten years later, and supply raced to keep up. Finding customers in this quickly growing market was relatively easy. By 2018, newcomers in the data set generated $40 billion from mobile, or eight times more than legacy publishers ($5 billion; see figure 5.1).

For years, mobile gaming had been a specialized, low-margin business, but with the success of the iPhone, it transformed into a thriving marketplace that carried the promise of success, especially for small developers. Compared with development for the console and PC market for

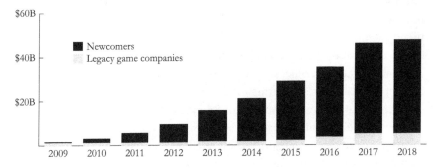

Figure 5.1
Mobile game revenue generated by legacy companies and newcomers, 2009–2018. *Source*: Data from company reports. *Note*: Although Apple initially launched the iPhone in 2007, it was not until 2009 that it allowed "freemium" monetization in its App Store, which resulted in a spectacular increase in consumer spending on mobile games.

which teams easily exceeded more than one hundred team members, suddenly anyone, even people with little to no programming experience, could release an app and, ostensibly, make millions. Following the financial crisis in 2007, a host of in-house designers and other creatives, who generally are among the first ones to go during layoff, had been looking for work. News media featured a steady stream of "accidental" app millionaires who had stumbled on an idea and subsequently made a fortune.[1] They all found their answer in the App Store. This platform provided access to a potential audience of millions of smartphone users without any of the usual obstacles associated with game development, including high barriers to entry, high quality demands from platform holders, and expensive software development kits. The successes of outfits like Lima Sky, known for its *Doodle Jump*, which saw almost a million downloads in a single month, fueled overall enthusiasm.[2] This type of success contributed to the idea that, at least on mobile platforms, a different set of economic rules governed mobile game publishing.

The repercussions were not immediately obvious. The sustained growth rate meant that new consumers were added to the marketplace daily, all looking for content to try on their new devices. Eventually, however, the app market started to become less accessible and much less forgiving. Despite its popularity, it would soon become more difficult to find success.

Consider, for instance, what happened to a puzzle game named *THREES*. After initially winning the hearts of consumers with its accessible, tile-swiped math game, the premium title quickly saw its fortunes reversed. The two-person crew behind it had spent about fourteen months in development, was well-respected among the broader development community, and even managed to win several industry awards, including the Apple Design Award in 2014. Within six days of its release, however, a slew of clones that closely resembled *THREES* popped up in the App Store with the important difference of being free-to-play rather than premium. Almost immediately, these free clones claimed the top-ranking spots in the App Store and pushed the original *THREES* into oblivion. By simply copying, or rather stealing, the game's mechanics and offering it for free, others like *2048* managed to out-earn the original version. Unfortunately, this was not an uncommon phenomenon. Other well-known indie titles like *Ridiculous Fishing* and *Flappy Bird* went through the same experience of seeing their formula copied and their revenue decimated.

Because of the low margins in the pre-smartphone era, creative firms that had relied on mobile and casual games markets historically also relied on outsourcing development. When the smartphone rose to popularity, a thriving industry of small development shops already was in place that could execute quickly and efficiently. Rather than coming up with an original idea, many of these contenders were quick followers that built their success on copying others and undercutting their offering. More often than not, this approach meant content was available for free. And because these firms focused on scale, they tended to be more experienced and have dedicated resources for marketing. These resources allowed them to claim the top spot in the app stores and surpass the original creators' effort. Lowering the barriers to entry to mobile game development meant that the bedroom coders in developed economies like the United Kingdom and North America competed with the sheer production muscle generally found in emerging economies. The accessibility of the app store also offered little protection for original work. Apple, with its rich history of indifference to the interests of content creators, put no stock in curating its App Store. The absence of an effective system to connect consumers to content meant that top-grossing titles were able to maintain their position and enjoy high visibility and a disproportionate share of overall spending compared with the smaller shops toiling in the ever-expanding long tail.

In addition to cloning, competing with free substitutes, and a cluttered App Store, mobile games also tend to monetize poorly. As a rule of thumb, between 2 percent and 5 percent of players actually spend money. Even if the total addressable audience consists of millions, the slice of paying gamers is generally quite small. It is, in effect, the ultimate form of price differentiation: audience members determine what they will pay for, and how much. This makes the addressable audience as large as possible but has an important disadvantage that most will pay nothing at all, which forces creative firms to compete over what is in reality a much smaller revenue-generating player base.

For most of the early years, having such a large contingent of non-spenders was no problem. A persistent influx of new consumers who were eagerly exploring the app store with their brand-new phones meant publishers had much less difficulty getting people to find and try their titles. Often fueled by venture capital, content creators initially focused on just building an audience and trying to extract revenue later. As long as millions of new consumers were coming into the ecosystem every day, ample opportunity existed for both small and large game makers.

But such a thing cannot last. The predominance of this model has had two long-term effects that increased the financial pressures in the market: first, it established the idea that mobile games are mostly free. Mobile gaming greatly expanded the worldwide audience for interactive entertainment by giving so much content away for free that new consumers were not accustomed to having to spend anything at all. Subsequently, only a small subset of players actually did, which meant game makers were forced to either compete with free content or copy the strategy. Only firms with existing success or vast capital resources can compete in these conditions. Second, it removed the ceiling on what so-called whales could spend. Dependency on this small subset of paying players resulted in companies having to push this select group to spend as much as possible. Relying on a narrow customer base carries a lot of risk. Despite claiming millions as active players, the paying player base for even popular titles includes only a small subset of the market and creates a distorted picture of a firm's risk profile. Unlike the typical product-based model in which players pay first and play later, the ubiquity of the free-to-play model on smartphones sits at the center of many of the market's challenges.

Note, of course, that success is relative. In an industry with thousands of small studios, even modest success can be meaningful. It was a team of only eight developers that released *Monument Valley*, a puzzle title that cost $852,000 and took fifty-five weeks to make but generated more than $14 million in its first two years.[3] Its polished and innovative gameplay set it apart from many of the other titles in the app store and it fit neatly into the overall aesthetic that Apple used for its devices. A success story in its own right, *Monument Valley* enabled its developer, ustwo games, to secure its future for years to come and expand its business. But for large multinationals generating billions in annual revenue, that degree of success is not meaningful and is difficult to replicate.

An important driver behind a game's success like *Monument Valley* is the visibility it receives by having Apple prominently display it in the App Store. In a crowded marketplace, platform holders may elect to actively promote specific content that they believe best represents the quality and type of inventory available to encourage consumer spending. In much the same way that in-store placement at the retail level had a positive effect on traditional boxed sales, prominent placement drives downloads in the App Store. This is an important consideration in helping consumers find worthwhile content on their devices.

During its earlier stages, novelty largely drove demand, as consumers eagerly looked for interesting experiences on their new phones. As the addressable market continued to grow, acquiring new users remained relatively cheap as publishers met a hungry audience that was willing to try new things (figure 5.2). But over time, this enthusiasm naturally subsided, and consumer expectations increased. In much the same way that people watch television, with an average household having access to hundreds of channels but regularly watching only a few, mobile games are abundant, yet few are played regularly. This scenario presents a critical distinction for a market in which virtually all of the available content monetizes through a free-to-play model. Individual titles rely on active engagement among a broad audience to successfully convert a small percentage to spending.

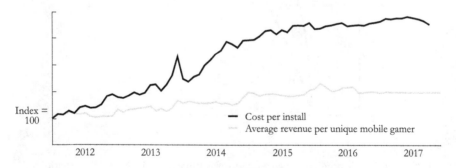

Figure 5.2
Indexed cost of user acquisition compared with revenue per unique mobile gamer, 2012–2017. *Source*: Data from SuperData Research.

Active engagement is key, but a million other titles are competing for attention. As a result, marketing costs have gone up significantly. To make matters worse, average spending has not.

The combination of these factors of a low monetization rate, growing cost and complexity of marketing, and high substitution risk resulted in a marketplace in which it is relatively easy to release a game but simultaneously difficult for content creators to become financially sustainable.[4] These pressures have an observable effect on design because they force creative firms to extract revenue from their player base at an increasingly aggressive rate. Figure 5.3 displays the fundamentals of mobile game monetization. With a given cost per install and profit point, the two separate players A and B monetize at different rates during their life cycle: player A takes less time to reach profitability than player B. Consequently, the developer is incentivized to accelerate monetization by incorporating "encouraging" mechanics into the experience. It follows that as acquisition costs increase, the time between players first starting a game and the moment they become profitable is prolonged, which encourages the developer to pursue more aggressive monetization. Ultimately, this pushes a creative firm to do whatever is

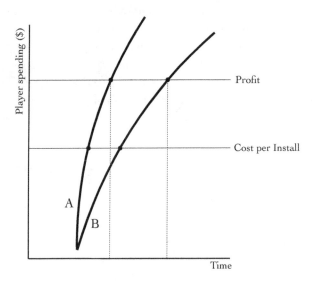

Figure 5.3
Different life-cycle progressions in a free-to-play game scenario. *Note:* The scenario assumes different players over the course of their respective lifetimes in a free-to-play game scenario, with fixed development and acquisition costs, and both players starting their life cycle at the same time.

necessary, including, for instance, releasing content updates to retain players long enough for them to start spending money, and persistently inundating players with sales notifications. Such an effort, however, can threaten the quality of experience. It is this dynamic that sits at the center of the debate on the merits of free-to-play gaming. Traditional designers often refer to it as developers being greedy. And that may be the case. It is also the outcome of increasing pressure to generate revenue in a crowded marketplace, and, for many, it is the only way to survive.

How then does a mobile game company ensure that it can retain a large audience that spends enough for it to be financially sustainable and at the same time insulated from competition? One answer is to build accessible multiplayer games that encourage people to play with others and connect with them through groups and tournaments. Network effects may facilitate an active community of players around a title and ensure that switching costs are sufficient to prevent people from playing a similar but competing title. To do that, however, requires some ingenious development. The kind that can be done only by seasoned industry professionals.

As it turns out, the realization of a successful creative vision is not necessarily the result of just having the best people work together. What often goes unnoticed is the need for a clear strategy and the cultivation of distinct company practices to accomplish success. In the years following the introduction of the iPhone, there was no shortage of aspiring talent. Organizing that talent effectively proved to be a critical business model innovation for Finnish game maker Supercell.

After selling their development studio in 2004 to mobile publisher Digital Chocolate, Ilkka Paananen and Mikko Kodisoja stayed on for another six years before founding Supercell in 2010. The firm's driving philosophy was to "get the best people to make the best games and provide the best environment for them to work in."[5] To accomplish this, they raised $12 million in funding and actively recruited talent from around the world. Supercell's vision was to create games that would both be financially successful and become part of the industry's rich history. Remarkably, it did. But before Tencent acquired Supercell for almost $9 billion in 2016 it would first almost fail, repeatedly.

The release of *Gunshine*, an online multiplayer role-playing game, on Facebook was a rather unconvincing result for a group with such talent and funding. Emulating the basic tenets of what had made *World of Warcraft* so popular, Supercell discovered that audiences for social network–based games were looking for less complexity and less depth. Initially, they had imagined the demand for social network–based games as being similar to that on consoles. They found out they were wrong. Despite a peak of half a million monthly active users, the game suffered a high degree of churn as players quickly got bored and moved on. Their initial strategy of emphasizing high production values had little success retaining players. This reality forced the company to focus on acquiring new users, which was expensive. And, finally, it struggled to effectively port *Gunshine* to smartphones because the game originally was developed for the PC. After trying for eighteen months and achieving only modest success, Supercell discontinued the game.

The failure of its first major release taught it several valuable lessons. For one, Supercell learned that users on social media platforms like Facebook craved a casual type of gameplay that was different from the multiplayer role-playing that *Gunshine* offered. This experience forced the company to rethink its original strategy of making games that people would play for years and across different platforms. Instead, it realized that it needed to develop games specifically for the mobile and tablet market.

It also made clear to leadership that it needed to rethink how it was organized: "We were really great at raising money, and we were great at hiring people. But all the games that we tried, nothing seemed to work."[6] Having the best team and resources alone was not a direct path to success. To succeed, they reasoned, they would need to try multiple things, see what worked and what did not, and learn from the experience. Most important, rather than pursuing a single project all the way to completion, Supercell decided to reorganize into smaller teams, or cells, that each would operate largely independently.

The initial feedback it received from the market resulted in establishing a company culture in which failure was part of the overall learning experience. This approach enabled its teams to look critically at their own games and discontinue their efforts whenever results did not match expectations. Supercell's success depended on its teams having the "freedom to fail."[7] Rather than getting stuck on a particular creative vision or succumbing to the pressures of office politics, the firm mitigated risk by embracing failure. To instill this mentality, the company celebrated whenever it shut down development of a game and acknowledged the hard work its team had put into the project and the lessons it had learned. "We aren't trying to pretend that failing is fun, because it absolutely sucks. We celebrate not the failure itself, but the learning that comes out of that failure."[8]

With this approach, Supercell instilled several key company practices. First, it moved decision-making downward and gave individual teams almost complete freedom to pursue a project. At regular intervals, it shared its progress and garnered feedback from the rest of the company. By establishing this culture of trust, people were able to work on their projects rather than working to satisfy any corporate administrative needs. Supercell's founder Ilkka Paananen is fond of claiming to be "the least powerful CEO in the world." Second, the firm exemplifies this trust by being unusually open about its overall performance. On a daily basis, it shares key performance metrics across all of its titles and company. Accordingly, people learn from everyone else's experiences and failures and incorporate those lessons into their day-to-day decisions. Third, the company actively encourages collaboration among teams. Once a year, the entire organization meets for a company retreat to bring together everyone from its various offices and establish familiarity and friendship. Fourth, Supercell also requires an extensive onboarding process for new hires. Understandably, the company's habits are uncommon, and to set new employees up for success, they are slowly educated on how the firm operates. This introduction includes a series of one-on-one meetings with senior people, all to break down any obstacles to speaking freely and being honest with each other.

The focus on transparency, honesty, and collaboration worked. By instilling a process of ongoing iterations and embracing failure, Supercell proved able to slowly perfect the handful of titles that eventually did see the light of day. After the disappointment of *Gunshine*, the company managed to launch not one but four mobile titles that each generated billions in revenue and attracted millions of monthly active players (figure 5.4). Creating games that appealed to broad audiences and simultaneously offered deep experiences proved to be Supercell's magic formula. To accomplish this, it had to formulate an innovative organizational approach that enabled it to realize its creative vision.

Another strategy to do well in this segment is less innovative as much as it is expensive: capturing share through acquisition. In this context, Tencent and NetEase are dominant forces. Having benefited from the Chinese government's regulations that forced foreign publishers to go through a local partner to sell their games to Chinese consumers, both firms are rich in revenue and data. In its 2010 earnings report, Tencent Chairman Ma Huateng stated: "To become a stronger player in the market, we need to significantly enrich the applications and content offered to users."[9] In addition to opening its platform to third parties, it also started investing in content providers and creative organizations. Tencent uses its vast resources to make many smaller bets. On one hand, this mitigates risk. The top-performing

Figure 5.4
Monthly active users for Supercell titles *Boom Beach, Clash of Clans, Clash Royale*, and *Hay Day*, 2012–2018. *Source*: Data from SuperData Research.

firms in its investment portfolio more than make up for the losers. More-over, each of its investments are handed a set of "best practices" that it is expected to integrate into their games, including encouraging players to connect their game to their social network profiles and explaining how to monetize effectively. From its early history, Tencent learned that the social layer serves as a centerpiece around which it builds its offering.

On the other hand, making multiple investments across different out-fits gives Tencent access to an unparalleled array of data. In cases in which performance metrics are generally off-limits, having a financial stake in a company, especially one that you've just vetted for performance and future promise, means that, in aggregate, Tencent has a lot of information avail-able about what moves the market. This information allows it to anticipate and seize opportunities. We find a comparable strategy with NetEase, which has established a massive global network of mobile game studios by acquir-ing well over fifty studios, all of which operate independently. It organizes regular demo sessions with an internal team that determines what games receive funding for its next development stage. Basically, it plays real-life *Battle Royale* with its studio subsidiaries. Both Tencent and NetEase's strat-egies require vast amounts of capital. Moreover, their ability to provide access to a billion Chinese consumers gives them leverage compared with regular investment funds, because it makes more sense for smaller firms looking for funding to go with a strategic partner like Tencent or NetEase than with a fund that can provide only capital. This strategy has allowed especially Tencent to offset the inherent risks in smartphone-based gaming and create artificial barriers to entry by simply outspending everyone else.

The Democratization of Mobile Gaming

An important question related to the popularization of mobile gaming and its lower entry barriers is whether it presents a more open market. On the basis of collected data, game companies that had previous experience with developing for browsers and the web ultimately were much more successful than legacy firms. The shift away from premium titles to free-to-play games removed the ceiling on what a game's biggest spenders could spend, which contributed to a new generation of organizations to emerge and claim their share.

This shift also posed a challenge to the conventional practices surrounding game development and publishing, in particular among legacy companies. Their tried-and-true approaches proved to be much less effective. When Nintendo released *Super Mario Run* in late 2016 and charged $10 for the full game, audiences were disappointed at the high price point, because they had expected it to be free. But the collaboration between Apple and Nintendo was clearly centered on providing content at a premium: during its big annual Apple event, Nintendo's chief game designer, Shigeru Miyamoto, took the stage to announce its upcoming mobile title. With the surprising success of *Pokémon GO* earlier that summer still fresh in everyone's mind, Nintendo initially seemed poised to make a huge splash, and this time with its most valuable franchise. Following the initial announcement, the Japanese firm steadily turned up the intensity of its marketing effort by releasing more details about the game toward its launch date. Where Supercell and Machine Zone managed to create notoriety by investing in ads during the 2016 Super Bowl half-time show—typically the most expensive commercial break of the year in American television—Nintendo took it one step further by having its North American CEO appear on the television show *Late Night with Jimmy Fallon* for a ten-minute segment to discuss the game in front of a live audience. To ensure its success, Nintendo employed a conventional wide release strategy to promote its upcoming game and announced a week after its launch that *Super Mario Run* had been downloaded fifty million times. Despite all this effort, Nintendo revealed during its 2017 earnings a few months later that the game had been downloaded seventy-eight million times, but that only five million actually had bought it. Revenue from the game "did not meet our expectations," stated Nintendo president Tatsumi Kimishima.[10]

So, perhaps then it is a difference in perspective between newcomers and legacy firms. Having held a dominant position in console and PC gaming for years, it was quite sobering for large incumbents to suddenly have to share the market with a new generation of creative firms.

To determine whether the mobile games market is accessible, we can look at the distribution of total downloads among titles. If only well-established games manage to reach audiences, smaller and newer titles should logically have a more difficult time building a player base. On the basis of the total downloads of the top one thousand mobile titles, we can observe a gradual shift. In 2013, the top-twenty titles accounted for 28 percent of total downloads. By 2018, this had declined to 18 percent. In particular, titles ranked fifty and up have come to claim a greater share. This is remarkable because, on average, mobile audiences play only a handful of titles and tend to be loyal. In aggregate, the top fifty titles by total downloads has declined from almost half (49 percent) in 2013 to about a third (37 percent) in 2018. At the same time, the share of remaining titles in the top one thousand has grown from 51 percent to 62 percent. This growth suggests that the mobile games market has indeed become more democratic in terms of accessibility and less top-heavy (see figure 5.5).

Of course, a variety of explanations are possible. The data, for instance, do not account for buggy titles that require a user to reinstall. This also fails to tell us anything about how much time people spend playing, or how frequently a single user downloads the same titles. For example, *Candy Crush Saga*, which was the top downloaded title in 2013 with more than four hundred million downloads, has managed to stay in the top ten throughout the entire period and without seeing its totals decline. *Subway Surfers*, in contrast, started off at a comparable position, but then dropped to about

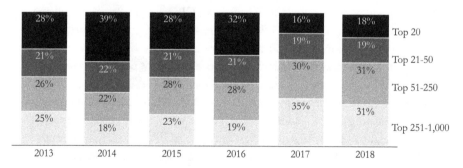

Figure 5.5
Share of total downloads among the top-one-thousand mobile titles, worldwide, 2013–2018. *Source*: Data from SuperData Research.

a third by 2018. Next, the top downloaded title in 2018, *Honor of Kings*, counted well over one billion downloads, or roughly three times the volume. This growth indicates that the mobile market has continued to grow with many new people continuing to come onto the platform and looking for games to play.

Contrary to the expectations created by the initial exuberance prevalent throughout the mobile industry and the degree of accessibility for newcomers, financial success has not been equally distributed. Legacy companies were slow to move on the mobile opportunity. Given their aversion to risk, this makes sense, of course. In 2010, Activision Blizzard's CEO, Bobby Kotick, stated: "We don't view the App Store as a really big opportunity for dedicated games," only to shell out almost $6 billion a few years later to get in on the action.[11] As a result of this hesitation among legacy firms, a new generation of companies came to dominate this emerging market. This dominance resulted in the establishment of a new top layer of disproportionally powerful firms.

The mobile market landscape has changed quite dramatically in a relatively short time period. Its spectacular growth has been an important driver of this change: overall growth of mobile game revenue among the top firms skyrocketed from roughly $2 billion a year around the introduction of the iPhone to $45 billion by 2018. Naturally, this attracted a slew of companies who all tried to get their share of the mobile millions. Newcomers who were by and large digital-only companies captured the bulk of the value: legacy publishers accounted for 11 percent of total revenue, about $5 billion, in 2018, compared with $40 billion for firms that did not exist before 2008.

This had at least two important consequences. First, the number of companies that control more than 1 percent of the total market has risen disproportionately, from eight in 2006 to twenty-five in 2018 (see table 5.1). Twenty-one firms made more than $500 million in 2018 from mobile games, giving them each a substantial war chest to invest in other projects. Second, the concentration of the overall market structure has dropped from being just shy of high concentration with a Herfindahl–Hirschman index (HHI) of 2,458 in 2008 all the way to being unconcentrated, with an HHI of 832 in 2018. That makes sense, of course, because of the influx of new participants and the sustained growth of the global market. It also makes mobile gaming the least concentrated market of the three when compared with the PC and console markets. However, the drop in the HHI in 2018 was largely the result of Tencent missing out on roughly $3 billion in revenue due to

Table 5.1

Top-twenty-five mobile game publishers, 1998–2018

	1998	1999	2000	2001	2002	2003	2004	2005	2006	2007	2008	2009	2010	2011	2012	2013	2014	2015	2016	2017	2018
Tencent													1,382	2,299	3,321	4,646	6,505	8,224	10,296	14,226	11,366
Supercell															78	777	1,814	2,177	2,572	Tencent	
NetEase												5	36	51	54	177	694	1,814	2,620	3,446	4,161
Activision Blizzard											237	244	184	167	164	629	433	418	1,674	2,081	2,175
Activision								90	164	65	Activision Blizzard										
King Digital													3	6	30	1,319	1,582	1,620	Activision Blizzard		
CyberAgent																	415	502	948	1,020	1,359
Niantic																			42	892	1,359
Mixi															63	60	57	961	1,777	1,763	1,202
Aniplex																		150	537	1,006	1,195
DeNA								27	61	134	281	356	455	1,066	1,386	2,148	1,915	1,715	1,360	1,359	1,150
Playrix																		39	209	537	871
Peak Games																		10	91	250	869
Softstar																				226	856
Long Tech Network																		6	141	268	852
37 Interactive																		71	219	455	810
Electronic Arts					150	147	100	124	636	612	915	424	469	448	270	337	527	504	617	660	792
NCSoft									2	7	8	8	32	11	52	60	61	57	69	622	781
GREE														510	1,360	1,316	1,097	830	602	575	673
Yotta Games																				49	666
Zynga															627	262	283	421	475	586	635
Nexon											2	28	193	194	288	260	202	342	397	471	518
IGG Inc.															2	25	138	124	154	299	501
Machine Zone																46	376	891	993	719	500
Ceasars														9	268	241	294	416	477	626	497
DianDian																			22	209	482
Netmarble																		251	350	567	468
Moon Active																				42	465
All others	47	64	66	118	179	180	158	341	543	415	728	674	806	1,032	1,305	4,588	5,829	8,500	7,990	6,967	6,755
Mobile revenue	**47**	**64**	**66**	**118**	**329**	**329**	**265**	**608**	**1,452**	**1,300**	**2,260**	**1,818**	**3,532**	**5,861**	**9,497**	**15,967**	**21,074**	**29,168**	**35,526**	**43,635**	**45,104**
C1	100%	100%	100%	68%	48%	45%	38%	27%	44%	47%	40%	24%	39%	39%	35%	29%	31%	28%	29%	33%	25%
C4				100%	100%	99%	97%	75%	85%	77%	86%	81%	79%	76%	70%	59%	56%	48%	49%	49%	42%
C10								100%	100%	100%	100%	99%	98%	95%	89%	81%	76%	67%	67%	63%	57%
HHI				5,666	4,443	3,018	2,695	1,694	2,555	2,644	2,458	1,779	2,128	2,138	1,760	1,272	1,260	1,028	1,063	1,227	832
No. of firms >1%	1	1	1	2	3	4	5	8	8	8	9	9	11	12	12	18	17	22	21	22	25

Source: Author's compilation based on company reports.

Note: Mobile revenue refers to the aggregate revenue for 2018 in millions U.S. dollars ($) generated from mobile game publishing activities by all companies in the data set. Industry structure metrics (e.g., C1, C4, C10, and HHI) calculated using all available company data across entire data set. HHI, Herfindahl-Hirschman index.

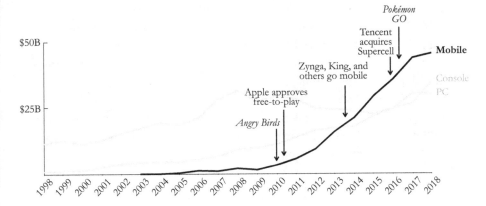

Figure 5.6
Mobile revenue for top game companies, worldwide, 1998–2018. *Source*: Data from company reports. *Note*: Revenue shown on *y*-axis in billions U.S. dollars ($). Callouts refer to related cases from this chapter and elsewhere.

its struggles with the Chinese regulatory agency that approves foreign content. Tencent was unable to benefit from the momentum behind titles like *PlayerUnknown's Battlegrounds* and *Fortnite*. Likely, its earnings would have been higher and up year-over-year without this issue and masks early indicators of market consolidation.

Toward the end of our analysis we can observe the first signs of change (figure 5.6). Consumer spending on mobile games has started to slow, suggesting the onset of market saturation. Even as growth in the total market is decelerating, the top firms continue to grow faster. On average, the top 20 mobile game companies grew 92 percent from 2017 to 2018. The total market increased only 4 percent. At the same time, mobile publishers faced an increasing set of challenges as a result of mobile's growth: low monetization rates, fierce competition, and the growing cost of marketing. The growth that drove initial success is now creating new challenges.

It is true that newcomers initially managed to capture most of the value in smartphone-based gaming. They were able to do so because their experience in making games for other markets allowed them to formulate creative strategies that gave them a competitive edge. Supercell's management had decades of experience in developing games and building and selling businesses, for instance. Tencent's unrivaled access to data and capital gave it a competitive advantage. By contrast, legacy firms had a more difficult time formulating a pricing strategy that suited the mobile audience, and they proved to be too attached to traditional marketing practices to accomplish the same level of success. For years after the introduction of the iPhone, the idea of the mobile millionaire persisted, and with it the notion that the mobile market remained open and accessible to anyone. The initial circumstances that cemented this idea have shifted quite dramatically. For now, the myth of the mobile millionaire remains alive, but for how long?

6

Greatly Exaggerated Death of the Console

In 2014, a firm called BOXER8 raised almost $9 million on the crowd-funding platform Kickstarter for its proposed OUYA console. Marketed as the "people's console," the device promised to be accessible both to audiences and content creators in a way that conventional dedicated gaming hardware never had been. Anticipated to be sold at a much lower retail price compared with incumbent consoles, this suggested that more people would be able to afford one. Its ostensible mainstream appeal promised to provide a massive user base at a fraction of the cost to development studios. And by leveraging Google's mobile operating system, Android, and its app store infrastructure, the OUYA significantly lowered the entry barriers to creative firms, who in turn would see to it that the device had ample content available. When, finally, Chinese e-commerce giant Alibaba invested another $10 million in the platform, it cemented the idea that the OUYA would not just disrupt but outright do away with the traditional console industry. Sony, the console market leader, had been put on notice.

In the preceding years, a string of media coverage and articles had started to openly speculate about the "death of the console." *Wired* magazine ran an article titled, "The Game Console Is Dead. What Will Replace It?"[1] CNN pointed at the poor performance of the Wii U to explain "why console gaming is dying."[2] Voices from inside the industry grew similarly skeptical.

One of the biggest trade publications, *IGN*, chimed in asking, "Are consoles dead?"[3] The prospects for dedicated gaming hardware were eroding because of the disruptive introduction of the iPhone. At the Game Developer Conference that year, industry veteran Ben Cousins presented a talk entitled, "When the consoles die—what comes next?"[4] In it, Cousins postulated the imminent decline of the dedicated hardware by drawing a parallel with historical examples of now-redundant technologies. Examples included the horse and carriage, which virtually disappeared following the introduction of the car, and the decline of the Walkman after the MP3 became available. His evidence included the decline in stock prices for big publishers and platform holders, combined with the turmoil at retail. The rapid growth for newcomers like Zynga, Facebook, GREE, and Nexon amounted to a revolution as the non-console business overtook the long-established way of playing games. Consoles were, according to Cousins, to suffer the same fate as the arcade because of a similar combination of bigger organizations entering the market and cheaper chipsets becoming available. The "invisible force" that served as a disruptive technology was the emergence of mobile.

Cousins's lecture serves as a proxy for an emerging school of thought in the industry at the time. Many senior executives felt the days of dedicated devices were numbered: president of Epic Games Mike Capps openly asked: "What's the point of next-gen consoles?"[5] According to Gabe Newell, "the notion of a separate console platform will disappear."[6] And the CEO of Square Enix, Yoichi Wade, simply stated: "In ten years' time a lot of what we call 'console games' won't exist."[7]

In fairness, the business was ripe for disruption. Just three industry participants controlled the console market. Each offered dedicated proprietary hardware for different use categories and kept prices comparatively high. Consoles were experiencing an unusually long hardware cycle. Historically, manufacturers had introduced new hardware generations every five years. The timeline for seventh-generation consoles, however, was much longer than earlier models. Instead of releasing new hardware, Microsoft extended the life cycle of its Xbox 360 with the launch of its peripheral, the Kinect. And Sony followed a similar strategy by developing upgraded versions of its PS3. Moreover, the disappointing sales of Nintendo's Wii U, which followed the spectacular success of its predecessor the Wii, further evidenced imminent doom. It all supported the idea that the conventional games business had become stale, slow, and ready for disruption. Even large publishers had growing skepticism about how much longer the console would dominate the industry landscape.

Incumbent content creators, too, were seemingly having difficulty. The challenge of adapting to the new reality of global, digital economics had put pressure on larger publishers. Activision Blizzard had tried to launch a modified version of one of its biggest franchises, *Call of Duty Online*, specifically for the Chinese consumer market. And Take-Two had established a 150-people studio in China to develop *Borderlands Online*. After much fanfare, these high-profile efforts fizzled out. Industry observers grew increasingly skeptical of the traditional console's ability to survive the new market conditions. In line with Christensen's basic theory around "disruptive innovation," several big firms like Apple and Google were entering the games market and the cost of chipsets was coming down, thereby opening up the console business to disruption.[8] Two underwhelming market entries added insult to injury: the introduction of a digital-only console called the Zeebo into Brazil, and the Pyrrhic victory of Xbox's entry into China.

The Emerging Market Solution

As digitalization started to open up territories that previously had remained inaccessible, high-growth emerging economies were in vogue. Among the most promising at the time was Brazil. Because the console business there historically had been absent, the country's broader prosperity proved irresistible. Up to this point, Brazil had been out of reach for both economic and tax reasons.

Piracy long presented a major concern for publishers. They remained hesitant to release their carefully developed content without a comparable level of protection they enjoyed elsewhere. One producer recalled to me seeing illegal copies of a game he had worked on being sold at a market: "I was devastated. After spending six years developing this game, they were selling it for the equivalent of $1." Further exacerbating the difficulties of entering the Brazilian market was the high tax rate on imported hardware. This tax rate affected hardware manufacturers in particular. In Brazil, a legally purchased Wii, for instance, cost about US$1,000 (R$1,750 Brazilian reals). This price was four times the average selling price in North America and well outside the reach of an average Brazilian consumer. By comparison, a pirated Xbox 360 or PlayStation 2 ran about US$250.

In 2008, a collaboration between Qualcomm, a U.S.-based provider of telecom equipment, and Tectoy, a Brazilian game and electronics firm, resulted in the launch of dedicated gaming tailored to emerging economies of Latin America: the Zeebo. A popular rationale at the time was the idea that up-and-coming economies would "leapfrog" technologies. Where consumers in North America and Europe gradually had upgraded from dial-up to fixed cable to cellular broadband, emerging economies were expected to jump straight to the most novel internet technologies. For this reason, the Zeebo was wireless and would not require cartridges or CD-ROMs. It aspired "to make a living-room gaming console for emerging markets that would connect to the Internet over wireless phone networks and sell at prices middle-class families could afford."[9] Launched at a comparatively low price point of US$170 (R$299) at retail, games were priced between $5 and $15. The hope was to have conventional game publishers eventually participate given that the Zeebo's wireless feature meant that piracy no longer would be a concern.

But this was not to be. A combination of shortcomings resulted in the Zeebo's failure. To establish an appealing portfolio of available content, hardware manufacturers need to ensure that creative firms can easily make games for their platform, or port existing ones. The Zeebo's hardware architecture was poorly designed and made development cumbersome and expensive. In addition, its manufacturers offered inadequate software support. With a limited content offering and largely uninspiring catalog, the device received a lukewarm welcome from Brazilian consumers. The Zeebo also lacked the backing of one of the incumbent platform manufacturers. Without sufficient market power and the necessary publisher relationships, it proved too difficult to gain traction. Microsoft, in contrast, had successfully launched its Xbox in Brazil two years earlier. Instead of building a device specifically for this market, it relied on its existing content inventory, brand recognition, retail relationships, and vast capital resources. To accomplish this, Microsoft built its own factory in Brazil, thus bringing down the price of its device and making it within reach for consumers. Despite the expense, the strategy paid off and proved to be hugely successful. It resulted in Microsoft claiming more than 80 percent of the Brazilian console market.

It was only a matter of time before the idea of a much larger, global audience proved too hard for Microsoft's executives to resist. Watching the success of the iPhone, Microsoft CEO Steve Ballmer determined in 2011 that it, too, should have a successful consumer device. As new markets in Asia emerged, the firm set out to launch the newly released Xbox One in China. According to conservative internal estimates, China had the potential to become the third-largest market for the Xbox after the United States and the United Kingdom. Microsoft was losing the console war against

Sony and needed a strong win. It sold roughly half as many units of its eighth-generation device as its Japanese competitor. Entering a new territory, especially one in which the presence of dedicated gaming hardware was virtually nonexistent, Ballmer reasoned, would allow it to claim massive share in the fastest-growing consumer segment for video games. The plan was to dispatch the same team that had conquered the Brazilian market to China and create a tailored device rollout.

It proved easier said than done. China is a difficult country to enter, because, well, it banned consoles. In June 2000, the Chinese Ministry of Culture made the production and sale of electronic game equipment and accessories to Chinese consumers illegal. In their view, the businesses of console gaming and arcades went against Chinese values, and they considered it to be especially bad for its underage population. In fact, it regarded the devices as a technological steppingstone to more nefarious acts and gambling machines. Console games by design sit in the center of the living room, a sacred, private space that could only become corrupted by the influence of a device meant for frivolous entertainment. Subsequently, Microsoft had to not just break into a new market, but to do so, had to overcome the negative perception the Chinese government held of game consoles. To make things worse, unlike the more open platform of the PC, consoles allowed regulators much less control over content. In addition, there was a broader cultural context that did not work in Microsoft's favor. For years, it was mostly Japanese firms, like Sony, Nintendo, Capcom, and Namco Bandai, that had dominated the global business (see chapter 4). It fueled the economic protectionism around its consumer audience. Its own gaming industry was still nascent at the time, but early market entrants like Shanda Interactive, Perfect World, Tencent, and The9 showed promise. In 2011, revenue for top Chinese games companies totaled $5 billion.

To gain access to this thriving economy, Microsoft positioned the Xbox One in China as a "lifestyle device" rather than hardware dedicated to interactive amusement. Unlike its marketing strategy in North America and Europe where it played up the processing power and title inventory, it took a different approach to placate Chinese officials by emphasizing four components: its functionality as a television, as a video-playing device, as a fitness device using the Kinect, and as a learning aide. It also downplayed its entertainment segment titled "curated gaming," hoping to win favor by de-emphasizing the Xbox's capacity as a gaming device and foregrounding other applications.

Microsoft realized, of course, that it also needed strong partnerships with local organizations to solidify its case. It entered into a partnership with the Shanghai Media Group/BesTV, a television content provider, in 2013. Ultimately, it won Microsoft approval to trade in the newly minted Shanghai Free Trade Zone. With this victory in hand, Microsoft reached out to its publishing partners to see whether they were willing to localize some of their content for China. A key point of consideration was that Xbox had to be competitively priced. Specifically, in a country that was accustomed to free-to-play monetization on the PC and mobile platforms, in combination with an existing gray market, consoles were comparatively expensive. Even so, Microsoft managed to persuade EA and Ubisoft to agree to a $30 price point for console games—half of what it cost everywhere else.

Among the most important lessons learned from the experience was undoubtedly the degree to which the Chinese government implemented a sluggish approval process for foreign content providers. Requiring publishers and platform holders to work together with a Chinese partner meant having to share revenue with firms that elsewhere were competitors. Moreover, the approval process proved entirely opaque—with no sense of timing or information about what censors look for. Even today, it still can take a long time before a game is finally released in China. Microsoft learned this the hard way as it tried to gain entry.

When it finally received approval in July 2013, the Xbox One had a significant lead-time on its closest competitors, making it the only available console system in China for almost a year. It also had compiled an inventory of more than seventy committed titles, nearly half of which were developed by Chinese organizations, and through its partnership with BesTV, it offered a host of premium television content. In total, it spent around $100 million on content and another $300 million on hardware development to build a device tailored to Chinese audiences, to subsidize and help localize quality content, and to invest in marketing just to gain access. At launch, it was initially hailed a success: it sold one hundred thousand Xbox One units on its first day.

Despite getting this far, the Xbox entry into China did not bring Ballmer the anticipated riches. Internal estimates anticipated Microsoft would sell more than two million units of the localized Xbox in China in its first year. After spending close to half a billion dollars and successfully getting a slew of industry participants to collaborate, the effort did not result in a significant increase in share or competitive power. To penetrate the market, Microsoft had overcome a range of obstacles that opened the road into China for Sony and Nintendo as well. Sony's PlayStation had continued to grow its install base, Apple's iPhone remained wildly popular with consumers, and the launch of Nintendo's newly announced Switch device was imminent. Successfully entering China had provided no competitive advantage.

In part because of the lower-than-expected results from both of these market entries, many industry observers held on to the idea that the console was dying. Even as the eighth-generation devices continued to sell faster than their predecessors, to many, these minor disappointments of the Zeebo in Latin America and the Xbox in China evidenced declining demand and questioned the suitability of the console as critical to the industry's future. To them, the business was clearly grappling with the new reality of digitalization and suffering from an inability to grow at the same rate as mobile gaming.

However, by this time, broadband penetration had become more common and offered a reliable, fast connection to most consumers. Looking to leverage this increasingly pervasive infrastructure convinced platform holders to abolish the idea of a dedicated gaming device and, instead, to diversity their offerings by adding services and other forms of amusement.

The Connected Console Solution

For decades, hardware manufacturers have sought to differentiate by using online services and gameplay. Virtually all of them have failed. Even so, a few deserve a moment of attention. Take, for example, Intellivision, which launched its PlayCable service through a joint venture in 1981 between Mattel and General Instruments. It featured a separate cartridge capable of storing downloaded games and access to a broader, digital library. Despite offering abundant and differentiating content that justified the purchase of the device, PlayCable failed. Even at its peak the service counted just ten thousand subscribers across the entire United States. The growing file size of games gradually rendered the cartridge useless as an adequate storage device for newer titles, and the PlayCable discontinued its service. Around the same time, another contender, GameLine, launched a competing offering: a platform-agnostic service of downloadable content. Emulating the arcade model in which consumers paid per play, GameLine limited access to a set number of plays. Without the support of big publishers, however, the service struggled to attract a critical mass of players, and when the industry collapsed a few years later, GameLine disappeared.

Then in 1994, Sega launched Sega Channel, a monthly subscription for the Sega Genesis available on cable television. Unlike previous services,

Sega Channel offered several big titles, including online-only games. As hardware demands increased, Sega discontinued the service when it moved onto the Saturn because, like its predecessors, it was unable to facilitate the growing file size of newer games. One last notable initiative came from Nintendo, which spent six years pursuing a multimedia service. The Nintendo Satellaview, which was available from 1995 to 2001, offered music and news in addition to games. This service was exclusive to Japan, and users could download interactive content only during certain times of the day.

We can find other examples of consoles exploring online connectivity and downloadable content as a differentiator. This idea is not new, which brings us to the question why the connected console only recently managed to gain traction among consumers. The simple answer is, of course, that many more people have access to the internet today: right as a growing number of skeptics started to announce the death of the console, the number of households with access to broadband reached critical mass, which finally allowed console manufacturers to expand their digital services.

As the market leader, the rumblings around disruptive innovation by newcomers meant that especially Sony had a lot to lose. By formulating a service-based strategy, it managed to stave off the anticipated decline in hardware sales and successfully embraced digitalization. Sony anticipated much of this early on. Already in 2006, it launched a content service called PlayStation Network. The free digital entertainment offering initially worked only with PlayStation devices, but eventually it also became available on smartphones, tablets, and smart television. It offers a range of different premium components, including an online marketplace (Store), a subscription to games (Plus) that counted ninety-four million active users as of mid-2019, movie streaming and rentals (Video), cloud-based television service (Vue), music (Music), and a cloud gaming service (Now). Collectively, the services available under PlayStation Network generated $13 billion in revenue for Sony in 2018. As consumers began to prefer digital services, Sony's leadership emphasized the need to add greater content diversity.

The Plus service gives us insight into the dynamic between content creators and platform holders. During a period when digital content was still very much a novelty for major publishers, Sony effectively asked game makers to populate their subscription service at a fixed price. Having them on board validated the service and increased the overall value of Sony's services to consumers. In return, a prudent strategy to "wait and see" determined the viability and value of a new distribution channel or platform. Being part of a service actively promoted by Sony meant greater visibility and free marketing for participating creative firms. At the time, Square Enix's *Just Cause 2*, for instance, was one of the bigger franchises available for free on the PlayStation Network. I asked a former executive of New York–based Avalanche Studios, which had developed *Just Cause 2* and was working on the series' next title, what the benefit was of giving content away for free. He explained: "Marketing. We make a small amount of money from the in-game micro-transactions. But it's mostly to stay top-of-mind with our audience, as we're working on the next one." Digitalization of the console had, at least at this level, done little to change the existing mutual co-dependence between platform and publisher.

To further drive demand, Sony invested in exclusive projects for its digital service to pull consumers across the line and commit to an additional monthly fee. A title like *Journey* by Thatgamecompany proved wildly successful as a direct download on PlayStation. Similarly, Square Enix initially released *Life Is Strange*, an episodic puzzle game that features a female protagonist with the ability to rewind time, on all digital platforms and earned twice as much on console than on PC. By mid-2016, the digital version had generated $10 million from online console sales compared with just over $5 million on PC. It was a full year later before Square Enix finally decided to also pursue a physical release.

In addition, Sony was an early adopter of cloud gaming. In 2012, Sony acquired Gaikai, a service that enabled consumers to play games in the cloud from their home devices, for $380 million. It did so to corner the market and to prevent competitors like Samsung and LG from taking significant market share. This effort eventually became the PlayStation Now service, which provides a selection of titles from the PlayStation 2, 3, and 4 available for play on the PS4 and PC. Next, in 2015, it also purchased OnLive, its main rival and owner of several key patents around the technology, only to shut it down. The expectation at the time was that as broadband became more ubiquitous, consumer demand for cloud-based content would increase. Unfortunately, at the time it did not. In early 2020 Sony announced it had 2.2 million subscribers to the PlayStation Now service, or less than 2 percent of its global install base. In the United States, only about 3 percent of PlayStation owners, roughly 800,000 people, currently subscribe to the service.

Sony also focused on diversifying its content. Online connectivity facilitated the expansion of online offering beyond just games and included more conventional entertainment, such as film and television programming. By bundling different content types, platforms managed to increase the value proposition for its user base.

Beyond building on its content offering, Sony also expanded its hardware offerings. Building on its strengths as a consumer electronics firm, it continued to further develop the original PlayStation 4 device. Releasing a Slim version, a Pro version, and a standalone PlayStation VR version allowed it to cater to different consumer segments at varying price points. Sony also increased the capacity of the hard drives in its consoles up to 2 terabytes to better facilitate downloadable content. Whereas smartphone manufacturers were in the habit of releasing a new generation of devices annually, consoles had multiyear cycles. By releasing updated models, both Sony and Microsoft started to match consumer expectation more closely and they were able to better cater to different consumer cohorts.

Closely related to this was the concept of bundling. Selling a special edition version of its console associated with a blockbuster title presented another component critical to growing the PlayStation's install base. It also enlarged the addressable market for its digital strategy. Of the total units sold in North America across the company's various hardware products, devices that were associated with a specific title accounted for 52 percent of total. Bundles like the *PS4 Uncharted 4 Bundle* and the *Limited Edition Spiderman* managed to perform well, selling around four million and one million units, respectively, across the United States and Canada by early 2019. For the PlayStation VR, Sony teamed up with id Software and Bethesda on the *Doom* and *Skyrim* bundles.

A combination of gradual hardware iterations and complementariness, bundling its console sales with top-selling titles and franchises, and expanding its digital content offering has allowed Sony to retain its leadership position in spite of newcomers looking to disrupt this market. The combination of extending the hardware life cycle by offering additional subscription-based services, side-stepping piracy, and allowing publishers more distribution choices, as well as the newfound viability of a broader range of game titles, quickly made the connected console strategy a success. By 2016, Sony's PlayStation Network reported ninety-four million active accounts compared with forty-nine million users of the Xbox Live services.

Digital Publishing

Accustomed to a model of building up marketing momentum to maximize the sales of a full game in the few weeks following its release at retail, publishers like Take-Two and Electronic Arts initially committed only their

back-catalog titles to online distribution. In 2011, the head of digital channels at a major publisher explained why: "We are experimenting by releasing some of our older, smaller titles digitally on consoles. But at least
initially we will focus on our lesser known games to see how things go
before we take a chance with our bigger franchises." Observing the success
of the more agile, smaller studios, the big publishers slowly started to adopt
some of these new digital practices.

An important driver of the digital success of incumbent publishers was
their adoption of online multiplayer gameplay. Certainly, previous devices
had offered this feature. But they had not been able to reach enough consumers to make the added expense attractive. Playing against others over
the internet had remained a relative novelty. But now, with the bulk of
households having access to a fast enough online connection, publishers
could rely on ample available players and thus moved their focus to making games to support online multiplayer mechanics. This transition offered
several advantages. For one, it greatly extended the life cycle of a title. The
online multiplayer component proved additive to the traditional single-
player campaign. After completing the "story mode," a growing number
of titles offered access to an online game mode in which players could
test their skill against others. Online gameplay quickly developed into an
entirely new category offering loads more content.

This categorization helped game makers combat piracy and the missed
income from used sales. As observed previously, GameStop did not cut
publishers in on the earnings from second-hand sales. By taking content
online, creatives were able to regain control by requiring players to enter
a unique code to access online features. Once used, that code would no
longer work, which greatly reduced a title's resale value. Understandably,
retailers were unexcited about the prospect of platforms delivering full
experiences directly to consumers. Simultaneously, publishers and platforms had no interest in alienating their retail partners. Having seen the
results of digitalization on music retailing, where institutions like Tower
Records went bankrupt as consumers switched to downloading music
online, a specialty games retailer like GameStop had no qualms about
leveraging its market power to slow the rate of adoption. According to a
former GameStop executive, the retailer plainly confronted platform holders with the message: "If you continue to pursue this digital strategy, we will
tell our clerks to promote your competitor's hardware over yours." Despite
resistance among some of the value chain participants, console gaming
was lurching toward adopting digital distribution. Now, even incumbent

publishers proved willing to increase their investment in this bourgeoning distribution channel.

One organization that successfully capitalized on the digitalization of the console was Take-Two. The 2013 release of its marquee title *Grand Theft Auto V* (*GTA V*) is among the most successful in entertainment history. Within its first three days, it generated $1 billion in sales, and, to date, it has sold almost one hundred and thirty million copies across digital and physical sales channels. But even before it was successful, critics had predicted its doom. As consoles started to push online distribution, investors were skeptical of the firm's ability to adapt. Known for an emphasis on delivering quality blockbuster titles, Take-Two has a comparatively limited portfolio. This presented a particularly risky profile: after *GTA V* spent six years in development, it was either going to be successful or tank the company. Naturally, investors questioned whether the company was capable of leveraging the affordances of distribution over the internet.

After building up a lot of excitement among consumers, Take-Two's initial switch to enable online multiplayer gameplay did not go as planned. Although the title had sold well at retail, the moment its online gameplay went live, its servers crashed. Players immediately expressed their discontent for *GTA V: Online* and investors returned to their prerelease skepticism. Despite stellar sales figures, the publisher seemed woefully incapable of embracing online gameplay. Take-Two had not appropriately accounted for what would happen when millions of its players went online simultaneously. The online component to *GTA V* remained largely inaccessible for several weeks, and to many, this evidenced a lack of preparedness in one of the industry's leaders and reflected poorly on the console business at large.

This view proved shortsighted, as Take-Two's server collapse proved merely a growing pain. Or, as one of its developers told me at the time: "We simply underestimated the impact on our servers of 25 million players all going online at once." Different from free-to-play titles on PC, which tend to build up audiences gradually and therefore can add the necessary server space as things progress, Take-Two had to manage a massive simultaneous influx of gamers.

The initial failure in online gaming proved to be a symptom of the game's success. Part of the reason it had been so successful was because the publisher had cleverly launched its biggest title toward the end of the seventh-generation console's cycle. The combined install base for the PS3 and Xbox 360 was at its peak. Most of its competitors were at this point building up buzz for their new titles to release on the next hardware generation. To them, it made no sense to invest in a market that was about to be replaced in its entirety by new hardware. In addition, as demand was approaching saturation, it attracted cost-conscious people who were looking for a good deal on a console and a cool title to play.[10] By successfully catering to the latecomers on the PS3 and Xbox360, followed by a release on the PS4 and Xbox One, Take-Two also managed to capitalize on the growth of digital distribution by building up a massive inventory of additional content that could be distributed in smaller updates over time. As part of its development process, developer Rockstar had created a lot of additional content, such as missions, side-stories, and vehicles. Rather than continuing development post-release, the development team had access to a vast resource of available add-on content and simply had to analyze in-game behavior to look for clues as to when to release the next expansion pack. By removing the strain on the production team and instead focusing on marketing intelligence, it could continue to incentivize players. In its first five years, *GTA V* generated almost $2 billion in additional content revenue across PC and console platforms. By comparison, it earned $746 million in full game downloads on both platforms during that same period (figure 6.1).

Looking at total consumer spending, we observe something remarkable: following a prolonged period of decline, the console segment has started to grow again. After several years of decline and reaching a low

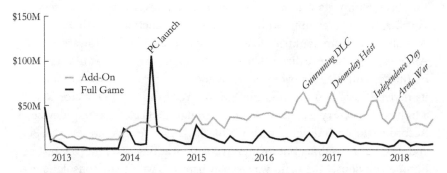

Figure 6.1

Total digital earnings for *Grand Theft Auto V*, full game and add-on revenue, PC and console platforms, 2013–2018. *Source*: Data from SuperData Research. *Note*: Add-on revenue refers to all money spent by consumers, including microtransactions and downloadable content.

point of $22 billion in 2015, console gaming has rejuvenated. Revenue among the top firms reached $35 billion in 2018, which rivaled the previous industry high point in 2008 when the popularity of the Nintendo Wii was at its peak. Despite the seemingly slow adoption of digital distribution among legacy firms initially, the console market has managed to successfully reinvent itself.

The landscape, however, hasn't changed much. The usual suspects continue to dominate: Sony, Nintendo, and Microsoft remain at the top of the food chain, followed closely by Electronic Arts and Activision Blizzard. Overall, concentration is now moderate as consolidation for the dedicated hardware business has been on a steady decline over the past two decades. The shares of the top firm and the four largest have gradually eroded. The share of the ten largest firms, in contrast, has not. Console gaming, the data indicate, remains reserved for a select group of companies that have managed to retain the bulk of the value in this market for themselves. Despite the initial calls for the death of the console, many of the legacy firms have survived and continue to do well today. The number of companies with a market share percentage greater than 1 percent (and therefore presumably capable of affecting the overall market structure) has remained more or less the same over the entire period at around 14.

Next, overall concentration has decreased (see table 6.1). The Herfindahl–Hirschman index (HHI) dropped from 3,106 in 1998 to 1,389 in 2018. At least according to antitrust regulation guidelines, the console games market has transitioned from highly concentrated to unconcentrated. Digitalization inadvertently allowed newcomers to enter this market. Today, we observe important newcomers like Epic Games, riding the success of *Fortnite*, and Wargaming with its mission to penetrate North America. As publishers from countries like China and Russia looked toward North America, they have realized that to reach audiences, they would have to be on the console. Following a tremendously successful rise to fame in its native Russia and neighboring Europe, Wargaming CEO Victor Kislyi admitted that entry was feasible only through dedicated gaming devices. According to an interview with CNBC in 2013: "Yes, we are on the PC and, yes, we are online, but for most of America, England and [the rest of Europe], obviously the main way to play games is with that [console] controller in your hands."[11]

Finally, it seems that the traditional barriers to entry in console gaming ultimately have protected legacy publishers and platform holders from disruption. The largest firm in 1998 claimed 53 percent of the total market,

Table 6.1

Top-twenty-five console game publishers, 1998–2018

	1998	1999	2000	2001	2002	2003	2004	2005	2006	2007	2008	2009	2010	2011	2012	2013	2014	2015	2016	2017	2018
Sony	6,187	6,376	6,158	5,817	6,487	6,887	7,046	6,237	6,772	8,047	8,999	7,545	9,016	8,414	7,682	7,224	6,792	5,103	6,468	8,373	10,191
Nintendo	1,744	1,876	1,376	1,766	1,928	2,413	2,118	1,896	2,992	6,172	9,184	7,017	5,749	4,361	3,228	2,017	2,067	2,092	1,797	1,883	4,294
Microsoft					108	250	387	470	649	1,104	1,260	1,232	1,473	2,188	2,172	2,237	2,723	2,873	2,959	2,916	3,863
Electronic Arts	736	900	840	954	1,503	1,974	2,471	1,795	2,003	1,974	2,877	2,699	2,327	2,669	2,751	2,314	2,643	3,013	3,312	3,532	3,395
Activision Blizzard											1,251	1,412	2,330	2,439	2,186	2,379	2,150	2,391	2,453	2,389	2,538
Activision	306	414	424	386	481	675	732	970	1,009	2,178		Activision Blizzard									
Vivendi (Blizzard)				1,253	1,496	788	594	566	649	776	Activision Blizzard										
Take-Two	169	286	322	104	103	147	70	796	179	137	41	79	1,168	776	87	2,019	898	201	246	339	1,841
Epic Games																			4	86	1,676
Square Enix	127	128	226	126	115	291	528	445	990	898	995	1,171	1,242	1,038	1,014	913	930	1,091	1,473	1,472	1,532
Eidos	270	258	207	119	69	202	133					Square Enix									
Ubisoft						512	605	554	788	1,177	1,335	1,089	1,156	1,221	1,347	1,364	1,305	1,163	1,317	1,465	1,488
Sega Sammy	377	578	645	700	338	1,025	1,584	1,139	1,127	1,041	1,174	1,262	1,294	1,294	841	995	861	808	792	836	745
Konami	269	272	248	351	966	451	1,000	875	948	1,038	1,362	1,146	1,279	1,374	1,070	844	726	703	683	628	654
Capcom				116	407	110	437	484	481	550	694	813	864	803	966	726	487	471	523	584	577
Disney							118	100	103	183	382	362	385	405	348	367	422	354	345	302	290
Bandai Namco			72	276	321	386	409	574	586	663	194	677	203	217	263	208	772	786	870	197	220
ZeniMax Media															100	67	67	209	339	228	201
Perfect World															8	20	19	97	124	148	150
AT&T																					130
WB Games											33	90	180	114	176	112	50	267	79	141	AT&T
GungHo															25	306	323	267	211	173	121
Leyou																			50	75	102
Koei Tecmo	37	38	34	30	36	41	51	42	39	43	53	114	148	154	151	129	110	94	102	99	101
THQ Nordiq																	4	5	7	12	90
Krafton																					88
Digital Extremes																27	44	43	58	74	86
Ubisoft																					63
Wargaming.net																	35	47	72	45	46
All others	2,101	2,247	1,600	2,728	3,296	2,752	2,660	2,611	2,793	4,041	1,629	792	688	781	251	154	181	401	478	533	250
Console revenue	11,746	12,699	11,519	12,967	15,609	17,335	19,484	18,554	21,149	28,187	31,463	27,316	29,470	28,246	24,667	24,421	23,608	22,482	24,764	26,604	34,734
C1	53%	50%	53%	45%	42%	40%	36%	34%	32%	29%	29%	28%	31%	30%	31%	29%	29%	23%	26%	31%	29%
C4	79%	77%	78%	75%	73%	71%	68%	60%	61%	65%	71%	68%	66%	63%	64%	58%	61%	60%	61%	65%	63%
C10	94%	92%	94%	94%	93%	90%	89%	84%	86%	88%	93%	92%	92%	91%	94%	91%	90%	89%	89%	91%	91%
HHI	3,106	2,864	3,134	2,414	2,148	2,016	1,747	1,504	1,481	1,515	1,865	1,659	1,568	1,450	1,519	1,368	1,350	1,155	1,260	1,505	1,389
No. of firms >1%	14	14	12	11	12	14	14	14	14	14	13	13	13	13	12	13	14	14	13	12	12

Source: Author's compilation based on company reports.

Note: Console revenue refers to the 2018 aggregate revenue in millions U.S. dollars ($) generated from console game publishing activities by all companies in the data set. Industry structure metrics (e.g., C1, C4, C10, and HHI) calculated using all available company data across entire data set. HHI, Herfindahl-Hirschman index.

which eventually dropped to 29 percent over the course of twenty years. In both cases, this firm is Sony. By welcoming innovations like free-to-play titles and expanding their digital offering, incumbents and platform holders like Sony and Microsoft successfully adjusted to their new digital reality rather than suffer its disruption.

In response to digitalization and the emergence of a generation of disruptors, incumbents in the console market formulated two strategies. First, they leveraged their vast capital resources and existing catalog to enter into new markets that promised accelerated growth. Microsoft's entry into Brazil and China, although costly, proved effective at growing their global install base. Second, embracing digitalization head on, by offering an array of downloadable content and complementary services, facilitated further revenue growth. Sony's adoption of new technologies and clever market tactics, in the form of bundling and releasing complementary hardware components like the PlayStation VR, resulted in its ability to maintain a leadership position. This paved the way for content creators to follow suit and invest further into new monetization models and releases.

Ultimately, the OUYA, despite its initial notoriety, failed to disrupt the console games business. Its software assets, totaling one thousand titles, were acquired by gaming hardware manufacturer Razer in July 2015, just three years after its spectacular entry. The challenge in disruption is to successfully convince consumers and not the industry. According to a former executive at GameStop's digital team, an internal study on consumer awareness of the OUYA proved to be "very, very low" and evidence of the fact "that the jump to mass market is a long one." One primary reason for OUYA's ultimate failure was its inability to commit a big enough marketing budget to its rollout. To show potential customers the benefits of the device, in-store kiosks need to allow them to play games right there and then. The expenses fall to the platform holder.

Even with these issues solved, the would-be disruptor still had to explain how it planned to make money. When it did finally launch, the OUYA managed to get no more than two devices in every Walmart outlet, falling short on its promise to claim significant share. In the two years following its release, OUYA sold an estimated sixty-eight thousand units in North America. A low price point of $99 and its reliance on a free-to-play monetization scheme made it difficult to establish the healthy cash flow it needed to invest in third-party support. Discontent among developers began to grow. Worse, the incumbent platforms ultimately proved to be in

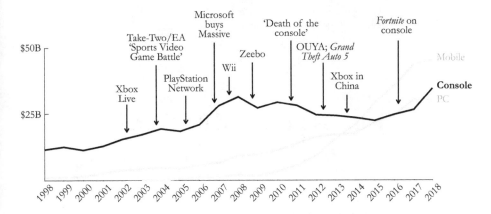

Figure 6.2
Console revenue top game companies, worldwide, 1998–2018. *Source*: Data from company reports. *Note*: Revenue shown on left *y*-axis in billions U.S. dollars ($). Callouts refer to related cases from this chapter and elsewhere.

a much stronger position to improve their appeal to independent developers instead, offering support and the opportunity to monetize a larger install base, and more overtly, to experiment with new revenue models (figure 6.2). Failing to recognize the ability among incumbent platforms to formulate new content and distribution strategies, the OUYA truly never stood a chance. Or as the GameStop executive had told me early on: "It will be business as usual."

7

Glorious Return of PC Gaming

The myth of the angsty artist is bullshit. Being creative is
not necessarily a unique virtue.

—RAPH KOSTER, CREATOR OF *ULTIMA ONLINE* AND *STAR
WARS GALAXIES*

Innovation tends to flourish on the fringes, outside the purview of incumbents. Perhaps because major publishers largely ignored the PC games market, it was here that firms with unorthodox approaches to business challenges were established. This chapter discusses some of the innovations that contributed to PC gaming both regaining its relevance to the overall industry and flourishing alongside mobile and console gaming.

Before digitization the physical PC business had fallen out of grace with major game makers. Executives had accepted the idea that dedicated gaming hardware had "won" the platform wars. Nintendo's success, combined with the market entry of Sega and Sony, had resulted in a massive growth spurt in the global install base, and many publishers were squarely focused on the console market. As the industry grew, so, too, had risk in game development, and especially large publishers found themselves unable to resist the economics of console gaming. Even a holdout like Trip Hawkins, who had started Electronic Arts in the expectation that the PC ultimately would become more popular, changed his mind and capitulated to the console.

Moreover, development for the PC had grown more complex than for dedicated devices. Unlike the console industry, which was centralized around the relatively rigid hardware specifications of its major platforms, hardware components varied greatly across PC devices. Consumers can select from among a broad variety of individual hardware components when purchasing a personal computer, including graphics cards, cooling systems, input devices and accessories, monitors, and processors. It makes it invariably more expensive to develop for PC because creative firms have to ensure their game will run properly on a wide array of available hardware setups. Consoles, on the other hand, offer universal hardware specifications among their entire user base, which reduces complexity. It also gives big publishers more control over the quality of the experience and minimizes the chances of players having a "buggy" experience.

Piracy also has been a much bigger issue for PC-based business compared with its counterparts. Because of its open nature, it is much easier to extract a title from its disc and distribute it over the internet. This renders especially large game makers hesitant to commit to the platform. Following the simultaneous release of *Max Payne 3* on both PC and console, Take-Two observed that its game was the top downloaded title on the well-known hub for pirated content, Pirate Bay, for two consecutive weeks, which resulted in a substantial financial loss. In response, big publishers tend to avoid or delay the release on PC until after console sales have started to slow.

For these reasons, the contribution to overall revenue for major firms from physical PC games sales has been anemic for years. In 1996, the market still was fairly equally split in terms of worldwide revenue between 41 percent PC and 59 percent console. But some twenty years later, that ratio had changed to 6 percent and 94 percent, respectively. Figure 7.1 provides a sense of the difference in scale in the physical PC market.

Digitization dramatically shifted the circumstances of the PC games market. As audiences came online, most large publishers clung to the lower risk profile in dedicated hardware. In particular, it was the smaller outfits that managed to come up with creative approaches to this bourgeoning market and managed to capitalize on the affordances of digital distribution early on and to drive growth in the PC games market from just over $1 billion in annual consumer spending in 1998 to more than $30 billion two decades later.

Perhaps the best example of a small innovative game studio from that initial period is id Software. Its best-known title *Doom* was the result of ingenious design and a visionary approach to crowd-sourcing development, as co-founders John Romero and John Carmack sought to overcome several of the challenges presented by the PC platform. During the

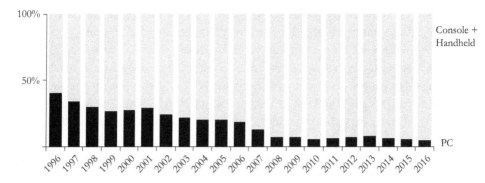

Figure 7.1
Revenue distribution of physical game software sales for PC and console (including handhelds), worldwide, 1996–2016. *Source*: Based on data found in Michael Pachter, Nick McKay, and Nick Citrin, "Post Hoc Ergo Propter Hoc; Why the Next Generation Will Be as Big as Ever" (Equity Research, Wedbush Securities, February 12, 2014).

mid-1990s, the computational power for an average PC was comparatively low, which forced developers to come up with clever workarounds to enable a game to run smoothly and offer a novel experience. In particular, Romero and Carmack's application of processing power to texture mapping, lightning models, scrolling, and other elements distinguished them from other designers at the time. By effectively solving key computational challenges, the duo created a realistic and immersive experience. *Doom* offered three-dimensional graphics, which was a new concept at the time. The game cast players in the role of a space marine fighting hordes of alien monsters and facilitated both single- and multiplayer mode (more on this in a moment). This feature allowed *Doom* to quickly rise to popularity among PC players.

Next, the developers released the first version of *Doom* under a so-called shareware license, which allowed anyone with free, albeit limited, access to the source code. Others could create additional content for the game, including levels and changes to its mechanics. This approach greatly expanded the available content for the game and established a thriving fanbase. Shareware quickly cemented *Doom* as one of the most popular and widely available PC titles. It proved to be another stroke of genius. Because of the unprecedented degree of access, in tandem with a bourgeoning developer community, no fewer than ten million people downloaded *Doom* within its first two years. This is arguably id Software's most important innovation: the extent to which it relied on amateur coders, or modders, to build levels and other assets. Instead of having only industry professionals create content, the studio recruited fans of the game to make levels and design maps by sharing the necessary source code. A growing community of PC enthusiasts at the time embraced the game and shared their creations. It was this open-sourced approach that ensured *Doom's* success and laid the foundation for a thriving developer community.

Last, unlike titles in the console market that focused on single-player game modes, *Doom* offered multiplayer gameplay on local networks. (I recall setting up LAN games by snaking an ethernet wire through the window to my buddy next door or just bringing the whole rig to someone's house.) The multiplayer feature caught the attention of an unlikely industry participant. After the end of the Cold War, the U.S. military faced a heavily reduced budget as global tensions had eased. In response, it changed its approach to both the way it trained troops and how it procured technology. For the former, it turned to distributed interactive simulations to facilitate training scenarios and practice routines. For the latter, it determined that rather than developing a new technology, it would call on the domestic amusement industry in which contractors competed for projects.[1] In return for the industry's technological expertise and financial savings, the military shared some of its own secrets. Following the 1996 release of *Doom II*, it made its own modification for the game publicly available, which subsequently propelled its popularity. The combination of these different innovative approaches—the technological finesse, the open-source strategy, and the multiplayer gameplay that won the support of the U.S. military—resulted in *Doom* being installed on more computers around the world than Microsoft's Windows 95 operating system.

Naturally, this did not go unnoticed. One of Microsoft's early employees, Gabe Newell, had been observing that most publishers were too singularly focused on console as their primary platform. In Newell's opinion, the PC was superior to the console because it facilitated more content diversity, had lower barriers to entry for developers, and allowed ongoing hardware upgrades rather than just once every five years. Newell needed evidence that would persuade more developers to adopt the PC. It was a novel idea at the time and few content creators were willing to invest in an unproven platform. To his chagrin, the PC had largely been a device used for administrative purposes and most available software consisted primarily of accounting and word processing programs. In the minds of most game company executives, the PC was a boring device compared with the console. To convince the industry of the contrary, Newell set out to "find the most technically advanced PC game and port it to Windows to show that there wasn't any reason for games not to be Windows apps."[2] He found his answer in *Doom*. Newell managed to persuade Carmack and Romero to develop a Windows version, and with the release of *Doom 95*, the world suddenly began to see the potential of the PC as a gaming device.

The Emergence of Digital Distribution

Having found tangible proof of PC gaming's superiority, Newell was inspired to leave Microsoft. Together with Mike Harrington, the two started a studio called Valve. Like id Software, it was difficult to overstate the contributions this one company has made to the overall industry. It has excelled in terms of publishing popular titles: among its best-known are *Half-Life, Counter-Strike: Global Offensive, Dota 2*, and *Team Fortress 2*, and each of these has generated the company billions in revenue. It also created a digital distribution platform that sparked a growth spurt and a wave of innovations in PC gaming.

Both early Microsoft employees, Newell and Harrington were among the first so-called Microsoft millionaires and had the financial resources necessary to run Valve without having to share control. This stability allowed the pair to implement several innovative strategies. In assembling their development team, they solved the issue we identified earlier about how to attract and retain experienced people. Having seen id Software's success with *Doom*, the two hired a mix of developers made up of industry veterans and modders. According to Newell:

> When we designed Valve, we said everything goes back to the question of how do we attract and retain the most highly productive people in the world?. . . Everybody was going in the wrong direction. There was a movement towards outsourcing. And outsourcing is essentially where can we find the lowest cost English language speaker somewhere in the world and we'll give them a job and they'll do it just as well for a lot less money. To us that seemed exactly the opposite of what you should be doing.[3]

At the core of Valve's formula of acquiring and retaining the best talent sits its management structure. Contrary to the hierarchical organization found in many large businesses, Newell institutionalized a flat structure. Employees can choose their own projects and compile their own teams around a specific effort. They also can determine their own work schedules and priorities. To emphasize employee agency over managerial supervision was a radical departure from the tight control traditionally held by creative firms. The notion of "un-management" had been applied successfully to other industries but never before to game development.

Unlike many of its peers, Valve was also able to prioritize creating great content over having to push out its titles to meet shipment dates. Or as Newell put it: "The whole point of being a privately held company is to eliminate another source of noise in the signal between the consumers and producers of a good."[4] Thus, despite having signed a publishing deal with Sierra, Valve initially missed several deadlines for its upcoming first-person shooter *Half-Life*. But it proved well worth the wait. It resulted in a game that went beyond the existing genre conventions of shooter title and featured innovative storytelling that addressed the player directly rather than showing cut scenes to move the narrative along. Its blend of immersive story-telling and action proved immensely successful: initially Valve expected to sell around one hundred and eighty thousand units over the game's entire life cycle, but *Half-Life* sold more than two hundred thousand in its first month and went on to sell close to ten million copies.[5] Insulation from hard deadlines and fiduciary obligations afforded by its founders' control proved key to Valve's success.

The market's response to the game also set the tone for the firm's creative strategy. It now could count on the enthusiasm and support of a broad audience of modders. By facilitating amateur programmers to design levels and additional content, Valve followed id Software's example, and with great success. A string of popular mods like *Day of Defeat, Team Fortress*, and *Counter-Strike*, each of which required consumers to buy a copy of *Half-Life*, continued its sales momentum. Observing the positive response to the three expansions, Valve promptly hired the modding teams and acquired the rights. It effectively replicated the model pioneered by Carmack and Romero and used its financial resources to scale the business.

Now overseeing the development of a growing portfolio of titles and their expansions, Valve faced another challenge: how to better facilitate content expansions and efficiently distribute updates to its titles. To maintain momentum for its online multiplayer game *Counter-Strike* (another *Half-Life* spin-off), an online solution was critical. And so, in 2003, it launched Steam, a digital distribution platform to automatically update its titles over the internet and reduce the growing anxiety about piracy and cheating. Having built a reliable distribution platform for its games that would allow it to better manage updates and the dissemination of patches to ensure seamless online gameplay, Valve had yet another idea. In addition to using Steam for its own content, Valve opened the platform to other developers. In exchange for a 30 percent cut, any creative firm was now able to make money without having to go through the lengthy process of acquiring console certification or the expensive exercise of dealing with physical retail. Combined with the success of its own titles, which ensured a growing consumer base, a string of game makers launched their titles on Steam. Within four years, other well-known publishers had started selling their titles through Steam to its quickly growing audience.

Valve's success and the rapid adoption of digital distribution channels by consumers finally galvanized smaller PC developers. Not in the least because of the low barriers to entry. For instance, making a game for distribution via Steam Direct costs a studio only $100 compared with making one for a console, which generally requires purchasing an expensive development kit and subjecting a game to an involved approval process. With no need for platform certification, this arrangement offered an average studio more freedom to realize its creative vision. Smaller developers, in particular, took advantage by pursuing eclectic or exotic titles that would not make the cut elsewhere. This approach proved quite successful and allowed even small outfits to generate income to further fuel their efforts. As Newell said, "We knew that people at other game companies had employees making more money being users in our framework than they were being employees at their company."[6]

The economics of digital distribution are not without challenges. An important trade-off is the inevitably crowded marketplace. In highly competitive markets like these, the combination of low marginal costs and fierce competition on price means a decrease in the general price level of games, or price deflation. As the available inventory of content grows, developers struggle to charge anything at all and often take enormous financial losses to build up a loyal following and overall awareness. Simply put, low barriers to entry result in excess supply. Because content production under those circumstances progresses exponentially and consumption moves linearly, the excess in supply inevitably depresses prices. We can observe this by looking at the number of title releases on Steam from 2008 to 2017. As prices spiked to $14, up from $10 a few years earlier, developers eager to self-publish flooded the PC games market with content. As the number of new releases began to increase around 2014, the average price started to come down. Excess inventory depressed average prices as studios tried to stay competitive. It also led to a steep decrease in average playtime (see

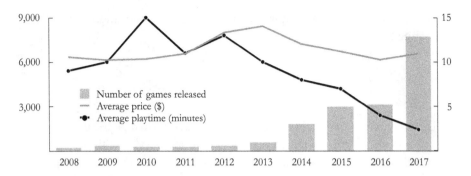

Figure 7.2

Playtime and average price for new games released on Steam, 2008–2017. *Source*: Data from Sergey Galyonkin, "Steam in 2017," Medium, April 5, 2018, https://galyonk.in /steam-in-2017-129c0e6be260. *Note*: Average price and playtime adhere to secondary axis.

figure 7.2). Consumers on the Steam platform simply had too much to choose from and became more price sensitive and shortened the length of an average play session. Steam had become the de facto digital PC platform. By 2014, small and midsize studios put out around fifteen hundred new titles annually via Steam, and by 2017, this number had more than doubled. The lowering of entry barriers to publishing on PC in combination with an audience eager for digital content resulted in Steam generating an estimated $4 billion in annual revenue by 2017.

The PC had gone from being largely ignored to facilitating some of the industry's most notable innovations. Years before any other publisher or platform had started to take digital distribution seriously, Valve created a market on its own terms and subsequently became the dominant PC distributor. Steam's success effectively reversed the trend of walled garden development and reinvigorated consumer appetite for PC gaming. Understandably, the big publishers wanted a piece of the action. As more people came online, it started to make sense to adopt distribution via the internet. Moreover, it forced publishers to decide whether to distribute a third-party like Steam or invest in the long-term and establish their own digital storefront. Larger firms like Activision Blizzard and Electronic Arts proved keen on vertical integration and created their own store fronts: Battle.net and Origin, respectively. Despite their substantial resources, however, none managed to reach the same level of success in terms of either the sheer number of active players or titles published. By moving away from the walled garden approach of the console, Valve managed to build (and dominate) an entire marketplace and helped foster innovation. It put PC gaming back on the map.

The End of the World of *World of Warcraft*

The momentum behind PC gaming that had faded when physical distribution was the norm started to build with the industry's digitization. This growth also opened opportunities to rethink how to cultivate, and charge, a growing online PC audience. Steady, monthly income is naturally considered a holy grail in an otherwise-hit-driven entertainment market. A successful title can make the difference between fortune and foreclosure. To establish predictable long-term income from a large audience base is an accomplishment in its own right and generally reserved for critically acclaimed content providers.

Despite the industry's reservations about the platform, it was on the PC that publishers first figured out the benefits of networked multiplayer gameplay. Subsequently, these publishers implemented gameplay on console and, later, on mobile, too. Specifically, as broadband penetration increased in industrial economies, publishers began to explore subscription-based massively multiplayer online role-playing games, or MMOs. Titles like *EverQuest*, *Asheron's Call*, and *Ultima Online* entered the relatively novel market to exploit its economics. The first experiences were promising: *Ultima Online* accumulated more than one hundred thousand subscribers each paying $10 a month within the first two months of operation. Their motivation was twofold: consumers were coming online and eagerly looking for content they could play over the internet, and the subscription-based revenue model meant a welcome relief from their otherwise strongly hit-driven and seasonal cash flow. As the momentum in the late 1990s grew, the MMO segment was in full swing by 2004 and counted more than three million paying subscribers worldwide.

Even so, the industry had only just begun to cultivate the potential of networked online play. It was the release of *World of Warcraft* (*WoW*) by Blizzard Entertainment in November of that year that served as a market catalyst and popularized the subscription-based MMO genre. It launched with a bang. Initially hoping to get four hundred thousand subscribers in its first year, *WoW* reached that number within the first month. What set this game apart from its peers was its ability to both claim significant market share and grow the addressable player base as a whole. *WoW* became a staple in PC gaming (see table 7.1).

Table 7.1

Major subscription-based MMOs by millions of subscribers, 1998–2016

	1998	1999	2000	2001	2002	2003	2004	2005	2006	2007	2008	2009	2010	2011	2012	2013	2014	2015	2016
World of Warcraft							0.5	5.5	8.0	10.0	11.5	11.5	12.1	11.32	9.78	7.89	7.9	5.92	4.83
Lineage I East								2.12	1.48	1.2	1.02	0.95	1.08	1.05	1.12	1.41	1.42	1.61	1.5
Aion: The Tower of Eternity											2.45	4.08	3.57	2.87	1.95	1.26	1.31	1.52	1.27
Runescape					0.01	0.04	0.2	0.39	0.88	1.01	0.92	0.92	1.04	1.06	0.73	0.6	0.69	0.66	0.61
TERA: Online														0.59	1.59	1.06	0.65	0.7	0.51
ArcheAge																0.58	0.85	0.45	0.46
Final Fantasy XIV: A Realm Reborn																0.6	0.38	0.37	0.37
Final Fantasy XIV Online																0.02			
Final Fantasy XI Online						0.2	0.5	0.51	0.5	0.5	0.5	0.46	0.39	0.39	0.43	0.5	0.47	0.38	0.34
EVE Online									0.146	0.19	0.24	0.32	0.36			0.4	0.33	0.34	0.33
Star Wars: The Old Republic															1.0				
Blade & Soul															0.36	0.23	0.26	0.31	0.28
Elder Scrolls Online																	0.64	0.31	0.26
The Lord of the Rings Online										0.22	0.23	0.23	0.23	0.29	0.27	0.34	0.35	0.26	0.24
Lineage II East								1.85	1.12	0.90	0.86	0.78	0.54	0.50	0.24	0.19	0.19	0.21	0.19
The Secret World															0.11	0.06	0.04	0.03	0.05
Wildstar																	0.20	0.05	0.03
RIFT														0.45	0.18	0.07	0.04	0.03	0.03
EverQuest II							0.36	0.33	0.18	0.11	0.07	0.06	0.053	0.046	0.036	0.031	0.037	0.029	0.028
Age of Conan											0.70	0.11	0.09						
Asheron's Call		0.05	0.03	0.11	0.11	0.09	0.06	0.03	0.01	0.02									
Asheron's Call 2						0.05	0.026	0.015	0.001										
EverQuest		0.05	0.176	0.320	0.42	0.43	0.425	0.485	0.25	0.175	0.145	0.122	0.105						
Star Wars Galaxies						0.3	0.29	0.27	0.21	0.11	0.09	0.07	0.05	0.02					
Ultima Online	0.1	0.11	0.15	0.225	0.225	0.215	0.23	0.165	0.13	0.11	0.1	0.1							
Other	0.01	0.01	0.019	0.085	0.237	0.613	0.6	0.831	0.837	1.052	1.972	1.325	0.942	0.407	0.459	0.055	0.073	0.009	0.007
Worldwide MMO subscribers	**0.11**	**0.22**	**0.37**	**0.74**	**1.0**	**1.93**	**3.18**	**12.5**	**13.74**	**15.59**	**20.81**	**21.01**	**20.54**	**18.99**	**18.27**	**15.3**	**15.83**	**13.18**	**11.35**

Source: Author's compilation based on company reports and SuperData Research.

Note: Subscription-based MMOs here defined as titles that require a recurrent purchase or subscription in order to gain full access to a game, product, or service, in addition to charging a premium for virtual goods or additional content. MMO, massively multiplayer online role-playing game.

Common theory on positive network effects dictates that an additional user of a service like an MMO increases the value of that service to others. By having more people to play with and, for instance, join as a party on a quest, online role-playing games benefit from having lots of active players at any one time to reduce wait times and deepen the social aspects of the online world. Blizzard masterfully used this to its benefit in several ways. Catering to mainstream players was its first strength. Up to this point, online role-playing games had been somewhat of an exclusive club. Titles were relatively expensive and hard to get into, especially for newcomers to the genre. Compared with its rivals, *WoW* offered more accessible gameplay, a polished experience, and a comprehensive tutorial for newbies. This approach critically removed key obstacles as new players familiarized themselves with the game's massive world and allowed them to explore at their own pace. In a lecture, Blizzard's chief creative officer Rob Pardo summarized the core of this strategy: "We really like to find those games that have a lot of hardcore loyalty, and then figure out what are the ways that we can make that game more accessible to a larger audience."[7]

Next, Blizzard spent it all. In its effort to appeal to the average gamer crowd, the publisher opted for high production values and a wide release in North America and Europe. *WoW* was based on the larger narrative universe that initially started as a real-time strategy game back in 1994 called *Warcraft: Orcs & Humans*. A decade of growing success around the franchise solidified the publisher's belief that there would be enough demand to be successful. To reach this level of success, the game spent four years in development and was the largest and most expensive project in the company's history. In total, Blizzard spent $100 million on development.[8]

Actively engaging its player base was a third contributor to *WoW*'s success. And as part of this effort, Blizzard employed offline avenues. In 2005, one year after *WoW* came out, it organized BlizzCon, an annual event for its fan base to showcase and celebrate its franchises. Whereas publishers were used to engaging their fans mostly at industry events like E3, Blizzard chose to break away from established conventions, at which it had to share the space with others, and host its own event instead. This exclusivity allowed it both to build a connection with its player base and to show off upcoming titles and content. For *WoW*, this also meant that Blizzard was able to test early versions of the game to see how people would react and build initial excitement.

The push to engage players on their terms also meant that Blizzard localized the game to better suit non-English speaking countries. Because role-playing games can be text heavy as players explore the main storyline

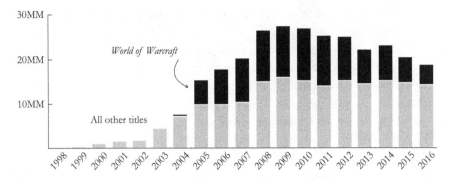

Figure 7.3
Number of active subscribers to subscription-based MMOs for *World of Warcraft* and all other titles, worldwide, 1998–2016. *Source*: Data from company reports.

and pursue quests, Blizzard made sure there were no language or cultural barriers. This global approach proved critical to its sustained success. After initially targeting Western markets, Blizzard set its sights east. There it was able to plug into the quickly growing online populations of China and South Korea who were eagerly looking for content in the otherwise-nascent domestic markets. China continues to make up about half of the game's player base.

By simultaneously targeting mainstream audiences, heavily investing in marketing and high production values, and prioritizing user engagement beyond the conventional confines of the genre, *WoW* grew to become a globally popular franchise and redefined the category (figure 7.3).

But where Blizzard proved successful in establishing a critical mass of players, a string of high-profile failures highlights the importance of accumulating a large player base. Titles like *The Matrix Online, Hellgate London,* and *Age of Conan: Hyborian Adventures* all carried promise but failed to deliver sustained success.

The success of online PC multiplayer games meant that legacy publishers started to make more money from PC games. Between 1998 and 2008, when the enthusiasm among consumers for MMOs reached its apex, the combined revenue from their PC divisions grew from just over $1 billion to $7 billion. As online connectivity continued to improve around the world, the player base steadily grew, and a new generation of game makers emerged. The next disruption that emerged from the PC market was an innovative new revenue model conceived in Asia called free-to-play.

In countries like South Korea and China, most people do not own a PC at home and instead play in internet cafés. In this region, online gaming historically has been different from in the Western Hemisphere in two important ways. First, instead of owning a copy, players usually purchase metered access from the cafés that charge them by the hour. To attract people, these cafés generally featured many different games, akin to the traditional arcade, to entice people to come in, spend some time, and play. Second, in the midst of the frenzied competitive environment, Asian publishers started offering their games for free, hoping to instigate the network effects that would provide a defensible position. It was a new way of doing things and quickly caught on throughout Asia and, not long after, in Europe and the Americas. Its rapid adoption by both audiences and publishers presents a remarkable shift in the way that the traditional games industry has operated for a long time. It challenged existing ideas on every aspect, including investment, distribution, and monetization. Executives at organizations from the product era asked: How do you make a billion dollars by giving your game away for free?

The basic premise of free-to-play is that players have access to content and can play without paying. They have the option, however, to accelerate their progress or customize their experience through microtransactions and in-game purchases. Titles will feature gameplay elements and aspects in the social layer that encourage players to spend money. This business strategy is antithetical to typical publishing, which centers on charging players upfront before they can play. In the free-to-play model, monetization starts slowly, but increases over time. It presents efficiencies for both the demand and the supply sides: consumers are able to play a game either in part or in whole at zero cost and are offered the opportunity to make purchases that enhance their experience. The free-to-play model removes any previous barriers for audiences that typically fall outside the addressable market in a premium model. Targeting a mass audience with free services emulates the general strategy found in the tech industry in which firms give away applications for free—a chat program, access to social network platform—to build up a critical mass of users. Once the supply side has successfully deployed, it allows monetizing users through the sale of additional functionality or customization and establishes an ongoing stream of revenue. The popularization of free-to-play presented an enormous challenge to the traditional business model in which users or players pay upfront to gain access to content. Western publishers suddenly found themselves competing against a free offering. The dismissal of the new revenue model, as was common among incumbents at the time, proved short-sighted.

Free-to-play also presents a new configuration of affordances and constraints to publishers: it allows for better risk mitigation against traditional industry characteristics, including seasonal sales patterns and the narrowing window to recoup on a title's investment immediately following launch. Adopting this model also allows for tailored content that is catered to different audience segments. Moreover, it opens new and more diverse markets that previously were out of reach. Overall, it facilitates an optimization of business and creative processes.

In the product-based publishing model, the costs for the publisher are largely fixed: after making an investment over the course of a few years, the game is ready for release. Then, it is up to the marketing team to ensure that as many people as possible buy the game. In this fixed-cost scenario, enough sales eventually allow a title to break even and generate a profit. For free-to-play games, however, this equation looks quite different. Players are acquired through spending on marketing—a fixed cost-per-install—and hopefully stay active long enough to eventually spend money and ultimately become profitable. In the traditional publishing business, designers were tasked with delivering a completed and polished experience, whereas the free-to-play model asks for ongoing iterations and recurrent expansions. The focus for a game company thus quickly shifts to retaining as many players as possible over time by offering incentives and an ongoing array of new content to explore. Table 7.2 summarizes the different components and financial considerations in product- and service-based publishing.

To maximize the chances of success for their largest releases, big publishers traditionally have competed with each other by spending heavily on marketing. During the race toward the holiday season, expenses increase and thereby lower the odds of success. A key weakness in the product model is the combination of high upfront development and promotional cost and a relatively short sales window during which consumers are willing to pay full price. Creative organizations leveraging a free-to-play model are capable of incrementally improving their offering over time, allowing them to side-step the cost structure generally associated with a product-based release. Through analytics and by monitoring player behavior, developers can pinpoint the most successful, or profitable, component of their game and optimize it across their user base. By feeding end-user information into the development process, a studio can optimize post-release and improve the player experience using data.[9]

Table 7.2

Comparison of title-level economics for product and service-based publishing

$MM (units in thousands)	Product-Based Publishing Business Case			Service-Based Publishing Business Case			$MM (users in thousands)
	Bear	Base	Bull	Bear	Base	Bull	
Units sold	**1,000**	**2,500**	**5,000**	**250**	**5,000**	**100,000**	**Installs**
				3	50	1,000	**Average daily active users**
Retail earnings	**50**	**125**	**250**	–	**7**	**145**	**Bookings**
Net revenue	**40**	**100**	**200**	–	**5**	**100**	**Net revenue**
				–	2	40	User acquisition
Cost of goods sold	12	30	60	–	–	2	Hosting, software, support
License royalties	–	–	–	–	–	–	License royalties
Developer royalties	–	5	30	–	–	28	Developer royalties
Total variable costs	12	35	90	-	2	70	
Gross profit	**28**	**65**	**110**	–	**2**	**30**	**Gross profit**
Marketing costs	10	10	10				
Developer advances	20	20	20	1	1	1	Developer advances
Total fixed costs	30	30	30	1	1	1	
Operating profit (loss)	**(2)**	**35**	**80**	**(1)**	**1**	**29**	**Operating profit (loss)**

Source: Based on Dan Sherman, "Video Game Deals" (College guest talk, The Business of Video Games, New York, May 2017).

Note: This comparison uses the following definitions and assumptions. For the Product-Based Publishing model Retail earnings refer to consumer spending via GameStop, Walmart, and others. Cost of goods sold includes payments to the platform holders (e.g., Sony, Microsoft) to print discs and the costs for packaging and freight. License royalties refer to what a publisher pays for the rights to an intellectual property holder. Developer royalties are expenses paid to the developer after any advances have been recouped. Developer advances are the amount of money a publisher paid a developer to complete a game. Marketing costs are expenses made to advertise and sell the game. For the Service-Based Publishing model Bookings refer to what consumers spend in the game. Net revenue is the money paid out to the publisher by platforms such as Apple and Google. User acquisition refers to the cost to grow the overall number of installs via advertising.

Another important aspect of this approach is that it affords a creative firm to release using a staggered rollout, publishing a game initially in a secondary test market like Canada or the Philippines to stress-test their back-end and improve on the experience iteratively. If done correctly, this practice makes developers progressively smarter at what they do and optimizes the user experience.

Free-to-play game design focuses on reaching the broadest audience possible. By tailoring the game to different consumers segments—by way of offering different sales to different users, for instance—a company is capable of servicing a heterogeneous player base. By widening its reach, a company can further mitigate risk and increase revenue potential.

Next, free-to-play game development is different from the way companies typically develop titles: instead of spending three to five years on the realization of a creative vision, an emphasis on data collection provides a game maker with information on what resonates with audiences and informs the active development process. This approach offers substantially lower fixed costs. But it also means lower entry barriers for competitors and drives a greater reliance on branding, intellectual property, and marketing. This, in turn, results in additional expenses post-release and requires an active team to provide customer support, analytics, live operations, and ongoing content development.

Finally, unlike conventional game launches that rely heavily on creating the maximum amount of buzz, free-to-play requires an ongoing development and promotional effort. Once out in the market, a title's health depends on the continued effort of engaging the player base and offering new items and content. A game's release does not stop its development and marketing. Rather, it marks an important second phase during which both developers and marketers have started to use player data gathered from their live operations to inform creative decisions and drive engagement. Marketing is an ongoing and, more important, variable expense as the cost of acquisition fluctuates over time.

Switching Costs

With no upfront risk, and an expanding global player base, demand for free-to-play multiplayer titles grew rapidly at the expense of the subscription-based MMO market (see figure 7.4). This scenario raised the question of whether, and how, titles like *WoW*, in particular, had to adjust

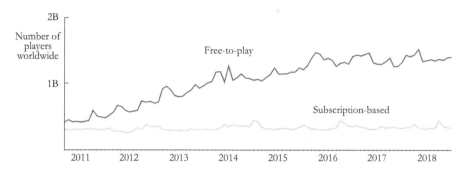

Figure 7.4
Worldwide player base for free-to-play and subscription-based MMO games, 2011–2018.
Source: Data from SuperData Research.

to this new market condition to remain successful: stay the course with a subscription-based model or switch to free-to-play?

The line of reasoning goes as follows: no longer charging an upfront fee for the base game fundamentally changes the economics. Presumably, by lowering the cost for consumers, more of them will start playing. More players become active in the game, which improves the overall network effects and, ultimately, the sale of in-game items. At the same time, however, a growing user base means a higher cost structure as a larger user base imposes on the back-end infrastructure and customer support services. All this makes it difficult to accurately anticipate the outcome of a switch to free-to-play. Nevertheless, a few titles have gone through this transition, with mixed results. At the high-end we find Electronic Arts' *Star Wars: The Old Republic* (*SWTOR*). From the start, it suffered from a high churn among players. The high-profile intellectual property (IP) and the caliber of the studio behind it meant *SWTOR* had a strong release and counted almost two million monthly active users. By its third month, however, it started to lose players as its ravenous audience had completed all of the available content and became bored. Just nine months after its release, the total number of players had dropped by two-thirds. In response, Electronic Arts switched to a free-to-play model to boost its player count.

Next, NCSoft launched *Wildstar* in June 2014. Its design team consisted of several former Blizzard employees, and the expectation was that their skill set would transfer well. To avoid competing directly with *WoW*, *Wildstar* was positioned as a sci-fi title aimed at younger audiences. At its launch, around three hundred and fifty thousand people played the game, roughly similar to *WoW's* start in 2004. But despite the similarities in terms of production qualities, its player base started to shrink to around forty-three thousand a year later, and NCSoft switched *Wildstar* over to free-to-play.

As a final example, *RIFT* by Trion Worlds was launched simultaneously as a game and television show. Now that the market for subscription-based titles had started to mature, marketing costs had gone up. By having a presence both in games and on television, executives reasoned, *RIFT* would benefit from a broader cross-promotional effort to attract players. Even so, here, too, we observe a decline followed by a switch to free-to-play.

Despite each having their own creative merits, these three games are comparable to *WoW*. Electronic Arts' *SWTOR* was an ambitious blockbuster production and built on preexisting IP, *Wildstar* was developed by former Blizzard employees, and *RIFT* focused on Western audiences by leveraging its existing marketing channels after spending $50 million on development (figure 7.5).[10] None of them proved capable of escaping the pressures of a declining user base by switching to free-to-play.

At best, *WoW's* closest comparable titles offer a mixed bag of results. Despite *SWTOR's* ability to hold off the decline in monthly income, financial success remained highly dependent on recurring expansions (note the spikes). Similarly, *RIFT*, with its clever marketing strategy, benefited initially from switching but shows an ongoing decline. *Wildstar's* targeted approach simply failed to turn the tides.

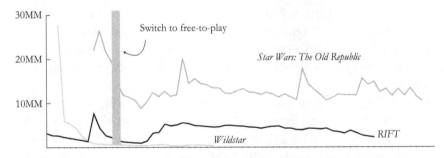

Figure 7.5
Monthly earnings before and after switching to free-to-play for *Star Wars: The Old Republic*, *RIFT*, and *Wildstar*. *Source*: Data from SuperData Research. *Note*: Revenue in millions U.S. dollars ($). Titles are lined up by month in which they switched to free-to-play.

The comparisons end here. The most important reason *WoW* did not immediately switch over to free-to-play was because of its dominant position. For the market leader to earn as much, or more, in a free-to-play scenario as it did with subscriptions, *WoW* would need to capture an unrealistically large portion of the addressable audience. The advantage of offering a game for free is the ability to reach many more consumers. A critical disadvantage is the low pay rate. On average, only about 3 to 5 percent of players convert to spending, which means that to capture comparable market value and earn as much in revenue as it did at its peak in 2010, *WoW* would need to claim at least two-thirds of the total free-to-play market. Instead, Blizzard opted for a *hybrid* model which offers the first twenty levels for free and requires players to spend before they can progress past that point. Over the course of its lifetime, *WoW* has generated more than $10 billion in revenue, which makes it one of the top-grossing game franchises of all time. It has managed to do so by cleverly exploiting network effects, catering to mainstream audiences, and avoiding falling victim to new monetization models.

Emerging Markets

An important affordance of free-to-play is that it allows publishers to reach consumers that were previously deemed "outside of the market." No longer requiring people to shell out $60 means a much larger audience will play a game. Known as demand heterogeneity, this strategy allows creative firms to monetize different customer types across their audience base. On the one hand, most users will end up paying nothing or very little. On the other, freemium also removes the upper limit in terms of what users can spend on a game. This tends to result in a small subset of players spending much more than what they otherwise would have spent on a traditional paid game.

Of course, the lowering of entry barriers also intensifies competition. Publishers aggressively pursue the largest audience possible and go well beyond traditional economic and geographic boundaries. Consequently, countries like Brazil, Russia, India, and China quickly have become favorite strategic territories for firms like Riot Games, Wargaming, and others. And for good reason: in each of these economies, there has been the absence of a strong console market and a relatively low percentage of PC ownership despite the presence of a large consumer base.

Digitization quite obviously resolves several key strategic concerns. Piracy, which historically deterred publishers from releasing their games in countries like Russia, is much less of an issue. Similarly, the fantastically high import taxes in countries like Brazil historically drove up the cost of a console, for example, to $2,000 for a PlayStation 2, and thereby was well outside the reach of an average Brazilian consumer.[11] And even after manufacturers were allowed to do business directly with the Chinese mainland, the penetration of dedicated hardware remained relatively low. Instead, games like *League of Legends*, which purposefully do not require a sophisticated PC rig, find adoption among large consumer groups in these countries.

It is a matter of perspective when it comes to determining which economies are emerging and which are developing. Wargaming's CEO Victor Kislyi described his point of view on the most important growth markets in the context of a free-to-play publisher in an interview about his company's strategy:

> U.S.A. is for us an emerging market. If you combine Canada you have over 400 million population, and we have, like nothing. In America it is a success financially, very successful. [But] in comparison to population ratio and *World of Tanks* popularity in Russia, America is nowhere. So, we still have 1,000-percent growth potential. So, only markets with potential are attractive. Take Brazil. You say, "yeah they don't have payment options and the internet is not that good," but if you are one of the first movers, there is less competition. There are no huge Brazilian organizations making free-to-play online games. So, it is only a bunch of Western firms that dare to go there to establish service. So, you can be the first Brazilian, or the number one Turkish game, which would make for good revenue for you as well, at least to offset the development cost.[12]

The gravity point of the global games industry has shifted from Western to Eastern countries. Where historically North American and European audiences spent the most money on video games, digitization has opened up new markets like South Korea, China, and Russia. Unencumbered by the typical product-based publishing model, creative firms from these countries proved to be adept at establishing a profitable business model around free-to-play. Developing around free-to-play monetization is common to game makers from, for instance, South Korea, which accordingly has developed an expertise in balancing in-game currencies, item sales, and stimulating user engagement.[13] Nexon, for example, managed to lay claim to an important part of the U.S. market. Initially launched in 2005, it found that its core PC title *MapleStory* proved tremendously popular especially among American teenagers. Despite the much lower broadband speeds in the United States relative to South Korea and requiring a hefty download of around 700 megabytes, Nexon managed to build up a loyal following. At an industry conference, Nexon's CEO for America, Min Kim, boasted: "In 2005, Nexon America's revenues were around $650,000. In 2006, when they added PayPal as a payment option, sales rose to $8 million, based on item sales. In 2007, once Nexon released its Nexon Cash cards to retail stores, revenue jumped to $29 million."[14]

MapleStory's success, however, was not unilaterally the result of a lack of competition. Nexon also understood its player base really well. In rolling out in the United States, it defined a strategy that contained two key components. First, Nexon needed to overcome the difficulty of monetizing what are known as the "unbanked" by offering prepaid game cards. Government regulation around the time had changed the minimum required age for anyone looking to open a credit card account to twenty-one years or older. And so, to allow these "un-bankable" players to spend money in the game, Nexon struck a deal with prepaid card vendors that allowed teenagers to put credits onto a card that they then could add to their game account.

Second, the publisher quickly figured out that despite the relatively young driving age in the United States, the bulk of its core audience would have a hard time getting to retail locations where they could purchase in-game credits. Consequently, Nexon focused its efforts on building a relationship with 7-Eleven, which in many suburbs can be reached by bike rather than by car. It removed the need for its distinct player base to ask their parents to drive them, and in so doing, greatly improved the game maker's ability to monetize its customer base. Not long after, competitors followed the example, and firms like Zynga started merchandising ice cream and other consumer goods sold at these specific retail points to further drive their marketing and user spending.

Previously, North America had been out of reach for Asian and European publishers. Digitization redefined how these digital-only publishers managed to capture value from their content and what an emerging market looks like. Suffice to say that digitalization has had a dramatic effect on the structure of the global PC industry. Since 1998, when PC gaming revenue among top firms was about one-tenth the size of console gaming, the segment has grown to a $30 billion a year market. Innovators like Valve and id

Software set the stage for large publishers like Activision Blizzard to accelerate growth and bring PC gaming to a much broader audience.

Because this market historically had much lower barriers to entry, the share of each of the top firms also was much smaller. In particular, in combination with the segment's growth, the top-grossing game maker consistently held roughly half as much market share, between 12 percent and 24 percent, compared with the console market in which the C10 was between 30 percent and 50 percent. The top-ten firms in this market saw a decline in their market power, initially controlling 94 percent, only to see this share decline to 66 percent by 2018 (see table 7.3).

Unsurprisingly, the HHI dropped from moderately concentrated (1,647) in 1998 to unconcentrated (838) two decades later. An important factor in this decline was the widespread adoption by consumers of free-to-play games, which allowed Tencent, Nexon, NetEase, Netmarble, Smilegate, and others from China and South Korea to claim their spot on a global stage. Unlike console and mobile, which were more hardware-specific and consequently governed by rules from regulators and platform holders, PC gaming benefited from the games industry's globalization, resulting in a more open market structure. This also facilitated an increase in the number of companies that controlled more than 1 percent of the overall PC segment: between 1998 and 2018 that number increased from 13 to 21.

In this case, legacy firms quickly lost control despite an initial growth spurt. Between 1998 and 2008, legacy firms grew their PC gaming revenue to $7 billion, but then digital-only firms took over. By 2018, digital game makers generated $22 billion in PC gaming revenue compared with $8 billion for legacy firms.

Innovation is generally described as something that happens to an industry rather than emerges from it. After gradually falling out of favor with major game makers, the PC market has regained importance through a string of new practices and approaches. Digitization and the effective exploitation of new modes of production, distribution, monetization, and market strategy have resulted in the growth of the PC segment. Several notable innovations from companies with a crazy idea allowed PC gaming to flourish. The success of *Doom* was the result of both a highly creative new type of game and a clever approach to distributed content creation. Valve managed to harness the efforts made by a growing consortium of independent developers. Blizzard reimagined the online multiplayer category and introduced new gameplay components with *World of Warcraft*. Even as it started to lose audience to a free substitute in the form of free-to-play

Table 7.3
Top-twenty-five PC game publishers, 1998–2018

	1998	1999	2000	2001	2002	2003	2004	2005	2006	2007	2008	2009	2010	2011	2012	2013	2014	2015	2016	2017	2018
Tencent													868	1,050	1,329	1,892	2,697	3,500	5,809	8,153	7,267
Riot Games																	1,313	1,628	2,124 (Tencent)	2,042	2,180
Activision Blizzard											1,294	2,200	1,555	1,731	2,200	1,252	1,418	1,499	2,124	1,856	1,835
Activision	78	105	107	153	147	125	174	273	223	304		Activision Blizzard									
(Vivendi (Blizzard))					641	338	254	243	278	332		Activision Blizzard									
Nexon	0.2	1	2	2	4	23	72	163	232	252	380	485	722	971	1,029	1,001	568	977	1,411	1,665	1,700
NetEase									38	58	87	526	757	945	970	1,156	1,236	1,194	1,268	1,612	1,655
Microsoft	179	219	238	537	976	1,000	904	1,098	1,515	1,656	1,260	1,232	982	1,459	1,448	959	1,167	1,231	1,270	1,424	1,332
Netmarble																				997	1,229
Smilegate														756		1,158	713	1,110	1,206	997	996
Epic Games																			4	80	891
Krafton																				763	859
Electronic Arts	412	503	470	608	836	700	602	560	478	564	688	424	682	749	935	924	1,345	879	916	893	774
Take-Two Interactive	42	72	81	220	605	763	926	117	521	575	1,107	522	112	80	703	438	80	882	1,168	1,441	727
Valve										1	1	2	3	31	94	232	421	602	719	862	707
Square Enix	68	69	122	68	62	157	284	209	450	415	452	540	573 (Square Enix)	479	468	421	429	504	680	680	638
Eidos	68	65	52	30	17	50	33						Square Enix								
Perfect World																		414	527	630	618
Ubisoft						173	205	204	162	242	106	113	108	54	35	84	79	168	231	352	592
Wargaming.net													1	101	405	532	523	498	541	572	485
Kingsoft							18	34	50	88	130	110	107	111	134	143	145	139	220	272	445
NCSoft	1	7	46	95	131	142	280	335	360	345	266	539	559	514	659	656	707	655	797	319	358
THQ Nordiq															81	111	117	111	29	49	307
ZeniMax Media														132	179	89	225	353	325	348	303
Mail.ru												61	100						159	234	300
37 Interactive																	20	504	394	319	290
Disney			168	270		256	274	232	239	183	382	362	385	413	356	375	422	354	345	302	272
Zynga												121	597	1,140	653	611	407	344	267	276	
All others	370	461	335	418	577	728	853	1,212	1,365	1,747	3,194	2,768	3,314	3,056	3,421	4,269	3,277	3,484	3,128	3,971	3,460
PC revenue	1,218	1,500	1,619	2,937	3,996	4,457	4,879	4,679	5,911	6,763	9,366	10,007	11,443	13,922	16,576	17,262	18,001	21,763	24,534	30,220	30,220
C1	34%	34%	29%	21%	24%	22%	19%	23%	26%	24%	14%	22%	14%	12%	13%	11%	15%	16%	24%	27%	24%
C4	64%	64%	62%	66%	77%	63%	56%	48%	50%	47%	46%	47%	37%	39%	36%	32%	38%	36%	43%	45%	43%
C10	94%	91%	89%	93%	93%	88%	85%	77%	77%	75%	74%	76%	71%	71%	66%	61%	68%	63%	69%	70%	66%
HHI	1,647	1,613	1,383	1,314	1,576	1,234	1,069	976	1,034	961	754	905	630	627	571	485	612	571	851	976	838
No. of firms >1%	13	13	14	15	12	16	16	18	17	19	20	22	20	18	21	24	20	21	19	19	21

Source: Author's compilation based on company reports.

Note: PC revenue here refers to the aggregate revenue in millions USD ($) generated from PC game publishing activities by all companies in the data set. Industry structure metrics (e.g., C1, C4, C10, and HHI) calculated using all available company data across entire data set. HHI, Herfindahl-Hirschman index

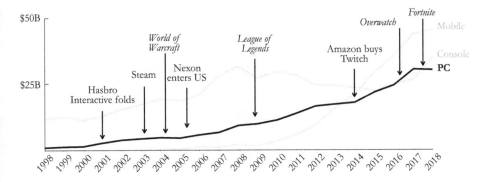

Figure 7.6
PC revenue for top game companies, worldwide, 1998–2018. *Source*: Data from company reports. *Note*: Revenue shown on left *y*-axis in billions U.S. dollars ($). Callouts refer to related cases from this chapter and elsewhere.

games, it managed to retain the lion's share of its player base and, instead, introduced a hybrid model that relied only in part on free access. And, finally, companies like Nexon introduced novel strategies tailored to their specific player base and figured out how to reach and monetize younger players long before any domestic publisher. Newell's ambition to make the PC the dominant platform ultimately resulted in it becoming a highly innovative market segment that has come to represent the avant-garde of interactive entertainment (figure 7.6).

3

Games as Media

8

Epic Quest for Intellectual Property

The most spectacular failure of licensing intellectual property (IP) to make a game must be *E.T.* for the Atari 2600. This game was doomed from the start. Steve Ross, an executive from Warner Communication, which had recently purchased Atari, offered to pay Steven Spielberg $23 million for the video game rights to *E.T.* His motive, however, was not to pursue a particular creative vision, but rather to build a relationship with the famous movie producer.[1] The purchase was a means to an end, and the creative effort lacked integrity. Despite the popularity of video games, many in the broader entertainment industry regarded the category with disdain and felt that it presented nothing more than a passing fad. Consequently, the allocation of only a limited amount of time to development illustrated the clear lack of respect for content quality. Predictably, consumers avoided the game. Amid a commodified market riddled with look-a-like titles, *E.T.* failed miserably and became a lesson in how even the biggest IP cannot compensate for poor execution.

The practice of licensing someone else's property as the foundation of a video game is common. It is a strategic alternative to developing your own IP. Taking this route takes a long time because it requires a grand vision, including fleshing out a main character, establishing a broader story universe, and creating a consistent visual aesthetic. It is time-consuming and expensive, and therefore generally reserved for experienced firms with deep pockets. Exceptions like *Minecraft* and *Angry Birds* defy common business strategy and confuse companies about what to expect when developing new IP. Large publishers may have multiple projects in development simultaneously but only release a single one at once to give it the support it needs to succeed. Electronic Arts, for instance, spent several years on *Anthem*, a new shooter franchise, and Ubisoft weathered through months of criticism for repeatedly delaying its fighting game *For Honor*. Both of these franchises have been only moderately successful. Even the most successful companies struggle with developing IP.

For our purposes, we will focus on two types of IP: (1) narrative universes and characters developed by game makers, and (2) IP borrowed by them from other entertainment categories. The former includes licenses that originate from the games industry. Examples include *Super Mario*, *Halo*, *Assassin's Creed*, and *Call of Duty*. Each of these presents a creative vision that offers a unique experience that distinguishes itself from content created by competitors. The latter covers licenses that come from other amusement segments, such as film, music, or sports, and that have been "made into" a game. Examples are *Guitar Hero*, *Dance Dance Revolution*, *Kingdom Hearts*, and *FIFA*.[2]

From a creative standpoint, a studio decides early in its design process to either invest in creating its own narrative universe with identifiable characters and a distinguishable experience, or to borrow someone else's. The role of IP is foundational to a firm's strategic approach: it either borrows IP to mitigate risk and reduce cost, or it takes an all-or-nothing gamble to develop its own for a much higher reward.

Licensing IP offers developers multiple benefits. Most obviously, it makes the creative process much more manageable. Creatives spend less effort on developing a compelling storyline, world, or characters. Using existing IP also answers any questions about a game's overall atmosphere and graphic style: franchise-holders ensure that a particular application of their license is consistent with clearly defined guidelines and does not deviate from the original. This emphasis on consistency means a game will fit into a broader range of available entertainment products, thereby lowering demand uncertainty and signaling value to consumers. An additional advantage is the ability to piggyback off of a broader marketing effort: simultaneously releasing a mobile game of the same franchise as a movie means more people will hear about it and thereby increases the total addressable audience. It is a common approach—most notably around large block-buster movie releases (e.g., *Star Wars*, *The Avengers*). Small studios benefit from the immense marketing push by large film companies. Finally, once a studio has "won" a license, it can use this experience to showcase its abilities in pursuit of future licensing deals and can build its own brand around it. As discussed in chapter 3, Electronic Arts did so by establishing itself as the go-to sports video game publisher.

Borrowing IP, however, is not without cost. In exchange, a developer is expected to make several concessions. The basic structure of a licensing deal contains a minimum guarantee: a payment from the licensee to the licensor that allows the latter, at a minimum, to recover some of its expenses. It serves as a safeguard for the licensor, because the initial capital investment by the studio incentivizes it to make the project a success. A minimum guarantee can take the form of a material percentage of anticipated revenue, generally between 5 and 7 percent, or a fixed sum, depending on the arrangement. In addition, competition around popular IP is often fierce. Because a licensor is careful in managing their brand and its underlying values, winning a bid is an arduous process. Generally speaking, several studios will compete over an opportunity in a "beauty contest" in which each hopes to win the contract. This competition invariably puts pressure on a studio's cost structure. Each of the contenders pitch a game idea and explain how they intend to deliver on their promises. Next, the complicated language involved that itemizes the various obligations for both parties means that the associated legal fees can be substantial. It creates a natural barrier to entry and safeguards licensors as a reduced, arguably more reputable, group of outfits will vie for its license. One executive explained this to me as follows: every year license holders and creatives come together at licensing shows to pitch and negotiate over IPs. It is an expensive event and requires that studios bring legal representation. Or, as it was told to me: "If you can't afford to bring a lawyer, you shouldn't be here."

Working with licensors can be challenging. They may impose creative restrictions and may allow a developer the use of only the broader universe of a particular franchise and require them to stay away from the main characters. In some cases that may be the result of a tight grip held by a license-holder; in others, it could be because of a media firm's agreement with a celebrity—to use their likeness would require renegotiating their contract. Worse, strict rules around IP may inhibit a designer from using game mechanics that otherwise would make a great title.

The main benefit for a licensor is the ability to draw revenue from products and services for which it has no expertise. For example, the *Bejeweled* franchise initially started as a web-based game in which players make combinations by swapping gems. As the game became more popular, the opportunity arose for its developer PopCap Games to build out the *Bejeweled* brand by selling licenses to its imagery and game mechanics to firms like Global Eagle Entertainment, which specializes in developing content for in-flight entertainment systems. It also proved easier to license *Bejeweled* to a Blackberry developer than it was to create the content in-house. This approach allowed PopCap to expand its brand's presence far beyond the boundaries of its entertainment expertise. Because the *Bejeweled* brand resonates well with an older, female demographic, its imagery also appeared on scratch tickets and slot machines in Las Vegas, which has an overlapping audience. To stand out in the commodified businesses for gambling and chance games, partnering with a strong brand is critical. The success of this cross-platform strategy by PopCap Games ultimately resulted in the company's acquisition by Electronic Arts for more than $1 billion.

So, what does successful IP look like? There is arguably no better example than *Pokémon*. In my experience teaching at New York University over the years, it became evident that preferences among my students are wildly diverse. They come from a broad variety of countries and have grown up in vastly different cultural contexts. They each have their own familiarity when it comes to movies, music, and celebrities. But universally they share a strong affinity for *Pokémon*.

IP with such broad appeal can dramatically reverse a studio's fortunes. When the relatively unknown developer Niantic released *Ingress*, an augmented reality game in which players use their mobile phones to collect items and strategic points on a real-life map of their surroundings, it was only met with mild enthusiasm. Despite the studio's backing from Google, the game generated only a few million dollars over the first couple of years after release.

The studio had considerably more success with its second title, *Pokémon GO*. With further investments from The Pokémon Company and Nintendo, the game grew to an absolute craze over the summer of 2016, with well over five hundred million downloads worldwide and earning around half a billion dollars in its first few months following launch. In this version, players compete with others to catch, train, and battle Pokémon, which can be seen by using a smartphone to scan their surroundings. Building largely on the game mechanics and software from *Ingress*, the experience combined Google Maps and the different characters from the franchise. Unlike Ingress, *Pokémon GO* caught on globally.

The success of a game does not depend entirely on how great of an experience or how well designed it is. An emergent market like mobile gaming matures over time, as consumers become more demanding in their expectations and creative firms develop increasingly complex content and formulate sophisticated marketing strategies. Over the two-year period between the release of the two titles, market conditions had changed. Among other things, the availability of content had grown exponentially, which made the market less accessible, especially for mainstream consumers. Releasing a game with a strong IP with broad appeal under these conditions is more effective as audiences seek value among the enormous inventory of available mobile games.

Moreover, because *Pokémon GO* encouraged people to roam their physical environment to look for Pokémon, it made sense to time the release during the summer because of better weather conditions. Consequently, crowds would gather around key locations in the game represented by real-world locations where rare Pokémon could be found, allowing others to wonder what was going on and drawing further interest. During the usual slowdown in news during the summer holiday season, traditional media outlets helped *Pokémon GO* become a highly visible phenomenon, sending film crews from New York to South Korea to capture the crowds gathering to play the game, and accelerating its popularity and success.

Even so, the combination of a crowded mobile games marketplace and the benefit of becoming a summer fad does not explain the enormity of its success. Certainly, Niantic's interpretation of the license and its application to augmented reality-style gameplay was brilliant in its own right. But the Pokémon franchise is not just a collection of cute-looking creatures. It is a well-designed and thought-out IP that has been carefully cultivated over the course of several decades. The franchise builds on an impressive marketing effort. Inspired by his childhood pastime of bug collecting, designer Satoshi Tajiri initially developed the franchise for the Nintendo Game Boy. The game consists of battling with your pocket monster (hence the name) against those trained by other players to determine the ultimate Poké-Master. It targets especially younger players with a colorful aesthetic and accessible rulesets. Beyond its array of cute-looking creatures, *Pokémon* is a deliberately crafted franchise, first as a title for the Game Boy and later as a collectible card game, that builds on several components that collectively amount to a clever business model innovation.

The wide diversity among its creatures is the first aspect of its innovation. Instead of offering a single protagonist, *Pokémon* offers a wide variety of creatures that all coexist within the same universe. This is done deliberately to allow fans to identify and connect with a specific *Pokémon*. Players can pick and choose their favorite creature and play style, which allows them to establish a strong emotional connection to the franchise. Even so, the complexity never gets in the way of individual enjoyment as *Pokémon* creatures are easily recognizable, even based on just their silhouettes.

Its gameplay revolving around providing its young audience with agency is another component. Its core demographic is between 6 and 12 years old, and made up mostly of children who, in fairness, have little decision-making responsibilities in daily life. On average, pre-teens have limited opportunities available to explore and express themselves. *Pokémon* tries to fill that void by making the experience accessible and inclusive. It is an important reason why the franchise released a collectible card game: to allow young players to create unique decks that easily could be brought to school and played during recess. Whereas other popular titles necessitate the use of a device that needs to be charged and that costs a lot of money, a card deck is perfect for a middle-schooler's backpack. The cards facilitate play during recess and further reinforce the game and the *Pokémon* as a social currency. Building a collection or card deck becomes an act of self-expression. Consider that one of the franchise's most popular taglines is "I choose you!" To young players, an important part of the appeal is being able to build a unique deck.

Finally, the game is also known for its relentless content creation as a key to its success. Today, there are no fewer than twenty-one full-feature movies, a comic book, an anime series, and a trading card game. According to one developer whose company worked on several trading card games for license holders, *Pokémon*'s broad reach across media channels was key to its success: "The Saturday morning cartoons are really a 30-minute infomercial teaching kids the rules of the Pokémon universe and how to play the game." Interactive entertainment experiences based on the *Pokémon* license have earned it around $13 billion.

The success of Niantic's *Pokémon GO* in the summer 2016 was the result of innovative game design with mainstream appeal. Using an overlay of different technologies, it offered a new and compelling experience. Considering the difference in commercial success between *Ingress* and *Pokémon GO*, which are largely the same experiences, it is the application of the license that propelled the game developer to the top of the charts.

Sports Video Game Battle

Licenses also tend to be the crux of competition between competitors. In 2005, two opposing game makers—Electronic Arts and Take-Two—tried to outmaneuver each other for control over the sports category. Central to both firms' strategies was to own an exclusive license to a sports franchise and build on the preexisting fanbase. Locking down exclusive rights to particular properties can be a useful strategy, particularly when it comes to content categories in which, at least on the surface, there are few ways to differentiate. In the mid-2000s, Electronic Arts had managed to acquire the exclusive rights to several of the major sports leagues: the National Football League (NFL) in the United States and the Fédération Internationale de Football Association (FIFA). Take-Two subsidiary 2K Games, on the other hand, held the license to the National Basketball Association (NBA). This set the stage for a flurry of punches thrown between the two firms.

In what one executive dubbed the "Sports Video Game Battle of 2004," Electronic Arts and Take-Two each went through a series of strategic decisions and price cuts to outmaneuver the other and claim the sports games segment for themselves. After Take-Two took over the publishing and distribution rights of Sega's line of ESPN video games in June 2004, it launched *ESPN NFL 2K5* for both PS2 and Xbox a month later and priced it at $19.99. Their approach was simple: to capture share by offering sports games at a significantly lower price and by releasing titles right before Electronic Arts came out with *their* versions. By comparison, in August, it put out its full priced football-based title, *Madden 2005*, for $49.99. Then two months later, Take-Two repeated the tactic with *ESPN NBA 2K5* priced at $19.99 at the same time that Electronic Arts pushed out *NBA Live* 2005 at $49.99. And it did so again in November with *ESPN College Hoops 2K5* priced at $19.99 versus Electronic Arts' *March Madness 2005* at $49.99.

Now, with three recently released, comparable games available and the holiday season in full swing, Take-Two's strategy started to pay off. Its line of sports games received higher ratings than those by Electronic Arts, and Take-Two managed to become a market leader in the segment on the Xbox console. To counter this success, Electronic Arts was forced to lower the price of all three of its titles to $29.99 to make the most of the sales spike around Thanksgiving. It momentarily seemed that Take-Two's strategy of "great games for a great price" had paid off and allowed it to become the premiere sports games publisher. Rather than competing on price, however,

Electronic Arts went all in and signed a five-year exclusive agreement with the NFL in December and followed it with a crushing blow by announcing a fifteen-year exclusive agreement with ESPN. Rather than competing on price and getting caught up in a race to the bottom, Electronic Arts acquired the exclusive rights necessary to box out its competitor and set its own price. But where the NFL gave Electronic Arts the exclusive rights, the NBA signed no fewer than five different publishers, each able to put out a game of their own. Take-Two, not to be outdone, managed to sign a seven-year agreement with Major League Baseball and the Major League Baseball Players Association, just before both Electronic Arts and Sony released their games in March 2005.

This type of aggressive price competition and pursuit of exclusive license agreements typifies the costs and associated risks of an IP-based strategy. Certainly, fans of the NFL will be strongly motivated to buy the latest version of *Madden NFL* each year. Even so, Take-Two tried to trip up Electronic Arts with an aggressive pricing strategy and forced its competitor to spend a lot of money to claim the space and increased the overall risk in Electronic Arts' portfolio. In the end, however, the *Madden NFL* franchise managed to sell more than one hundred million copies and has earned Electronic Arts more than $4 billion.[3]

Another approach is to acquire IP as the basis for innovation and further insulation from changes in the market. Even well-known firms at the peak of their success, however, have found that this is not a waterproof approach. As video games became more popular in the late 1990s and started to present a notable competitor to the toy business, Hasbro changed its strategy. After several years of licensing its toy IP to others and having third-party publishers and developers take on most of the risk of creating games, Hasbro launched its own game publishing group: Hasbro Interactive. As the industry started to grow in size, the toymaker's executives also became more ambitious. Developing and publishing their own titles, they reasoned, would strike the ideal balance between their exposure to risk and ability to generate revenue.

At first, Hasbro was right. Relying on its existing retail relationships, it was able to get its games placed in lots of stores. And despite the absence of any blockbuster successes, the new division managed to generate income right away. In 1997, revenue more than doubled year-over-year from $35 million to $86 million. To keep the momentum, Hasbro's leadership increased its spending and invested heavily in obtaining licenses like *Jeopardy* and *Wheel of Fortune*. It also acquired a string of development studios, including Avalon Hill (for $6 million) and Microprose ($70 million). It worked: by 1998, Hasbro Interactive posted $196 million in revenue.

The initial success encouraged its executives who had started to dream of $1 billion in annual income. To make this possible, the division formulated a strategy centered on acquiring more licenses, hiring more product developers, and expanding to all gaming platforms. It also set up a sports division and even toyed with the idea of acquiring Electronic Arts. This move gives insight into the degree of ambition that had captured the group's decision-makers because Electronic Arts had earned over $1 billion that year. Signals from the market were encouraging, too. Archrival Mattel had just acquired The Learning Company for $4 billion, and the broader economy was enjoying massive tailwinds as tech firms and the popularization of the internet heightened expectations. Hasbro Interactive was aiming for the moon.

Generally, it makes sense to double down on what works and to invest heavily in a growing segment. Particularly, in the absence of in-house expertise, as in the case of Hasbro Interactive, it makes sense to emphasize acquiring talent and IP to ensure continued growth and success. Unfortunately, Hasbro's strategy had fatally overlooked two points. First, the string of acquisitions and obtained IP resulted in a managerial nightmare. With many of its components moving independently, Hasbro's management structure had difficulty establishing obvious synergies and efficiencies. Its financial reporting structure quickly became convoluted and ultimately failed to accurately forecast earnings. In turn, the lack of transparency exacerbated trust issues between both the subsidiary and its parent company, and internally between management and creatives.[4]

Second, Hasbro Interactive was financially exposed. As part of its aggressive investments and acquisitions, its profit margin had started to decline: on the $196 million it earned in 1998, its profit was $23 million. One year later, it managed to grow revenue to $237 million (an increase of 21 percent), but it suffered a loss of $74 million. Understandably, this did not sit well with the rest of Hasbro. Of course, at the time, the interactive group may have been able to remedy this precarious financial situation. But then the dotcom bubble burst, and everything came undone.

With the wind no longer in its sails, Hasbro Interactive hung together with improved financial diligence and the fortunate success of titles like

Roller Coaster Tycoon. But it was not enough. By the end of 2000, French publisher Infogrames acquired the division for $100 million. Its fate ultimately offers a warning for organizations that think they are impervious to broader market trends because of a reliance on trusted IP.

Instead of leveraging IP to exclude others, like we saw in the example of the sports licenses, or to fortify vulnerabilities to a broader economic environment, some organizations also formulated strategies around the management of game mechanics and rulesets. One example comes from Wizards of the Coast (Wizards), which brilliantly managed to become synonymous with the role-playing category by making its IP available to others.

First released in 1973 by TSR, *Dungeons & Dragons* (*D&D*) is a role-playing game in which a group of players creates individual avatars and goes adventuring through a fictional world that is narrated and controlled by a single player, the Game Master. This person handles all of the necessary in-game accounting concerning battles, exploring, narrative components, and the results of player actions. Generally regarded as somewhat of a fringe activity, the game mechanics' underlying paper-and pencil-based role-playing have been hugely influential in many well-known franchises that are popular today. Central to this category is the publishing of rulebooks and narratives that help govern a larger fantasy universe.

Because paper role-playing games are relatively easy to make, the market had long consisted of many smaller development outfits. Low barriers to entry mean that anyone with enough time to construct a narrative can create their own role-playing adventure game, and as the category gained in popularity, the overall market landscape became highly fragmented. To compete effectively, most designers would formulate proprietary, closed-game systems. By locking players into a particular ruleset, developers would be able to build their own audiences and continue selling expansions and additional adventures. From a strategic perspective, this was meant to increase switching costs for players, discouraging them from abandoning one and going to play another. Moreover, it posed significant difficulty for new entrants to acquire customers. As a result, the role-playing market consisted of many small outfits with a low headcount and low profitability throughout the early years of its history.

As substitutes started to emerge throughout the 1980s and 1990s in the form of video games and trading card games, the market started to decline. Developer TSR released several different editions of *D&D* to make the experience more intuitive and to emphasize the social aspects of collaborative play over the increasingly cumbersome administrative effort required to make decisions and actions. As a result of the combination of internal conflict and the backdrop of a declining market, TSR struggled.

In 1997, Wizards of the Coast acquired TSR. It reviewed the firm's offering and reached the following conclusion. First, D&D had too many worlds. To appeal to a broader base of players, TSR had created a myriad of narratives in a largely confusing universe. As the number of "worlds" inside D&D increased, the player count for each declined, resulting in fragmentation and lower sales. Second, D&D lacked a unified, central system that governed all of its different series and supplements. Rules were often contradictory and lacked uniformity, forcing players to spend more time figuring out the appropriate rules during gameplay instead of actually playing. Third, Wizards determined that the franchise had become opaque to new players who confronted a steep learning curve to participate.

To remedy these problems, Wizards rebuilt the game from scratch and implemented several strategic changes. To start, it created a series of introductory D&D products for new players. Acknowledging the need to revitalize its player base, Wizards published products specifically targeting newcomers. It also streamlined the experience and addressed troubled aspects of the overall play mechanics. Game Masters, for instance, had suffered a growing amount of time pressure on their role as gameplay sessions became more complex. In response, Wizards created several playing aids and reorganized the game to bring its focus back to collaborative play.

By far, the most innovative approach to establishing itself as the authority in the category was to make its game system available for free. Wizards published a ruleset that incorporated the basic tenets of roleplaying by which players determine actions in the game, which in this case, centered on the use of a 20-sided die, or d20. This move streamlined the overall game experience and made it more accessible. Next, taking a page from the playbook in software development, Wizards created an Open Gaming License that allowed anyone to use their d20 game system as long as they acknowledged doing so. This open system enabled other developers to make their own content, quests, and characters that were compatible with the larger D&D universe. By effectively giving their IP away for free, Wizards succeeded in solidifying its own position and reinvigorated the overall market by encouraging innovation from smaller participants.[5]

Mobile IP Strategies

Strong IP signals value in commodified markets. In a digital marketplace with low entry barriers like mobile gaming, we have observed an ongoing increase in available inventory. This availability goes hand-in-hand with a decline in market transparency as consumers increasingly struggle to find content that interests them. IP plays a key role in negating the challenges of excess supply. Initially, during the early days of mobile gaming, IP holders were mostly hesitant to issue licenses or develop titles. The industry remained divided on the smartphone's long-term success, and publishers had little interest in having their franchises compete in a novel marketplace. The emerging category of mobile gaming had yet to prove itself to be sustainable over a longer period and most legacy firms merely monitored the market and remained unwilling to put out smartphone-based versions of their best-known franchises. For instance, it took Nintendo until late 2016, almost a decade since the first iPhone, before it released *Super Mario Run*. Others, like Take-Two and Electronic Arts, merely ported some of their existing older games. Even as mobile gaming grew, many incumbents still would not commit. Admittedly, it made no sense to risk devaluing their IP by closely associating it with what remained a segment dominated by up-and-coming content creators. Putting a premium franchise next to the work of a measly startup would bring value to the latter and add very little to the former. The success of smartphones and the insatiable demand for content eventually turned the tides. As the segment grew, it also became more crowded, and the growing inventory became increasingly less accessible to consumers. To circumvent the challenges, companies formulated different IP-based strategies with varying degrees of success.

An obvious strategy was to acquire a portion of a license of an existing franchise and leverage the shared marketing effort. In anticipation of the next installment in the *Star Wars* saga in late 2015, a slew of game makers sought to capitalize on the mounting promotional push and acquired a license from Disney to publish a smartphone-compatible version. Hoping to claim a portion of the inevitable consumer spending that would come with the release of a blockbuster movie like *Star Wars: A Force Awakens*, a rash of mobile games and applications across the mobile ecosystem leveraged the property. Examples included *Star Wars Commander* by Electronic Arts, *Angry Birds Star Wars* by Rovio, and *Star Wars Knights of the Old Republic* by Aspyr Media.

Looking at the revenue distribution among *Star Wars*–based games by title, a familiar pattern emerges: only a handful of firms manage to claim the lion's share of consumer spending. The top-earning game, *Star Wars Commander*, generated almost two and half times more money during the month leading up to the movie's release than the next runner up, *Star Wars Force Collection* by Konami. Organizing the sales data by publisher provides a similar distribution: Disney claimed approximately 48 percent of all income generated, not including earnings from minimum guarantees and other licensing fees.

Even if a licensed title helps to generate income, it may still be a liability. For a publisher like Konami, at that time, this meant that about 12 percent of its monthly earnings (i.e., around $12 million) was based on a Disney property. By comparison, another licensor, Kabam, earned $23 million in the same month, which represented roughly 3 percent of its total monthly income from smartphone gaming. And Rovio generated just 1 percent of income using the Star Wars brand (figure 8.1). This distribution illustrates how this strategy can both help boost earnings and simultaneously present a clear risk of building a financial dependency on someone else's IP. It goes

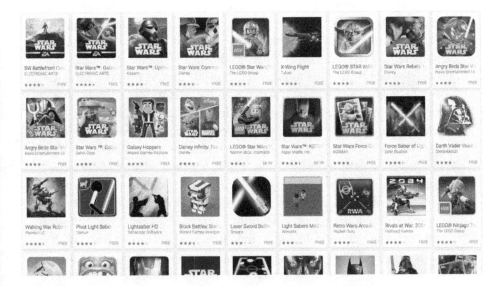

Figure 8.1
Top-selling titles on the Google Play Store one week before the release of *Star Wars: A Force Awakens*. *Source*: Screenshot taken by author on December 11, 2015.

against the general assumption that licensing strong IP is a safe bet because experienced firms like Disney manage to retain most of the value.

Another affordance of contemporary gaming is that it caters to regular consumers. Or so many studios thought. As discussed in chapter 4, the gamer audience is both much larger and more diverse than it has been in decades. This constitutes a second approach to IP in mobile gaming. Developers can leverage a broader range of celebrities and existing media properties as the differentiator for a new release. Previously somewhat limited to well-known athletes and perhaps a movie star or two, contemporary game makers have discovered that using the likeness of celebrities beyond those categories works well, too. One company in particular, Glu Mobile, struck gold when it contracted Kim Kardashian West.

The firm, which earned it stripes as a mobile developer before the popularization of smartphones, first released *Stardom: The A List* in 2011 only to relaunch it two years later as *Stardom: Hollywood*. The object of the game revolved around players achieving fame by carrying out tasks like dressing up and making red carpet appearances. It managed to achieve only minor financial success. That changed when Glu Mobile signed an agreement with socialite Kim Kardashian West to lend her likeness and voice. It took the game off the market and then rereleased it as *Kim Kardashian: Hollywood*. It was an instant success. Instead of just using her likeness, Glu actively involved the starlet in promoting the title, too, by making regular references to it in her television show *Keeping Up with the Kardashians* and sending regular notifications on social media. In an interview, the celebrity states, "The whole idea was to make it feel as live-time as possible. I would give [Glu] bikinis and be like, 'Hurry up and mock up this bikini, because I'm going to wear it, and then you can have it live in the game!"[6] As a result of the involvement of the high-profile celebrity, *Kim Kardashian: Hollywood* exceeded all expectations with more than eighteen million monthly active players at its peak and grossing around $284 million in lifetime earnings by late 2019.[7] Of course, watching the game's success led Hollywood agents to an obvious conclusion and a deluge of mobile titles developed around the public persona of celebrities followed. Musicians like Britney Spears, supermodel Kendall Jenner, and celebrity chef Gordon Ramsay all lent their likeness to developers, but none came close to Glu's initial success. Rapper Fetty Wap collaborated on a racing game called *Fetty Wap: Nitro Nation Stories* that carried his likeness but failed to reach the top rankings despite his musical success at the time. Nor did a match-three game called *Love Rocks* developed by Rovio in collaboration with singer

Shakira leave a lasting mark. In fact, the celebrity licensing strategy proved largely unsuccessful for everyone else. Even Glu Mobile was unable to replicate its initial success despite having convinced itself to formulate a novel business strategy around licensing celebrities. Its late-2015 release of *Katy Perry Pop*, a game around singer Katy Perry, failed to gain traction and Glu shut it down barely a year later. Despite having almost twice the number of followers on Twitter at the time, *Katy Perry Pop* earned only about $82,013 in its first nine months compared with the $89 million generated by Kim Kardashian West's game.

How can we explain the success of *Kim Kardashian: Hollywood*? Certainly, novelty was on her side. The sheer fact alone that someone like Kim Kardashian West would be part of a video game met an insatiable curiosity from audiences that only recently had started to play games at all. By the time other celebrities made their appearance, the initial shine had worn off.

A more cynical interpretation is that companies poorly managed these celebrity licenses. Observing Glu's success, a slew of firms eagerly jumped on the bandwagon and pushed out a string of low-quality titles. The success of a celebrity-based strategy depends heavily on an intuitive integration of game mechanics and a celebrity's persona (figure 8.2). It is easier to imagine Kim going to red carpets for photo opportunities than to visualize Shakira playing a gem-swapping game. A license only truly contributes value if it closely matches the entertainment property in spirit. Merely marrying a few things that happen to all be popular at the same time is a poor strategy. In addition, the positive network effects between celebrity-based mobile games is limited. As one executive pointed out: "Taylor Swift fans

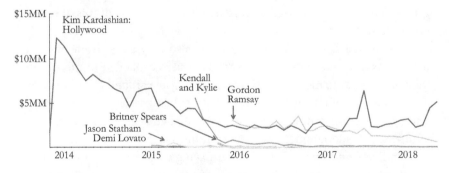

Figure 8.2

Monthly revenue for select celebrity-based mobile games, 2014–2018. *Source*: Data from SuperData Research. *Note*: Revenue in millions U.S. dollars ($).

will want nothing to do with Kim Kardashian." Cross-promotion, which had been critical to the success of Zynga and other game makers focused on the mainstream consumer, is far more limited between the loyal fan-bases of different artists and celebrities. Despite the possibility of licensing a broader inventory of franchises and famous people, it did not evolve into a sustainable strategy. Rather, a one-off success seduced a host of other industry participants to quickly release poorly developed games and in doing so became the very thing they sought to avoid.

It is understandable, of course, that conventional media firms are not always easy to convince of the merits of a new platform. As a third licensing strategy common to mobile, television properties are closely guarded, and their owners generally have a strict set of practices in place. The popularity and setting for a hit-series like *Game of Thrones* by HBO, for instance, would at first glance make for a great opportunity as a fantasy role-playing or trading card game. But this proved not quite so obvious in reality. One key obstacle is the absence of a clear arrangement with many of the actors in the series concerning the use of their likeness. To build a mobile game around any of the major characters consequently would involve having to renegotiate existing contracts with actors who came into the prime of their fame as the show gained popularity. This would result in unusually large financial concessions to release a property on a medium that, according to many media executives, would still be of only secondary importance. Or as one HBO executive told me: "There's no way they are going to pay that much to get approval from the major characters to use their likeness to make a mobile game." Because most traditional television executives only recently came to regard smartphone-based gaming as a meaningful market, contracts with actors today still do not necessarily take the rights for mobile games into account. This omission generally results in the dismissal of any proposed IP-based project.

Opposition from senior management also may come from internal inertia. As a former producer at A&E Networks explained to me, "Even though it is clear to me that we should make a game around *Duck Dynasty*, it remains difficult to get internal support, because games don't make sense to the old guard of executives." On one hand, the financial metrics of interactive entertainment, such as monthly active users, conversion rate to spending, and average spending per paying user, resemble a vastly different monetization model than the "cost per thousand" advertising jargon that is more familiar to the bulk of the organization. On the other, internal resistance comes from a generational difference: a senior professional with only a few years left before retirement is unlikely to take a chance on a model that is difficult to understand, not wanting to jeopardize their personal position on the way out. In particular in media organizations that produce television shows, an outdated mental image of what the gamer audience looks like persists.

Still, in other cases, it can be difficult to even find a suitable developer for television properties. Examples include Endemol Shine, a media firm known for shows like *Big Brother, Biggest Loser*, and *MasterChef*, and FremantleMedia, known for *The Price Is Right* and *Family Feud*. These two rivals spend a lot of effort trying to get reputable game studios to commit to one of their properties. Often a studio will insist on a media company leveraging its existing marketing muscle. Here, too, however, a project runs into the limitations presented by existing relationships and practices. Speaking to a former licensing manager at one of these organizations, I learned: "It is incredibly difficult to line up a marketing campaign that promotes the game around a show, because it eats into our ability to sell that airtime to advertisers instead." Without a dedicated promotional effort, especially the larger, more desirable game makers are a lot less interested. Moreover, for smaller television properties the minimum guarantee can be a deal breaker for major publishers, especially if the contract also requires them to invest in development and marketing. For these license holders that means having to do more handholding throughout the process and exposing themselves to working with firms that may not be as well known by their senior leadership, thereby increasing the perception of risk. In the case of FremantleMedia, it was no surprise then that they acquired Ludia, the studio that initially had developed the mobile game for *The Prize Is Right*. Having found a suitable partner for the development of its properties, it made more sense to reduce risk and remove the need to build relationships with other studios by vertically integrating. We thus find that IP is not a clear-cut path to success as key decision-makers struggle to see the value in the games category and refuse to surrender control over their IP.

What motivates the relentless push to developing and obtaining IP is the incredible value it can create. If we have so far mostly discussed the circumstance of a game company licensing someone else's IP, there arguably exists no better example than Finnish mobile developer Rovio to illustrate how much developing a successful proprietary franchise can change a studio's fortunes.

To understand how meaningful *Angry Birds* is for Rovio, we have to first look at the company's history. Started by four friends with a background in software development, Rovio initially followed a common path. Typically, the life cycle for a studio starts with a disproportionate, if not exclusive, number of work-for-hire projects. This lowers the amount of risk for the developer but also reduces its potential upside. Risks include working under the strict deadlines and requirements imposed by a license-holder or client; competing on the cost of development with many comparable contenders; having no guarantee that upon completion the next project will be waiting; and, in the case of a revenue share, having no certainty of a financial pay-off. This risk creates a tension between ensuring that the studio's clients are happy and meeting the studio's desire to "save up" and pursue its creative projects wherever possible to ultimately create a financially successful game and achieve more creative freedom.

After initially successfully growing to about fifty people doing contract work for major firms, including Electronic Arts, Namco, Nokia, and Real Networks, Rovio found that game development for devices that predated the smartphone ultimately was not sustainable. Before the introduction of the iPhone, mobile development required presenting handset manufacturers and telecom providers with a working version of a title for every single handset in their entire offering. That meant more or less having to develop, test, customize, and quality check the same game several hundred times. Consequently, Rovio downsized to about a dozen employees in the mid-2000s and was ready to give up when it made a last-ditch effort to develop something for the new iPhone.

Angry Birds almost did not see the light of day. One of Rovio's early hires, who oversaw marketing at the time, told me: "It was only because of persistence that we pulled it off. The design team spent the weekend improving on it and changed the game from just catapulting birds to giving the birds unique strengths and capabilities. When we came in on Monday, we had every intent to shut it down, but instead we found ourselves hooked on the improved gameplay."

In addition to *Angry Birds*'s appeal, Rovio also had to go through marketing channels and other gatekeepers to get people to play it. To raise the title's visibility among industry press, its marketing team visited every country in Europe and identified the top websites in each that reviewed mobile games. After weeks of travel and "sending invites and promo codes translated in every language with Google Translate," the game eventually ranked among the top-ten mobile games across Europe.

The success across Europe motivated the studio to push its publisher Chillingo to get the game featured in Apple's App Store. It found the ideal partner in the handset manufacturer. Apple had seen initial success with its smartphone, but for many consumers, the use of a touchscreen interface remained relatively new. *Angry Birds* provided a clever way to showcase the device's features, and with Apple's help, it quickly became one of the iPhone's most notable titles. Designed to be easily recognizable, requiring no tutorial, offering self-explanatory game mechanics and short play sessions, and appealing to a worldwide audience because of the deliberate absence of language, *Angry Birds* grew to become a massive hit.

After years of creating value for someone else, Rovio had done something few firms accomplish. It successfully escaped the turbulence of being a small development studio and reversed its fortunes by building an asset from which it could earn revenue through licensing. Even so, initially it did not pursue a licensing strategy. To run such a business is quite different from game development, and Rovio did not immediately recognize the opportunity. But after some experimenting, the organization's new strategy was clear: "As a test we ordered 30,000 plush toys. But after we sold out our entire inventory in under 20 minutes, we realized we had a brand on our hands."

Beyond lunch boxes, stuffed animals, and candy, Rovio also collaborated on a feature film in 2016, *The Angry Birds Movie*, which proved to be one of the most successful game-based movies of all time by pulling in more than $400 million in box office revenue. The franchise also has legally (and illegally) licensed theme parks, and a two-season cartoon series on Netflix. What makes Rovio's success particularly enviable from an industry perspective is that most game studios generally find that they have to prove they are worthy of handling someone else's IP. Licensors hold all of the cards and can make a lot of demands, whereas the licensee seeks to carve out a small profit, hoping that adding a visible IP to its portfolio will lead to bigger opportunities. Rovio managed to reverse that dynamic by developing its own IP, allowing it to finally exit the project-to-project death spiral of game development and pursue a licensing strategy of its own.

What makes licensing a tricky strategy is a lack of transparency. We do know, for instance, that Electronic Arts' decision to corner the sports games category worked out well, but typically little information is available to ascertain whether IP-based titles yield better results than original content. At the same time, it is obvious from our Star Wars example that the license holder ultimately manages to retain most of the value. Even so, most of the available data are anecdotal. Data on mobile games, however, allow us to take a more rigorous look into how a license strategy compares to creating original content.

On the basis of an analysis of the monthly top-one-hundred grossing mobile titles in the United States from 2014 to 2017, we can make the following observations (see table 8.1). First, over the course of this four-year period, the combined revenue for IP-based titles doubled to $2 billion. This growth was consistent with an increasingly crowded marketplace in which IP serves to better communicate value of content to consumers.

Second, organized by licensing category, we observe that casino-style titles generate the most revenue: $810 million in 2017, up 38 percent from 2014, and roughly twice the size of the next runner-up. Television-based games like *The Price Is Right* ostensibly connect well with general audiences, as this segment grew from $134 million to $484 million during the same period. Three categories that generally have served the conventional business well—Hollywood licenses, game franchises from other platforms, and sports—remain relatively small. Each generated a few hundred million annually. Sports-based titles grew the fastest, from $28 million to $156 million. Finally, as in the case of Glu Mobile, celebrity-based titles peaked early and then dropped, declining from $55 million annually to $5 million.

Even so, combined, these IP-based strategies make substantially less money compared with original content, which generated almost $4 billion in income in 2017, up 36 percent from 2014. In particular, titles like *Clash Royale* managed to earn billions and are uniquely developed for smartphones. In absolute dollars, original mobile titles accounted for 71 percent in 2014 and have since dropped to 64 percent of the total by 2017; nevertheless, this remains by far the most lucrative approach (see figure 8.3).

One key characteristic that generally stands perpendicular to the cultivation of successful IP is market consolidation. Large firms that rely for the bulk of their income on existing licenses and franchises tend to take fewer risks on new properties and instead prefer to reinvest in existing IP that has been proven in the market. Consequently, acquiring IP outright through acquisition and takeovers reduces the risk profile but generally is reserved for large companies with deep pockets.

In this context, the proliferation of additional platforms and a broader variety of available content options to consumers generally is explained as an overall improvement. When it comes to cultural expression or sources of information, more is generally regarded as better. With video games becoming a popular form of entertainment, it begins to serve as a shared mode of social exchange. Games express ideas.[8] Ostensibly and hopefully, games both widen the available channels that permeate society and contribute to the range and types of available content. Games industry creatives have an

Table 8.1

Total revenue for different licensing categories on mobile for top-one-hundred U.S. grossing titles, 2014–2017

	2014		2015		2016		2017	
	Revenue	No.	Revenue	No.	Revenue	No.	Revenue	No.
Original Content	$2,686	1,476	$3,823	1,230	$3,473	1,100	$3,731	1,125
Licensed Content	$1,111	822	$1,953	1,043	$1,942	1,149	$2,098	1,150
Casino	$588	452	$968	451	$825	504	$810	488
TV	$134	45	$138	68	$310	119	$484	171
Hollywood	$225	194	$371	231	$424	196	$334	136
Game	$82	76	$285	215	$214	247	$311	254
Sports	$28	43	$132	52	$147	64	$156	91
Celebrity	$55	12	$58	26	$21	19	$5	10
Total	**$3,797**	**2,298**	**$5,776**	**2,273**	**$5,414**	**2,249**	**$5,830**	**2,275**
Share original (%)	70.7		66.2		64.1		64.0	
Share licensed (%)	29.3		33.8		35.9		36.0	

Source: Author's compilation based on SuperData Research.

Note: Analysis based on the monthly revenue in millions U.S. dollars ($) for the top-one-hundred titles on both Android and iOS for the period from January 2014 to December 2017. Data collected from SuperData Research and organized into the following categories: Mobile Original (here defined as games that were developed for mobile platforms and not based on any existing intellectual property elsewhere), Casino (e.g., social casino), TV (e.g., quiz shows), Hollywood (e.g., movies), Game (e.g., video game franchises from PC and console), Sports, and Celebrity. Total does not add to 2,400 for each year due to illegible or missing titles in the original data set that were omitted.

Table 8.2
Overview of industry structure for mobile, console, and PC gaming, 1998–2018

	1998	1999	2000	2001	2002	2003	2004	2005	2006
Mobile									
Global revenue	47	64	66	118	329	329	265	608	1,452
C10								100%	100%
HHI				5,666	4,443	3,018	2,695	1,694	2,555
No. of firms >1%	1	1	1	2	3	4	5	8	8
Console									
Global revenue	11,746	12,699	11,519	12,967	15,609	17,335	19,484	18,554	21,149
C10	94%	92%	94%	94%	93%	90%	89%	84%	86%
HHI	3,106	2,864	3,134	2,414	2,148	2,016	1,747	1,504	1,481
No. of firms >1%	14	14	12	11	12	14	14	16	14
PC									
Global revenue	1,218	1,500	1,619	2,937	3,996	4,457	4,879	4,679	5,911
C10	94%	91%	89%	91%	93%	88%	85%	77%	77%
HHI	1,647	1,613	1,383	1,314	1,576	1,234	1,069	976	1,034
No. of firms >1%	13	13	14	15	12	16	16	18	17

Source: Author's compilation based on company reports.
Notes: Revenue in millions, U.S. dollars ($). HHI, Herfindahl-Hirschman index.

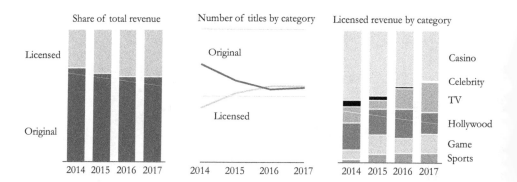

Figure 8.3
Breakout of top-grossing U.S. mobile titles (Android, iOS), original and licensed content, 2014–2017. *Source*: Data from SuperData Research. *Note*: Analysis based on the monthly revenue for the top-one-hundred titles on Android and iOS from January 2014 to December 2017. Data organized into the following categories: Mobile Original (i.e., games that were developed for mobile platforms and not based on any existing intellectual property elsewhere), Casino (e.g., social casino), TV (e.g., quiz shows), Hollywood (e.g., movies), Game (e.g., video game franchises from PC and console), Sports, Celebrity, and Other.

2007	2008	2009	2010	2011	2012	2013	2014	2015	2016	2017	2018
1,300	2,260	1,818	3,532	5,861	9,497	15,967	21,074	29,168	35,526	43,635	45,104
100%	100%	99%	98%	95%	89%	81%	76%	67%	67%	63%	57%
2,644	2,458	1,779	2,128	2,138	1,760	1,272	1,260	1,028	1,063	1,227	832
8	8	9	11	12	12	18	17	22	21	22	25
28,187	31,463	27,316	29,470	28,246	24,667	24,421	23,608	22,482	24,764	26,604	34,734
88%	93%	92%	92%	91%	94%	91%	90%	89%	89%	91%	91%
1,515	1,865	1,659	1,568	1,450	1,519	1,368	1,350	1,155	1,260	1,505	1,389
14	13	13	13	13	12	13	14	14	13	12	12
6,763	9,366	10,007	11,443	13,922	16,576	17,262	18,001	21,763	24,534	30,364	30,220
75%	74%	76%	71%	71%	66%	61%	68%	63%	69%	70%	66%
961	754	905	630	627	571	485	612	571	851	976	838
19	20	22	20	18	21	24	20	21	19	19	21

opportunity to realize ideas, narratives, and protagonists that other media cannot, or will not, fund for whatever reason now that a broad audience has adopted and is engaged with this novel form of expression. We may ask, following its digitalization do we have a broader, more diverse industry structure today?

To answer this question, most scholars historically have relied on establishing a concentration index for relevant markets to determine whether or not the availability and variety of content is in jeopardy.[9] Previously we saw that each of the main segments—mobile, console, and PC—presents different market structures (see chapters 5, 6, and 7). Organizing the revenue data collected for publishers by each of these platforms produces concentration indexes as shown in figure 8.3.

Over the course of three decades, concentration levels have declined in all corners (see table 8.2). The console segment initially dropped, but it climbed again following the success of the Nintendo Wii in 2007 and the 2008 Activision Blizzard merger. In particular, the influence of the latter should not be underestimated. Because it took place across different segments, the combination of Activision and Vivendi (Blizzard) resulted in the emergence of a juggernaut among Western publishers, both in terms of market control and its ability to create successful franchises like *World of Warcraft* and *Call of Duty*. After that, concentration in the console games market decreased, but it started to go back again in recent years.

PC gaming, in contrast, has always been less concentrated, and consolidation is a relatively new phenomenon in this segment of the market. This low concentration, in part, was the result of the dominance of Tencent and its appetite for new content to serve to Chinese consumers who favor the PC over consoles. Moreover, successes like *League of Legends*, *Fortnite*, *PUBG*, *Roblox*, and *Overwatch* managed to entice mainstream players and benefit from the growth in this audience segment. In 2018, the PC segment counted seven organizations that generated more than $1 billion in annual income each.

And, finally, mobile started off as highly concentrated, as is to be expected during the early years, and then quickly dropped (and continued to do so) until 2015. Here, again, we observed a spike as a result of Tencent's acquisition of Supercell in 2016 and the continued success of firms like NetEase and Niantic.

In aggregate, the games business has become less concentrated over the past twenty years. Large organizations have a persistent appetite for acquisition, however, and giants continue to drive consolidation. In the current lead-up to the ninth generation of console hardware and, a bit farther out, the advent of cloud gaming, incumbent platform holders have started to make more aggressive acquisitions to ensure themselves of premium content as a complementary. In 2018, Microsoft went through a string of purchases, including Ninja Theory, Playground Games, Undead Labs, Compulsion Games, Obsidian, and Double Fine Productions.

The broadening of the video games audience occurred in tandem with an overall diversification of its industry landscape. Today, more firms are making games than were doing so twenty years ago, and both incumbents and newcomers are successful. Organized by platform, however, we observe distinct differences between the three major segments. In the console space, in particular, platform holders continue to retain a strong grip on the overall market, in which PC and mobile remain less concentrated and populated by a broader group of successful firms (those that have more than 1 percent market share).

The short answer to the question of whether digitalization has made game development more democratic is, well, yes. The longer answer is that after a period of super-growth of a more than 12 percent annual increase in consumer spending on average, the industry has entered a next phase in which it has reestablished a stable market structure. Costs inevitably are going up among platform holders, who are developing new hardware, and publishers, who are confronting a crowded digital marketplace that demands a growing investment in marketing. We already have seen the first signs of an increase in consolidation in the most recent years: since reaching a low point, all three markets have started to increase again in concentration since 2014 (figure 8.4).

In sum, the use of, or reliance on, IP in gaming offers a false sense of security. As exciting as the success of *Pokémon GO*, *Angry Birds*, or *Star Wars–based* games is, each is an exception and is fraught with risk. For one, it is expensive. Despite initially losing out on the sports video games category, Take-Two and Sony forced Electronic Arts into spending a fortune to obtain the FIFA and NFL licenses. This worked out for Electronic Arts, but over time, it also eroded the firm's overall portfolio to the point at which it now relies for almost 80 percent of its annual income on the ability to extract revenue from sports licenses.

Spending a bunch of money on different IPs also brings obvious risk. In Hasbro's case, a combination of unchecked ambition, a lack of control, and an imploding market decimated its interactive ambitions almost overnight. Spending millions on obtaining IP and development studios without

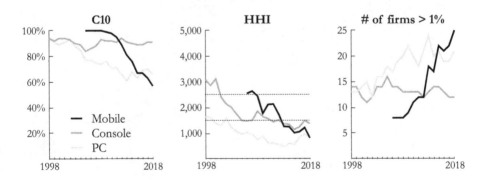

Figure 8.4

Market concentration in mobile, console, and PC games 1998–2018. *Source*: Data from company reports. *Note*: Dotted lines in middle figure (Herfindahl-Hirschmann Index) indicate thresholds established by the U.S. Department of Justice's Antitrust Division. See the appendix for more information.

a coherent managerial structure and brand strategy quickly results in a catastrophic degree of financial exposure, especially when markets do not go your way.

Novelty, too, plays a critical role. Especially in crowded segments, new and unexpected crossovers can create value and recognition among consumers. Here, too, however, game makers struggle to effectively replicate or maintain initial success. An effective strategy around IP, owned or licensed, requires an organization-wide vision that is consistent and focused. It is not, unfortunately, a simplified formula for success.

The quest for IP demands equal parts creative design and business strategy. In the end, going the long way around and developing your own IP appears to offer the best of both worlds: it provides the most creative control and is more lucrative. In particular, the launch of a new platform presents an opportunity to establish a new IP, as we saw in the example of *Angry Birds*. Even then, however, it remains a challenging strategy that cannot be phoned in. Just ask E.T.

9

Watching Other People
Play Video Games, and Why

Watching people [play] games was boring, but now people like to see how people play games. It's content of games, not games per se.

—LIN SONGTAO, VICE PRESIDENT, TENCENT

When Amazon acquired the live-streaming platform Twitch in 2014 for $970 million, it accomplished two things. First, it snatched a key strategic asset away from Google, which allegedly also had been in talks; and, second, it cemented with a single purchase the commercial viability of people watching other people play video games. Twitch's growing success was a direct challenge to the long-held belief among entertainment executives that online videos were inferior to traditional broadcast television and film production.

Previously, YouTube had enabled millions of amateur filmmakers to upload and share their work. Its online presence grew as consumers flocked to the platform and shifted the perception on what resonated with audiences. Preferring the newly emerging format, a growing number of younger viewers started to abandon broadcast television in favor of digital streaming services.

The appeal of gaming video content to an otherwise-difficult-to-reach consumer group is an important part of the current momentum behind sponsors', publishers', and investors' efforts. For years, broadcast television and radio have been losing their ability to attract people between the ages of eighteen and thirty-four, a key age-group for brands. In markets like the United States, around 15 percent of U.S. adults are so-called cord cutters (i.e., the consumers who used to have a cable or satellite television sub-scription but no longer do) and cord-nevers (i.e., those that never did). An additional 9 percent of Americans never even had a subscription to these type of amusement services in the first place. Instead, a growing portion of audiences turns to online streaming channels for their entertainment rather than traditional television. Predictably, fewer eighteen- to twenty-six-year-olds have a cable subscription (65 percent) than thirty- to forty-nine-year-olds and those who are over fifty (83 percent). Among those who cut the cord, three-quarters own a smartphone, 58 percent have a home broadband connection, and 27 percent are smartphone-only.[1] Succinctly, the emergence of gaming video content must be understood both in terms of its merits to deliver a novel experience and in the context of a decline in conventional media's ability to capture audiences.

Even so, YouTube posed only a moderate threat to more traditional entertainment business because it did not offer live television. Without the ability to draw a large number of simultaneous spectators, online video remained of secondary interest to advertisers. Its ability to attract viewers is where Twitch differs: it centers on the real-time broadcasts from a grow-ing group of content producers that is available online to anyone with the appropriate bandwidth. Originally started in 2007 as an online destination where people could broadcast video online about anything, its founders soon realized that the most popular category was gaming. By 2011, it spun off this entire segment and established a new site called Twitch.tv. Amazon's rationale for the purchase just three years later was to combine it with its growing presence in gaming retail (see chapter 3) and a broader strategy of creating original content. Around the same time, it also founded Amazon Game Studios with the intention of dominating every aspect of this enter-tainment market's value chain.

This new category, live-streaming, has since evolved into a critical component in the way that game companies market their content to audi-ences. It has emerged as a viable career option for a generation of video game fans and eager talent. Today, more than 2.2 million people are stream-ing on the platform to a daily audience of fifteen million unique visitors.[2] After music, which is the most popular type of content on platforms like YouTube, audiences like to watch videos and live streams of people playing or discussing interactive entertainment. One estimate puts the worldwide audience for gaming video content at 850 million viewers. The top-two platforms globally are Twitch with 183 million viewers and YouTube with 594 million viewers.[3] In markets like the United States, Germany, and the

United Kingdom, audiences are on average thirty-four years old, and the gender distribution is 65 percent male and 35 percent female. This desirable consumer group is increasingly difficult to reach through more conventional media channels like broadcast television and radio. With so many people worldwide now regularly watching both prerecorded and live-streaming videos of others playing games, the phenomenon has disrupted how publishers market their titles and opened up new avenues for advertisers to connect with young audiences.

In this chapter, we identify two major developments: we first discuss the emergence of gaming video content and the role live-streamers have come to play in the way interactive entertainment caters to its audiences. As publishing moved away from the product-based business model, both small and large creative firms have started to devise new communication strategies to reach players. This is changing the configuration of relevant marketing channels. Second, we look at esports. Game companies leverage tournaments and competitions to increase audience engagement and grow additional revenue streams. Initially dismissed as a novelty, competitive play has managed to cement its presence in the industry and now represents a common component to contemporary publishing. Esports presents an emergent form of entertainment at the intersection between the business practices surrounding traditional sports and technology and video games.

Gaming Video Content

Even the most seasoned media executive must have scratched themselves behind the ears when they watched a blue-haired twenty-seven-year-old named Tyler "Ninja" Blevins make his appearance on *The Ellen DeGeneres Show*. An avid gamer from Illinois, Ninja had managed to become the top streamer on Twitch with an average of fifty-three thousand concurrent viewers during broadcasts. He had hosted a play session with rap musician Drake that attracted a record-breaking six hundred thousand concurrent viewers on Ninja's channel, was making millions of dollars in ad revenue, and had successfully broken into mainstream television. Unable to recognize the new format and talent, media executives asked, Why would anyone watch someone else play video games?

To anyone who grew up playing video games, the answer was deceivingly simple. Gamers have always watched each other play in arcades and living rooms. To them, witnessing a friend, roommate, or sibling beat a particularly difficult level or break a high score is common. This is not unique to video games, of course. Through watching others, we learn more about a title's mechanics (e.g., What does this rule mean?), gain a deeper understanding of the meanings associated with a particular game, and identify with particular groups of people. Games are a universal, social activity. This is common knowledge to the average social scientist, but, as it turns out, it's brand new information to media professionals.[4]

An important catalyst behind the growth in gaming video content is the popularization of free-to-play games. In the absence of buyer's remorse, titles that rely on a slow drip toward monetization found that an abundance of available videos with epic moments and hilarious commentary had a seemingly positive effect on the acquisition and retention of users. Live streams broaden the experience and allow consumers to become more deeply involved and familiar with the intricacies of strategy for titles like *DOTA 2* or *League of Legends*. Many of these games can be quite complex. Consistent with a microtransaction monetization strategy, many different heroes are available, each with their own unique skill set and characteristics. Seeing how others play with them demystifies the game, improves overall awareness, and extends the average player's life cycle. Tencent subsidiary Riot Games, for instance, recognized this fact early on. Almost since its inception, the firm has emphasized hands-on support to the development of user-generated video coverage and has promoted content creation by hosting and supporting tournaments and channels. It learned that viewers flock to online video both to spectate and learn new tactics. In an interview with ESPN, CEO Brandon Beck stated that such viewership has become an "integral part of the experience."[5]

A second driver behind the popularity of gaming video content is the change it facilitates in the dynamic between large multinational game companies and the journalists who review the games they bring to market. We previously discussed how a product-based market forces consumers to negotiate a significant risk when deciding to pay $60 for a game. Before their purchase, they know little about it and largely hope it will be worth their money and time. To mitigate this tension, consumers have long relied on magazines and reviewers to decide what to buy.[6]

At the center of this dynamic, we find conventional games journalists. These professional reviewers carefully balance the tension between their reliance on the industry for access, on the one hand, and the need to remain objective, on the other. They depend heavily on being sent copies of upcoming releases and consoles before they are available to the broader consumer market. Having early access builds up their social capital and allows reviewers to become a trusted source of information. In exchange for providing access, publishers and platform holders hope to garner positive feedback and positive critiques to boost their overall marketing efforts. Journalists are flown around the world, put up in fancy hotels, meet famous game designers and hardware engineers, and are privy to embargoed product announcements. This is key to a games journalist's credibility. But to keep this access, they ultimately are limited in their ability to be overly critical of an upcoming release. Large, publicly traded firms whose stock price can depend on the positive outcome of a big launch naturally seek to influence tastemakers and gatekeepers.

As an example of how this tension can manifest, we can look to the case of Jeff Gerstmann. As the editorial director of GameSpot, a gaming website, Gerstmann refused to adjust his review of an upcoming title, *Kane & Lynch*. After its publisher EIDOS had spent significant amounts of money on advertising on the GameSpot site, it complained about Gerstmann's review and rating of the game. Unwilling to compromise his integrity, his employers prioritized EIDOS' interests and fired Gerstmann. In response, several other high-profile resignations followed from the GameSpot staff. One of my colleagues, David Nieborg at the University of Toronto, refers to this dynamic as the political economy of games journalism.[7] Succinctly, the financial pressures on reviewers force them to rely heavily on ad revenue to keep up their traffic and circulation numbers. This inevitably creates a murky circumstance in which it is increasingly unclear whether they truly serve the players in their need to know about what games to buy or whether they are on the side of the corporations that fund their efforts.

Live-streamers bypass this pressure of large corporations trying to influence an individual reviewer to a degree and, more important, allow consumers to see a game in detail before committing to it. This neutrality has resulted in viewers growing loyal to a particular personality or player and wanting to watch them play online. It is not unlike radio personalities: listeners tuned in to a specific disk jockey they liked, but who otherwise had access to much of the same music as every other radio professional. Live-streamers occupy a distinct position in the industry: they are both celebrities with their own following, and tastemakers who meaningfully affect consumer demand for a new title. Gaming video content has quickly evolved into a key component to the value chain and plays an important role in marketing new releases: today, online videos influence what 46 percent of PC and console gamers under the age of twenty-five play in a major market like the United States.[8]

The impact of a well-thought out campaign involving live-streamers compared with a more traditional approach is tangible, as Electronic Arts discovered in 2019. Despite putting most of its weight behind building momentum for the release of its new sci-fi shooter, *Anthem*, another one of its own titles, free-to-play Battle Royale shooter *Apex Legends*, stole the spotlight. Electronic Arts positioned *Anthem* as a blockbuster release and leveraged mostly traditional marketing channels. Simultaneously, it permitted *Apex Legends* studio producer Drew McCoy to independently determine its own marketing strategy and content rollout schedule. The studio paid celebrity streamer Ninja an alleged million dollars to play the game for one day on Twitch, which resulted in many other streamers also switching over to the new release. From there, the game went viral: several of the most-viewed streamers played *Apex* for another two weeks. *Apex Legends* quickly dominated the viewership rankings and managed to even push past the top title at the time: *Fortnite*.[9] After playing *Fortnite* for months on end, Ninja and others were eager for something new and continued to play *Apex Legends* without receiving compensation. This signaled the game's value to audiences and resulted in roughly twice as many people playing the underdog than the anticipated favorite, *Anthem*. Despite generating roughly the same amount of revenue during their launch month, consumer attention for the blockbuster release dropped quickly in the second month. Meanwhile, *Apex Legends* managed to outperform *Anthem* in terms of total hours viewed on Twitch and monthly revenue (see figure 9.1). Predictably, unit sales for *Anthem* dropped off postrelease, but *Apex Legends* continued to drive viewership, playership, and revenue. Nine months following both releases, *Anthem* had earned Electronic Arts about $200 million in revenue compared with the $362 million generated by *Apex Legends*. By leveraging gaming video content as an effective marketing tool, the underdog had outwitted the favorite.

Beyond promotional activity, large well-known studios have started to rely on gaming video content as part of their creative process. According to a senior producer behind *Horizon Zero Dawn* at Guerrilla Games, YouTube videos acted as "an extremely qualified feedback loop, that we can use to improve the game and check if it appeals to the community."[10] Handled well, design takes place with an unprecedented degree of insight into what resonates with audiences. Historically, developers have relied

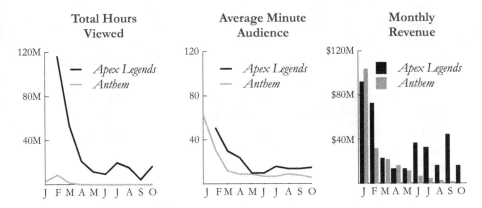

Figure 9.1
Live-streaming viewership and spending for *Anthem* and *Apex Legends*. *Source*: Data from SuperData Research. *Note*: Average minute audience refers to the average amount of viewers watching specified content at any given minute each month.

on focus groups or inviting a select group of people to come play-test a title before its release. This practice had been reserved for those firms that could afford it, because asking consumers for their feedback in person is costly and time-consuming. Monitoring video content and live-streaming, in contrast, enables creative firms to gather consumer feedback and add or remove aspects of a game to maximize its chances of success at launch. Unlike magazines, gaming video content presents a real-time feed of what audiences are playing and watching.

Smaller outfits similarly benefit. Independent developers leverage live-streaming to outmaneuver larger publishers and their considerable marketing budgets. Because overhead usually takes up the bulk of their financial resources, small developers generally have no money left for promotion. Instead, they send free copies to popular streamers in the hopes that they will dedicate play-thru video to it or give it a glowing review. According to designer Davey Wreden, it was his encouragement of players to post play-throughs on YouTube that helped him sell one hundred thousand copies of his title *Stanley Parable*.[11] In its current state, gaming video content acts as a powerful equalizer.

Not everyone has been onboard, however. Nintendo initially took an aggressive stance on having people make videos of its games, and in 2013, sought to enforce copyright on streaming video of its products. The firm demanded that YouTube pay it a percentage of the ad revenue collected on user-generated videos. But after facing public condemnation for their apparent misreading of the value created by the YouTube community, Nintendo relented and moved from a restrictive policy on video content to one of conditional support.[12] Similarly, Square Enix initially struggled with its position on streaming. In 2015, it released guidelines that heavily emphasized various restrictions and the use of imagery and music, rather than encouraging content creators to broadcast an upcoming title and drive its popularity. Square Enix also required streamers to display a copyright notice. And Atlus, another publisher, went so far as to threaten streamers to suspend their accounts if they broadcasted a recent release of *Persona 5* past a certain point in its storyline. The Japanese firm argued, "Simply put, we don't want the experience to be spoiled for people who haven't played the game. Our fans have waited years for the game to come out and we really want to make sure they can experience it fully as a totally new adventure."[13]

Despite the initial resistance by some, watching people play video games has evolved from a relatively obscure content category to become a key component of marketing and monetizing new titles.

Celebrity Gamers

The ability to attract audiences and reduce overall demand uncertainty among consumers has resulted in substantial revenue growth among gaming video content creators. For instance, PewDiePie made well over $7 million during his peak year in 2013, up more than 400 percent compared to the previous year.[14] And Ninja earned around $10 million in 2018. Much of their financial success comes from being regarded as more honest than other paid forms of marketing. These "kids in bedrooms" sharing their experiences with a worldwide audience appear to be, ostensibly, a more genuine way to learn about games compared with reading magazines and reviewer websites. They are perceived as more authentic.

Unfortunately, the influx of marketing dollars also seduces this category of influencers. Most of the gaming video content available is the result of a deliberate effort by large media corporations. Here, too, business interests challenge creative independence. To understand this, we must look at how live-streamers make money. Unlike magazines and television channels, and their substantial upfront capital expenses, streamers usually start as a single individual setting up a channel and then building up an audience over time. This part is relatively easy to do and, more important, it is free from the financial stresses that plague more traditional outlets. As a streamer becomes more popular, access to a broader variety of revenue sources opens up.

Initially, money tends to come mostly from donations. Platforms like Twitch encourage viewers to subscribe to a channel. In exchange for a monthly commitment of a few dollars, viewers can participate in real-time chat, use custom emojis, and remove ads. At this stage, the size of a following tends to be rather modest but dedicated, because they really like either the person or a specific type of niche content. Viewers spend an average of $4.64 a month on donations.[15] Popular broadcasters claim the lion's share, however, and earn thousands of dollars even from a single donation. They account for roughly one-third of Twitch's annual revenue. For beginning channels, donations tend to represent the bulk of their monthly income. Channel-specific revenue sources like "Bits" on Twitch also allow viewers to "cheer on" their favorite streamer for a small fee. So, right from the start, it is conceivable for anyone to make money from streaming on Twitch.

Provided that things go well, and a fan base starts to grow, a next revenue source becomes available: advertising. This is a significant step up in terms of earning potential, but it also requires a process of authentication and agreeing to terms on Twitch or YouTube. To participate in ad revenue, platforms impose quotas for streamers to qualify for affiliate and partnership programs. This includes a minimum number of broadcasting hours, unique broadcasting sessions, concurrent viewers, and followers. Once accepted and set up, advertising revenue increases as popularity grows, and platforms tend to negotiate better rates with top-tiered content creators. On YouTube, for instance, earnings tend to vary widely and range roughly between $0.50 and $5.00 for every thousand views depending on the size of the fan base and channel exclusivity. YouTube keeps 45 percent, which means that a video with one million views, on average, earns a channel around $1,500.[16]

Beyond donations and advertising, several other revenue sources are available. With growing popularity, it usually makes sense to invest in additional derivative revenue sources, such as merchandise. Over time, streamers may identify a particular catchphrase or come up with an image or visual that uniquely identifies their channel (think of PewDiePie's "bro-fist"). Selling branded hoodies, t-shirts, or stickers is a common way to complement primary income sources and offers a way for viewers to "help the site stay alive." Sponsored content is yet another revenue source in which a channel dedicates time to do game or product reviews. These can be lucrative, especially around the release of a blockbuster title, but they are harder to come by and rarely provide guaranteed income throughout the year. Sponsors also will look to optimize their reach or focus on a specific type of streamer: for instance, someone who exclusively plays PC games. Finally, access to sponsors and successfully negotiating a fair price in exchange for displaying their logos or discussing their products is a time-consuming effort. At this stage, a channel usually has grown into a small production company that includes both a team in front of the camera and one behind it that handles production and business operations. Last, streamers make money by receiving a percentage of sales from games they feature or discuss on their channels. First launched in the spring of 2017, Twitch started offering its streamers 5 percent of its sales. Initially met with great enthusiasm, the devil is in the details, as only streamers who are part of the partnership program are eligible and only a small number of publishers currently participate.

This diversity in income sources, combined with the ability to connect directly with a fan base, has contributed to the idea that streamers and content creators differ from traditional outlets because they are free from the editorial influence that comes with a corporate paycheck. Instead of getting paid to say what they say, they retain, at least in theory, a degree of objectivity and personal freedom to speak their minds. This, in turn, is what appeals to audiences that know that publishers actively try to persuade them to buy their games. Financial pressures are changing the market structure for gaming video content and are presenting a challenge to the perceived authenticity of its creators. Increasingly, streamers have to make a decision between retaining their objectivity as reviewers and accepting financial compensation. In 2016, Warner Bros. settled with the U.S. Federal Trade Commission on charges that it had purposefully misled consumers during the marketing campaign for its upcoming title *Middle Earth: Shadow of Mordor*.[17] It failed to disclose having paid online influencers, including PewDiePie who at the time had fifty-three million subscribers on YouTube, to post videos that spoke positively about the game. In this case, PewDiePie had already come under scrutiny a few years earlier when it came out that his production company earned $4 million through indirect revenue from subscribers. For many, a for-profit pursuit contradicted the candid nature of his channel and raised questions regarding his credibility. *Shadow of Mordor*'s questionable deal terms faced swift criticism from gaming video content creators. After they posted the terms of this shady sponsorship agreement, broadcasters quickly voiced concerns. According to one, "It is the worst-case scenario in which a company withholds review copies to maximize potential exposure while keeping critique at bay. It's about as anti-consumer as it gets."[18]

More broadly, in response to the popularization of streaming video, different governments have begun to formulate regulations that obligate channels to acquire broadcast licenses, adhere to local content stipulations, and publicly disclose commercial relationships, among others. The German broadcast authority, the *Landesmedienanstalt*, determined that streamers are akin to radio broadcasters and therefore are required by law to obtain a broadcasting license.[19] In that same vein, the United Kingdom and China have issued similar directives.

Next, the platforms started to raise barriers to entry. To protect the interests of advertisers, YouTube began enforcing a "demonetization" policy: for videos containing "footage of natural disasters, tragedies, violence, promotion of drugs, sexually suggestive content, political conflicts, war-related subject matter and profanity" advertisers can pull their ads, thereby affecting a channel's ability to earn. One manager was quoted: "If you're seeing fluctuations in your revenue over the next few weeks, it may be because we're fine tuning our ads systems to address these concerns."[20] In particular, channels that feature shooter games like *Call of Duty* saw their earnings diminish, in many cases unfairly.

The costs of producing and maintaining a channel present additional business challenges for both established names and newcomers. Long gone is the charm of watching someone play from their basement. To stand out, content creators stay online for hours a day and go to great lengths to stand out and build their audience. Certainly, production values and audience expectations have gone up. But so, too, has the need to constantly produce new content or stay "live" to remain relevant. In aggregate, this mounting financial challenge has forced live-streamers to look for safety in numbers. If we organize the top-250 channels in this category on YouTube, the following pattern emerges (see figure 9.2). A handful of global media conglomerates dominates the category on YouTube: media firms account for 84 percent of total video plays, compared with agencies (8 percent) and game publishers (3 percent). The remainder consists of independent YouTube channels: a paltry 6 percent of viewership goes to independent channels. The top-five organizations are Bertelsmann, The Walt Disney Co., AT&T (through its recent acquisition of Time Warner), Groupe Marc de Lacharrière, and Omnia Media. By itself, the German firm Bertelsmann alone

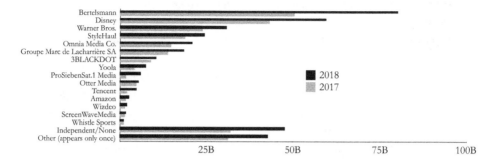

Figure 9.2
Market share distribution, total video plays among the top-250 YouTube gaming channels, by parent company, 2017 and 2018. *Source*: Data collected from YouTube. *Note*: Data recorded in January 2017 and 2018. Number of video plays for each of the top 250 channels from the gaming category on YouTube aggregated by parent company.

accounts for 31 percent of total video plays with more than one hundred billion compared with the second runner-up, Disney, at fifty-nine billion and 17 percent of total. Following the acquisition of Time Warner in 2018, AT&T took the third-largest share with 16 percent. Despite the fact that it is largely their games that are discussed and shown on many of these channels, relatively few channels are associated with publishers. Tencent, Nintendo, Take-Two, Electronic Arts, and Ubisoft generate billions in sales but account for only a fraction of total viewership.

Consolidation around gaming video content has raised the question whether YouTube is a positive or a negative development for game developers and publishers. A small consortium of media conglomerates controls the bulk of this market. Despite low entry barriers and an absence of overt editorial influence over creatives, gaming video content has evolved into a marketing channel that struggles with familiar pressures. As a broader category, the practice of people watching other people online playing video games is now a key component to contemporary development and publishing. Unsurprisingly, several notable firms have entered the market. In late 2016 Microsoft acquired streaming platform Mixer and later poached several high-profile streamers from Twitch. Sony entered the space in 2020 with a $400 million investment in Chinese entertainment company Bilibili. And in China, Tencent increased its overall participation in this industry through the purchase of roughly a third of Huya's shares and 50.1 percent voting stake for $262.6 million. For major platform holders this type of content has emerged as a critical component to capture contemporary audiences, market new titles, and establish ad revenue.

One category, however, among the millions of live-streamed feeds differs from the rest.

Esports

In 2013, the U.S. government granted a P1 Professional Athlete visa to competitive video game players. It baffled journalists and sports media professionals alike, as they struggled to come to terms with the idea of video gamers as professional athletes.[21] Many were quick to dismiss the idea. To them, it was inconceivable to reconcile the moniker of professional athlete with an activity that had long been associated with the familiar stereotype of a pale, lazy, and predominantly indoor demographic. People like John Skipper, who was ESPN's president at the time, proclaimed at a conference that competitive video gaming was "not a sport; it's a competition," and compared it instead to chess and checkers.[22] Video games, according to this view, had nothing in common with physical stick-and-ball sports. And, of course, they don't. But to look at esports through a lens of conventional sports media practices is to miss the point entirely. In this second part of the discussion about this emerging category of gaming video content, we find competitive gaming. Organized around teams playing against each other, this segment presents an initial proof point for a larger investment by content firms in the phenomenon of people watching other people play video games.

Esports as we know it today first emerged in South Korea. In the late 1990s approximately half of all Koreans played online games in the internet cafes throughout the country. This practice provided the necessary popularity to transform competitive gaming into a spectator sport. The country's high broadband penetration and comparatively fast internet speeds created the perfect circumstance for people playing games against each other, and esports thrived. Seeing the success and how well it aligned with its broader agenda of transitioning to a new information and technology-based economy at the time, the South Korean government founded the Korea e-Sports Association in 2000 to further stimulate the growth of competitive play. The stimulus worked, and triggered the first growth spurt. By 2005, no fewer than 278 tournaments were held in South Korea, quadrupling numbers from just six years earlier. The practice became so popular that dedicated cable channels like OnGameNet and MBC Game emerged, which collectively generated $203 million in advertising revenue in 2007.[23]

But these were the early days. Many continued to regard the phenomenon as an oddity. Esports had long been almost exclusively a practice found in South Korea, even if the number of tournaments throughout the world had started to grow. To most television executives and advertisers elsewhere, the notion of people playing games competitively and selling ads to support it remained a strange novelty. In their minds, the phenomenon was a statistical outlier in global entertainment and largely confined to Asia. Worse, after the initial momentum in the early 2000s, the introduction of smartphones meant that audiences began to move away from PCs to mobile screens, rendering the future of competitive gaming uncertain. Consequently, advertisers lost interest and pulled their budgets. With ad money gone and audiences adopting smartphones en masse, the foundation collapsed.

The story did not end there. Around this same time, a novel business model came into vogue among a new generation of game companies. Free-to-play titles like *League of Legends* amassed millions of players in a short amount of time. To encourage positive network effects, free-to-play publishers employed a variety of tactics to acquire and retain players. Active investment in organized tournaments proved to be an important marketing tactic for free-to-play publishers, both to create excitement and as part of cultivating a community around their titles. Esports owes a great deal of its momentum to the rapid popularization of this new type of entertainment. With lots of titles entering the market and audience competition, the emphasis on an underlying revenue model for the bulk of game companies has shifted from making an initial sale to cultivating a thriving user base and monetizing more gradually. With the popularization of free-to-play gaming, esports emerged as an important hallmark of publishers willing to invest in the community around it and, hopefully, benefit from positive network effects. A title like *League of Legends* depends heavily on competitions to keep its massive audience of one hundred million players engaged and subsequently has invested heavily in tournaments and world championships as part of its broader business strategy.

It is nothing new for game makers to host and organize professional tournaments. In fact, the practice goes back a long time. In 1996, Wizards of the Coast launched the *Magic: The Gathering Pro Tour* circuit, a series of highly competitive weekend-long tournaments with large cash prizes to promote its trading card game *Magic: The Gathering* and to recruit new players. According to one of its designers, Mark Rosewater, the company had identified organized play as a second act building on the *Magic: The Gathering*'s early success.[24] The effort came from the realization that Wizards "was not just selling a game, but rather an entire experience. What good is a game if there's no one to play with?" Similarly, the collectible card game *Pokémon* long held an extensively organized play system, now called Play! Pokémon, which is composed of leagues, tournaments, and high-level events, including national and world championships.

Across the industry, organized play is a common practice and a central component to business model strategy, because it offers a myriad of benefits. Events are an opportunity for fans to congregate and socialize, to promote the game, to serve as a key component in a user acquisition strategy, and—in particular for more complex titles—to substantially lower the barriers to entry for new players. By actively hosting tournaments, publishers provide a place and time for a community to exchange ideas and helpful information on how to play or explore new strategies. Cultivating an active community also keeps people involved even when their interest in the game wavers, making it a critical component to retention strategies.

What is new today is that audiences will sit and watch others play competitively. Although the phenomenon has existed for years, until recently, it had not attracted a global audience of viewers and it remained largely a niche form of entertainment. Even so, it is a mistake to equate esports audiences too closely with traditional sports viewers. Initial research into the motivations behind this behavior suggests that esports fans are different from their traditional counterparts. One study found that audiences that watch competitive gaming actively look for "escapism, acquiring knowledge about the games being played, novelty and eSports [*sic*] athlete aggressiveness."[25] That is quite different from watching a perfect performance in gymnastics or watching a soccer game in the hope of a dramatic turnaround. Its findings, for instance, indicate that "the enjoyment of the aesthetic aspects" scores low as a motivation.[26] In a relatively short time, esports has grown into a common element in contemporary interactive entertainment and manages to draw large audiences. Titles like *Counter-Strike: Global Offensive*, *League of Legends*, *Hearthstone: Heroes of Warcraft*, *Dota 2*, and *Overwatch* have accumulated hundreds of millions of viewing hours on streaming platforms like Twitch and YouTube every month. For these games, esports is a key ingredient to their success.

How a publisher defines its esports effort as part of a broader strategy determines its earnings potential. When I first spoke with Ubisoft's esports manager in 2014, right as the phenomenon started to become more common, I was told that it was "costly to organize events and the return on investment is not immediately obvious." Consequently, two different schools of thought emerged about its application as part of a broader strategy. On one hand, some publishers regard it as a promotional tool and an attempt to both reach a broader player base for their games and encourage customer loyalty among its existing fans. For Take-Two and Electronic Arts, two firms with a substantial part of their overall games portfolio built around existing sports franchises, such as the NBA and FIFA, live streaming extends their existing marketing effort. In this context, Electronic Arts prefers the term "competitive gaming" because it implies a more casual experience, consistent with a large part of its audience buying each annual edition of their favorite sports video game. In this regard, esports generates more awareness and improves the overall engagement of its existing player base.

On the other hand, a publisher like Activision Blizzard is actively investing in esports with the goal of eventually charging media rights and licensing fees from teams, much like the traditional sports business. The centerpiece in this strategy is its *Overwatch League*. Leaning on its experience from organizing *Star Craft* tournaments and BlizzCon, Activision Blizzard's approach entails the following components. First, the league features city-based teams that compete globally. Borrowing a page from traditional sports, establishing a connection between a local fanbase and a team is key to attracting sponsorships. Generally speaking, about half of a traditional sports team's earnings comes from local advertisers. Second, by having a more organized league system, Activision Blizzard can protect players. Under this agreement, teams sign players to a one-year guaranteed contract, a minimum salary of $50,000 annually, insurance and retirement savings plans, and a performance bonus.[27] By professionalizing competitive gaming, teams are better able to attract and cultivate talent, in addition to ensuring a reasonable schedule for top players.[28] To participate in the *Overwatch League*, teams have to pay a license fee, which includes them in the overall marketing effort behind the game and provides a share of ad revenue. In return, Activision Blizzard retains the right to both sell media rights to its league and sell sponsorship packages to major advertisers.

Esports viewership has subsequently emerged as a key strategic component for contemporary game makers. It both creates greater awareness among audiences and extends the overall experience for existing players of a title. Novel innovations that have emerged in this context are crowd-sourced prize pools and the league system. Here, again, we find Valve leading the charge. One of its top earnings titles, *Dota 2*, has a monthly active user base of eleven million players. The game, a free-to-play multiplayer online battle arena, competes directly with *League of Legends* for players and viewers. To draw attention to its title, Valve established a prize pool for its biggest annual tournament, The International. Hosted by Valve, it brings together the best teams from around the world for a showdown to determine the world champions. As news media discovered esports, their reporting often focused on *Dota 2* for two reasons: the enduring novelty of watching others play competitively and the disproportionately large prize pool.

Valve made brilliant use of the momentum and enthusiasm among its player base by introducing an offering to its preferred fans in 2013 called The Compendium. For $10, avid fans get the chance to win event-related items in the game, earn a vote for the tournament player awards, and gain access to the event's statistics and predictions. But most important, a quarter of the earnings generated by The Compendium goes toward the overall prize pool. This last piece, in particular, gives an indication of how deeply engaged *Dota 2*'s player base is. In 2014, the total prize money was $11 million, and it since has increased to $26 million in 2018 and $33 million in 2019. Keep in mind that the company puts in only $2 million, and you have a good sense of the level of engagement of the game's fanbase. Table 9.1 provides an overview of three of the most popular titles in competitive gaming, their annual revenue, average monthly active user base, and prize pools for their respective world championships. By providing fans the opportunity to contribute, *Dota 2* historically has offered the largest prize pools, driven entirely by their contributions. Valve has not increased its sponsorship amount. By allowing fans to directly influence overall winnings, Valve succeeded both in creating an additional avenue for retention marketing and in gaining free press. With many watching tournaments online rather than in person, The Compendium has become a central component to the promotional effort behind *Dota 2*. By comparison, the total prize pool for the biggest annual event for *League of Legends* in 2018 was $6 million.

The growing appetite for interactive content by advertisers further benefits from two broader developments. The development of competitive gaming presents an answer to the growing interest among contemporary media audiences to attend live events and share their passion with others.

Table 9.1

Prize pools, annual revenue, and monthly active user base, 2011–2018

Title	2011			2012			2013			2014		
	P	R	M	P	R	M	P	R	M	P	R	M
Dota 2	1.6	n/a	n/a	1.6	13.6	1.1	2.9	85.4	4.6	10.9	232.8	8.9
League of Legends		85.3	5.6		376.8	25.6		818.3	52.1	2.1	1,313.4	76.3
StarCraft II		75.0	3.9	0.3	39.9	2.9	0.3	86.7	5.2	0.3	40.9	3.5

Source: Author's compilation based on company reports and data from esportsearnings.com/games, last accessed February 2, 2019. Monthly active user base and annual revenues are estimates from SuperData Research.

Note: P, prize pools for world championship tournaments; R, annual revenue; M, monthly active user base. All figures are in millions. Excluded from this table is *CS:GO* (Valve), which has multiple world champion events, each with their own prize pools and organizer.

Fans congregate, watch some of the best players in the game battle each other, and get a chance to meet their heroes. Esports are to video games what live performances are to music. Cross-pollinations are obvious. The 2018 annual championship for *League of Legends*, for example, featured an augmented reality performance by (G)I-DLE and live performances by U.S. artists Madison Beer and Jaira Burns. Activision Blizzard's first Grand Finals for its *Overwatch League* in 2018 were held in Brooklyn and counted 22,434 spectators over the course of two days. And the first world championship of *Fortnite* held in 2019 in New York attracted more than two million concurrent viewers across YouTube and Twitch and included a live performance by musician Marshmello.

Moreover, the number of viewers for traditional sports is declining and the remaining audience is aging. For instance, the average age of a loyal Major League Baseball (MLB) fan is fifty-three years old. And the MLB has been consistently losing audience: the biggest baseball event of the year, the World Series, drew thirty-four million viewers in 1988, but this has since declined to fourteen million in 2018. It makes these audiences less relevant for advertisers that instead are looking for younger consumers who are not yet set in their purchase behaviors and brand preferences.

Contrasting the enthusiasm and monetary investment made by these large publishers is the sobering realization that esports is not a mature media segment quite yet. Following several years of excitement around esports, it currently is going through a period of business model rationalization as the market seeks to establish an equilibrium between demand and supply.

2015			2016			2017			2018		
P	R	M	P	R	M	P	R	M	P	R	M
18.4	311.2	11.2	20.8	371.8	13.0	24.8	405.8	12.5	25.5	338.0	10.3
2.1	2,130.5	91.9	5.1	2,946.6	98.5	5.0	2,030.8	96.7	6.5	1,677.0	86.6
0.3	109.8	3.4	0.5	71.6	4.7	0.7	15.0	5.3	0.7	9.0	2.6

In short order, a string of events belies the bigger ambitions held by publishers and platforms. First, one of its most visible and famous financial backers, former professional basketball player Rick Fox, threatened to leave his esports organization Echo Fox because of a racist shareholder.[29] This obviously sets an unpleasant tone in an otherwise-optimistic entertainment category. Next, a flurry of issues with opportunistic contracts, especially among younger streamers and esports players, led to a high-profile and public spat between celebrity streamer Turner Ellis Tenney, known as Tfue, and FaZe clan.[30] In addition, the departure of Overwatch League Commissioner, Nate Nanzer, to Epic Games implied challenges ahead for Activision Blizzard in its ambition to grow esports as a revenue stream.[31] Finally, a devastating article on the absence of reliable metrics and measurement in esports laid bare the lack of a necessary infrastructure for brands and advertisers to be able to commit to the category.[32] Combined, these incidents create a comparatively high level of uncertainty that may deter investment in esports.

The industry around people watching other people play video games is still young. The phenomena of gaming video content as a general form of entertainment and esports as a specific category are reshaping the relationship between publishers and players of games. The games business now largely adheres to a service model, and online video and live-streaming play an integral part in acquiring and retaining new users. Building a loyal community and establishing a worldwide audience that will watch tournaments and matches among professional gamers is no longer a novelty.

The outbreak of the coronavirus in early 2020 triggered an increase in online viewership across major markets. As billions of people remained at home for weeks and traditional sports leagues around the world cancelled live events, Covid-19 accelerated the change toward broader adoption. Demand for live streaming exploded and it pushed video games to the foreground. Up until that point, advertisers and brands had already been experimenting with this new content category to reconnect with the younger audiences that had disappeared from more conventional media channels. As millions of consumers found themselves stuck at home in response to the virus outbreak, they turned to gaming video content. According to one source, viewership on Twitch jumped 10 percent and YouTube 15 percent in March.[33]

The long-term expectation is that brands and advertisers, in their desire to reach younger consumers interested in games, will play an increasingly relevant part. The size of the global audience for interactive entertainment and the pervasiveness of online games suggests that the phenomenon of people watching others play video games will become even more widespread and can potentially develop the current trickle of indirect revenue into a more significant source of income. After digitalization enabled publishers to sell in-game items through microtransactions and to distribute content and subsequent updates and expansions over the internet, the popularization of video games has opened up a third revenue model. The next chapter will discuss this in more detail. However, the appetite for watching others play is not just going to affect how games are marketed. It also will have an indelible influence on their design. Now having to satisfy two demands, namely, having to be fun both to play *and* to watch, designers are facing a new challenge: how to make a game that appeals even to audiences that don't play it.

10

Next-Gen Revenue Models

In the near future, we'll have games that don't depend
on any platform.
—HIDEO KOJIMA, CREATOR OF *METAL GEAR* SERIES

Now that video games are a mainstream form of entertainment, the underlying economics that drive this industry have shifted. Geographic boundaries and homogeneity of its audience no longer restrict game companies. We may ask: does this newfound status and broader cultural visibility enable revenue models that previously were unsustainable?

So far, we identified two distinct eras in the games business. Starting with selling boxed titles through retail and tying software sales closely to the hardware cycle of consoles, interactive entertainment has been a product-based business since its inception. The production of physical goods that are distributed and sold through stores characterizes this period. Consumers paid a single, one-time fee in exchange for access to content, which, as we saw, sits at the very foundation of the razor-blade model of hardware manufacturers. The need for content curation and quality assurance facilitates both overall growth and the emergence of entry barriers for creative firms. This, in turn, allowed a small group of highly successful industry participants to dominate the most lucrative categories. Electronic Arts' strategy to simultaneously corner the market for sports licenses and establish a global sales force resulted in it claiming a dominant industry position for years.[1] Across the board, legacy publishers took on the capital risk associated with the production and marketing of blockbuster releases.

Success in this model consequently was expressed as the total number of units sold. By leveraging control over the value chain, publishers maximized their ability to sell as many copies as possible at the highest possible price.

With the advent of the internet began a second era: the digitalization of video games. In the aftermath of the dotcom bust, game makers quickly established themselves among the de facto suppliers of valued, novel content in an expanding digital universe. As incumbents wrestled with the poor economics of digital distribution, which allowed them to capture only accretive revenue, a new generation of companies emerged focused on attracting mainstream audiences through lightweight gameplay, accessible distribution, and novel revenue models. Firms like Nexon, Riot Games, and King Digital benefited from formulating innovative business strategies and came to characterize the digital industry. They popularized a games-as-a-service revenue model in which the measure of success consisted of the average earnings per user. This evolution triggered enormous growth and transformed the industry into a mainstream leisure activity that now caters to a global audience. The lowering of entry barriers resulted in many small developer outfits connecting with users directly and facilitated an artist-led model that previously had been unsustainable.

The industry's progression has not stopped there. With two billion people actively playing games across mobile, console, and PC devices, publishers and platform holders now are exploring two prospects for what may soon become the next relevant source of income: indirect revenue (i.e., advertising) and recurring revenue (i.e., subscriptions).

Advertising

Unlike firms in every other entertainment category, game companies have been largely unwilling and unsuccessful in generating indirect revenue. At best, the effort to connect advertisers to their audiences is nascent. We can explain this in part by the broadly accepted perspective among creatives that money corrupts the art of making games. The tension between creativity and commerce has been prevalent throughout this book but perhaps nowhere as pronounced as in the context of ad-sponsored games. Product-based titles historically spent years in development before a publisher had a chance to promote it to consumers. In this scenario, anticipated revenue became a priority only in the lead-up to its release. By and large, creatives were not concerned about the financial outcome of their efforts until a title was fully developed. This allowed them a financial vacuum in which they honed their craft in pursuit of the best possible experience. Having to insert a monetary component into the design process introduces a new constraint on the overall creative endeavor. Zynga is an example of this. Its early success resulted from constantly measuring how well specific items performed in its virtual store. By relentlessly analyzing what worked and what did not, Zynga managed to optimize its development effort accordingly. Data, of course, were geared toward maximizing the amount of money that people spent on the game. In response, many held Zynga in low regard, arguing that instead of publishing true creative experiences, it merely designed its content to funnel players through a never-ending monetization loop. This approach deviates strongly from the traditional emphasis on creativity and delivering immersive experiences.

In entertainment, games have long existed on the fringes and have presented an odd business to media executives. It has been a long-held belief that advertising and video games do not mix. Ad revenue historically has played only a marginal role in interactive entertainment, despite a much greater prominence everywhere else. When online connectivity facilitated building a network that enabled dynamically integrating ads into games, the time for in-game advertising seemingly arrived. Microsoft found out exactly how incompatible games and advertising were when it acquired an in-game ad network called Massive in 2006. The software giant's rationale at the time provides valuable insight into a failed business model innovation.

Initially, Massive's business model showed great promise. By adding a few lines to a game's source code, it was able to insert ads into the experience through the internet with the intent of becoming the intermediary between the two company types. In return, it would take a slice of the revenue. Massive's CEO Mitch Davis quipped that its solution added "$1–2" to a company's bottom line per unit sold.[2] As we saw earlier, development had started to become more complex and costlier. The interest for in-game ads surfaced between 2004 and 2006, around the same time the industry started to introduce games at a considerably higher average selling price to offset the investment in developing titles for the new hardware generation (see figure 3.3). Adding a few bucks for each copy improved the risk profile and profitability.[3]

Massive raised a total of $8 million in funding. Advertisers were excited and spent an estimated $414 million annually on media buys in video games at the time. Despite a slow adoption rate among publishers for whom this was new and unfamiliar territory, Massive succeeded in establishing a network that included several notable early adopters like Atari, Codemasters, Eidos, Funcom, Konami, Sony Online Entertainment, THQ, Ubisoft, and 2K Sports.[4] This initial success was enough to convince Microsoft of the long-term benefits, and it promptly acquired Massive in 2006 for an estimated $200 million.

It is not immediately obvious why Microsoft, which is mostly known for its enterprise software, would buy an in-game ad company. There were no clear synergies. More broadly, however, its relevance had started to suffer as competitors like Google managed to build billion-dollar businesses on the internet. Consequently, an important part of Microsoft's rationale had to do with its insecurity around losing online audiences to a new generation of tech firms. It was not alone in this, and the purchase coincided with a broader industry trend of big media conglomerates looking to "get into gaming" through acquisition. That same year saw a string of similar merger and acquisition activity: Viacom spent $102 million buying XFire, an online social network around video games; NewsCorp bought IGN Entertainment for $650 million; and Google acquired Adscape, an ad firm that specialized in integrating in-game advertising. Other competitors at the time included IGA Worldwide, Double Fusion, Extent Technologies, Navigate, Engage, and Greystripe, all of which fixated on the idea that the time for a marriage between interactive amusement and advertising had come.

Another aspect of Microsoft's rationale originated from its broader strategy to increase the use value of its device for consumers by positioning the Xbox at the center of the living room. Microsoft held a formidable portfolio of development studios that included Bungie, Carbonated Games, Ensemble, FASA Interactive, Lionhead, Rare, Turn 10, and Wingnut Interactive. Integrating the ad network in all of these studios meant it would control access to their aggregated audience. As we read in chapter 6, Microsoft also started adding a string of services to its platform in the hope of pushing competitors out of the living room and becoming the primary device used by consumers to access content. Part of Microsoft's reasoning was to sell ads against this aggregated audience.

But this move was not to be, and in 2010, Microsoft shut down Massive. In its enthusiasm, the software giant critically overlooked several things. For one, game developers had never before considered advertising as a relevant revenue stream, and they had no interest in sitting through a meeting with an ad platform to hear about the merits of their offering. To creatives, the idea of adding a bit of third-party code to a game they had spent years developing was blasphemy. According to one executive: "The account manager would work with the publisher after which the integration fell to the developers. Generally, this happened toward the end of the production of title, leaving us with little resources. Devs would come back to us saying they couldn't do it because they were out of memory." Technical and operational limitations forced Microsoft to dispatch last-minute client support, which made the effort cumbersome and largely unprofitable.

Massive's executive team also critically lacked the necessary experience. Although many of them had held positions at large media firms and consultancies, few had any games industry credentials. As a result, their entry point into creative firms generally was through the corporate teams at game publishers. Executives reasoned that in-game advertising added realism to the experience. According to Kevin Johnson, Microsoft's co-president of Platforms and Services (and who would later become the CEO of Starbucks), a racing title like *Tokyo Race Driver 3* "is obviously a great place to advertise car insurance like Progressive. What you get a sense for is the ability to drive better consumer excitement, because they get more realism. You can drive rich, immersive advertising."[5] This approach, according to Johnson, made consumers "happier." But that, too, turned out to be a horrible misconception. Players, in fact, were upset that their games suddenly showed ads. In this context, ads were new and invasive without offering any benefit to the player. In a similar vein, intellectual property holders were uninterested in having their properties sit alongside commercial messages, especially if they had no control over the type of ad. To them, this could only lower the value of their carefully cultivated franchises.

A final reason Massive failed was that, ultimately, it competed directly with its acquirer Microsoft. On top of a botched integration process that crippled Massive's ability to grow, the parent company insisted on facilitating in-game ads, in particular for the studios and titles it already owned. Worse, big publishers like Electronic Arts started running in-game ad networks inside key franchises like FIFA, for which ads conceivably would be perceived as contextually relevant. This proved fatal to Massive's momentum, and Microsoft shut down the division.

Despite all of this activity and investment, advertising income never grew large enough to become relevant. Simultaneously the market had started to move away from display ads to search-based ads, which further exacerbated Massive's circumstance. Observing the failure of even a large multinational like Microsoft, we may ask: Why would advertising as a revenue stream for game companies work now?

To establish a reliable two-sided model that allows publishers to efficiently connect brands to their audience, the industry needs a broad and diverse consumer base. As discussed in chapter 4, that is now the case. This need is a first reason why ads now take on a more meaningful role. Like broadcast television, radio, newspapers, and magazines, video games attract billions, which positions this business to claim a piece of the billions of dollars spent each year by advertisers. Globally, advertisers spend around $650 billion on media and entertainment. In the United States, the second-largest market after China, television generates $70 billion a year in ad sales, compared with $15 billion for print media, and $14 billion for radio. As these audiences continue to age and decline in size as people move to new technologies to consume content and those that remain tend to skew older, advertisers have started to turn to gaming. On paper, this makes sense: gamers are tech savvy, highly engaged, and early adopters, which makes this consumer group valuable to advertisers.

Second, the more recently emerged generation of game makers takes a different approach to indirect revenue. Unlike legacy publishers to whom this represents only a modest revenue stream in comparison to the income generated from their top franchises, newcomers are open to the idea of accepting money from advertisers. In their view, the relationship between ad-based revenue and a creative agenda is less tenuous and central to their economics. Rather than imposing, they argue, it frees them from revenue obligations and having to aggressively monetize their players.

Following the tremendous success of *Pokémon GO* in the summer of 2016, Niantic CEO John Hanke went on to explain that ad revenue was beneficial and allowed his studio to focus on its creative pursuits. According to Hanke, advertising presented a viable alternative monetization strategy because integrating microtransactions "exerts a lot of pressure on game design that can lead to games that are not very much fun to play even if they make a lot of money."[6] Instead of aggressively monetizing through microtransactions, Hanke reasoned, it was more intuitive to drive traffic to specific real-world locations and charge retailers for it.

This proved to be remarkably successful. During the height of its popularity, the firm struck deals with several notable retail chains, including McDonalds and GameStop. In Japan, *Pokémon GO* featured fifteen hundred McDonalds' restaurants as poke-gyms and successfully increased foot traffic at those locations. In the United States, GameStop had a similar arrangement and saw a spike in the number of people visiting its stores. As a result, it managed to upsell visitors on battery packs and data plans.

According to Niantic, the initial ad campaigns had been so successful that it was only the beginning as a growing number of companies and brands contacted the firm for comparable campaigns.

Another mobile giant had also come to appreciate the opportunity of ad revenue, despite having walked a different path. At the height of its success in 2013, King Digital had initially sent an email to its advertising partners that explained why it would no longer rely on them for income. According to the email, the firm's commitment to providing "an uninterrupted entertainment experience" meant it was going to remove all advertising components from its games.[7] This was not surprising as the success of its titles like *Candy Crush* meant that advertising income represented only around 1 percent of total earnings (see table 10.1). Nevertheless, as an organization with deep roots in both social network–based and mobile gaming, both of which are characterized by their ad-heavy nature, this was a shock to many. King's success meant that it did not need to rely on indirect income and could monetize its audience directly through microtransactions.

This proved to be only a temporary abstinence. Following its acquisition by Activision Blizzard, King saw its momentum decline and came under pressure to make its earnings goals. It had suffered a disastrous initial public offering and had to confront the general slowdown in its business as competitors swept in and audiences moved on. Increased competition also put pressure on King's ability to draw revenue from its existing player base. King readopted the model. Its monthly active user count had declined, but King still reached such a massive player base that it was well worth it to embrace advertising again in 2017.

Of course, only the disproportionally popular titles like *Candy Crush* and *Pokémon GO* have managed to establish meaningful revenue from advertising. We already can see, however, a rough outline of how the broader adoption of this income may play out. Across the ecosystem, we find other initiatives by large firms that push in this direction. Google's cloud gaming solution, Stadia, offers game publishers a 30/70 revenue split in addition to a cut of ad revenue generated by video content featuring their titles. Facebook similarly is enticing publishers, hoping that gaming content will drive traffic and engagement. And Tencent used ads to offset the decline in revenue it suffered in 2018 as a result of its government shutting down the approval process for new titles to be released in China. The success it initially enjoyed as a result of the market protectionism enforced by the Chinese government has proven to be a limitation in more recent years. At the height of the success of titles like *PlayerUnknown's BattleGround*

Table 10.1
Game company ad revenue and share of total revenue, 2008–2018

	2008		2009		2010		2011		2012	
	$	%	$	%	$	%	$	%	$	%
Zynga	14.1	73%	35.7	29%	22.8	4%	74.5	7%	137.0	11%
Glu Mobile							2.4	3%	8.7	8%
King (Activision Blizzard)							7.7	12%	16.4	10%
Gameloft (Vivendi)										
Group Total	**14.1**		**35.7**		**22.8**		**84.5**		**162.1**	

Source: Author's compilation based on company reports.
Note: Revenue in millions U.S. dollars ($).

(*PUBG*) and *Fortnite*, Tencent saw itself unable to monetize because of a government reorganization that, ultimately, sought to purposefully stall the approval processes before titles could be monetized in China. To make up the difference and continue its growth, Tencent triggered a reorganization that, among other efforts, united the firm's advertising operations into a single division in order to increase ad revenue and lower its exposure to the volatility in its gaming group.[8] Moreover, according to Yang Yu, the head of Tencent Cloud Gaming Solution, the firm plans to rely on in-game advertising to monetize its cloud services. The average hourly spending among Chinese consumers in 2018 was Rmb2.2 ($0.30) compared with the Rmb5 ($0.70) cost of streaming games over the internet.[9] Given their dominance, vast data resources on users, and strong relationships with advertisers, these firms will notably influence the industry's move to design around an ad-based model.

With games becoming a viewable form of entertainment, live streaming and esports continue to further strengthen the interaction between game makers and advertisers. Activision Blizzard's success with its Overwatch League (a professional esports league) relies on its ability to persuade large advertisers to commit to long-term, league-wide sponsorship deals. In its ambition to cater to a diverse, mainstream audience, Activision Blizzard faces the still-substantial challenge of creating a clear path to market for sponsors and advertisers. In an interview, one of firm's senior ad executives acknowledged that, "gaming is new for a lot of advertisers, (so) we've really tried to make it as simple as possible." In the same breath, however,

2013		2014		2015		2016		2017		2018	
$	%	$	%	$	%	$	%	$	%	$	%
113.7	13%	152.8	22%	174.0	23%	195.0	26%	191.7	22%	232.2	26%
6.6	6%	14.6	7%	13.1	5%	10.3	5%	30.9	15%	43.9	15%
18.8	1%							50.0	2.2%	70.0	3.5%
				5.5	2%	12.7	4%	42.7	15%	40.0	13%
139.2		**167.4**		**192.6**		**218.0**		**265.3**		**386.1**	

the executive repeated the exact words that previously evidenced the disconnect between the creative and commercial sides when it comes to in-game ads, claiming that they "can even improve the concept of the game."[10] Even as the technology has advanced and audiences have evolved, some of the old ideas around the relationship between games and ads persist in the minds of decision-makers. Economic pressures and the popularity of video games incentivize top companies in the industry to formulate and explore innovative revenue models. Advertising presents a credible candidate for how interactive entertainment will generate money in the future.

Subscriptions

A second revenue model that recently has started to become viable involves audiences paying a recurring fee in exchange for access to a content selection. It emulates conventional models of, for instance, cable television and print publishing. With interactive entertainment having reached mainstream status, and the contemporary challenges of a global market saturated with digital content, video game subscriptions present an emerging approach to capture value.

We can distinguish among different types of recurrent revenue models. Subscriptions around specific titles or access to a single publisher's catalog in exchange for a monthly fee have been around for quite some time. Many failed to attract large audiences, however, until the cost of online connectivity started to come down. We already discussed *World of Warcraft* and how it led the charge as online role-playing took off and successfully proved that millions of players were willing to pay a monthly fee for continued access. And even before that, there were also several casual PC-based services that had accomplished something similar. In the early 2000s, casual game maker Big Fish Games, for instance, offered packages for $4.95 a month or $29.95 annually in exchange for discounted access to premium downloadable games and a range of other content features. Audiences were coming online in droves even at a time when dial-up internet was still the norm. Access to a broad inventory of casual titles that were relatively small to download quickly proved popular with consumers. In combination with a curated content strategy, which included its best-seller series *Mystery Case Files*, Big Fish Games managed to grow revenue from $9 million in 2005 to $100 million in 2008. It managed to do so by distinguishing itself through an abundance of available content. Key to this approach was its aggressive content acquisition strategy. For years Big Fish Games was a top-tier sponsor of casual gaming conventions in order to set up hundreds of meetings with small creatives and acquire fresh content for the Big Fish catalogue.

Next, platform holders offer content subscriptions. Most obviously, it increases their earnings potential per customer. We previously covered PlayStation Plus and Xbox Live in the discussion of strategies that allowed the console market to sustain its presence as mobile became more popular. Hardware manufacturers successfully expanded their offering (and grew revenue) by upselling their user base. In addition to improving the return on investment made by selling hardware at a loss, capturing additional value through the sale of software by charging users an additional monthly fee is quite lucrative, because there are no incremental costs of goods. This is doubly important toward the end of a hardware life cycle, when market saturation sets in. Because gaming hardware resets every several years, consumers generally are aware that a new generation of better consoles is just around the corner. Existing owners will naturally become increasingly reluctant to invest in new games for an aging platform. Offering them a low-risk monthly commitment that provides access to a host of titles they otherwise would not have tried creates additional value for both sides.

For example, Microsoft's release of the Game Pass, a monthly subscription of curated titles, successfully reinvigorated earnings for its gaming division. When first introduced, the program received positive reviews and Xbox owners readily adopted it. According to Microsoft, there were fifty-seven million active Xbox Live users in 2018.[11] Having lost the console war against Sony's PlayStation, Microsoft doubled down on its services offering and subsequently acquired a string of studios to satisfy the growing appetite among its user base for content. In the financial quarter that followed, the firm reported a 36 percent year-over-year increase from its software and services division.

Elsewhere in the industry subscriptions appeal to distinct user segments and are central to catering to different audience cohorts within a platform's ecosystem. Apple, for instance, introduced the Apple Arcade, a $5 per month subscription that carries only premium titles and no microtransactions and no in-game ads. Once Apple approved freemium titles on the smartphone, the category exploded. A decade later Apple launched its subscription service to also cater to specific audience segments like parents who have little interest in free-to-play titles. More broadly, microtransactions had started to lose their appeal among platform holders and regulators in 2019; loot boxes and aggressive monetization strategies had sourced consumer sentiment. Apple moved to distinguish itself by offering dedicated, exclusive content available for a single monthly fee.[12]

Cloud gaming is a relatively new area in which we see subscriptions emerging. With consumer broadband increasingly ubiquitous, it gradually is becoming feasible for people to play high-end video games on their local devices while the graphics processing is handled remotely. Referred to as cloud gaming, this technology carries the promise of disrupting the current industry landscape, in particular among platform holders. One ultimate vision among cloud gaming providers is to one day soon have what Microsoft CEO Satya Nadella termed the "Netflix of games," a service that provides people access to a buffet of interactive content on any device for a fixed monthly fee.[13] A cast of well-known technology firms including Google, Microsoft, Amazon, and Facebook, aims to provide an average person with access to high-end content through an online service on any device. For consumers, this means they no longer will be restricted by the limitations of their favorite device to gain access to experiences with high production values. Now able to play console titles on their smartphone, this technology ostensibly will remove all boundaries that traditionally have existed between devices. Of course, in its current state, many of the available services merely provide access to a souped-up PC in the cloud, and consumers still have to purchase titles separately. The appeal for publishers is that cloud gaming expands their addressable audience. Until now, it had only been the console players who spent money on the high-end titles from legacy publishers; the removal of technical limitations promises to extend this reach. In particular, services that work on smartphones carry the promise of reaching many more people than previously possible.

It is currently unclear how this will affect content creators. In the context of a subscription, titles are a line item in a platform's cost-plus pricing strategy, which means that individual games receive a fixed fee or, as in the model popularized in the music business by Spotify, an amount based on the number of "plays" by subscribers. Why would a publisher commit to an exclusive arrangement when it otherwise could make money from both the Xbox and PlayStation ecosystems? We find a partial answer in microtransactions. In negotiating with game makers, Microsoft, for instance, will argue that because a title is now available for play at zero risk to the consumer, the chances of them playing titles that otherwise would fall by the wayside are much greater. By limiting the overall offering of the Xbox Game Pass to a selection of curated titles, the overall quality expectation is much higher, which, over time, will draw a larger audience. This, in turn, increases the chances of at least some of those "free" players starting to spend money on microtransactions.

The jury is out on whether or not the popularization and globalization of games will afford companies the ability to generate meaningful earnings from sources like advertising and subscriptions. In the first scenario, content providers look to capture value by selling their audiences to advertisers. It emulates the two-sided business model familiar from television, radio, and other forms of entertainment. In the second, platform holders seek to establish an ongoing monetary commitment in exchange for unlimited access to a content buffet. Because both of these monetization strategies originate from conventional amusement categories, we can characterize this next era of games as media. Both approaches rely heavily on establishing a critical mass in audience and herald a different configuration of financial pressures and operational affordances that will govern the overall creative process. An obvious consequence from a third revenue model in gaming will be the need to accurately express and measure success as it affects creative efforts. During the period in the industry's history when physical, product-based revenue dominated, the core metric used by publishers, retailers, and investors centered on total units sold. Publishers dominated the value chain after disintermediating from hardware manufacturers and independently producing and distributing content across platforms. Following digitization, however, the focus shifted to "earnings per user" as audiences only gradually converted to spending. An important benefit to this artist-led approach is the increased control over user data by creative firms to inform their design agenda and marketing tactics. Now, with the emergence of advertising and subscriptions as increasingly viable monetization strategies, financial pressures will shift again. In this games-as-media model, content is largely platform-agnostic, and its appeal centers on playability both in terms of access to them and the degree to which average consumers can easily pick up and play them. This need for playability heavily emphasizes the degree of overall engagement as the amount of time spent becomes more significant in the economics for game makers and platforms. In this regard, we can anticipate a hybrid monetization strategy that is both direct (subscriptions) and indirect (advertising) and that ultimately leans on a two-sided business model in which creative firms intermediate between audiences and advertisers (see table 10.2).

To a degree, these different approaches in interactive entertainment can coexist and allow the industry to simultaneously serve different audiences. We have observed a comparable blend of these models in music, where people still buy CDs, listen to the radio, and pay a monthly fee for a music streaming service. Now that games are a mainstream form of entertainment, the underlying economics have shifted, although not in favor of one business model or another. Audiences in North America undoubtedly will continue to show a preference for premium content compared with

Table 10.2
Recurrent revenue models in interactive entertainment

Model	Description	Example	Monthly Cost
Publisher	Access to one or more titles from a single publisher	*World of Warcraft*, Big Fish, GameClub	$5–15
Platform	Complementary content services (e.g., games, video, music, live entertainment) or functionality	PlayStation Network, Xbox Game Pass, Apple Arcade	$5–50
Franchise	Regularly occurring content expansions or releases	*FIFA*, *Fortnite Battle Pass*	$10–60
Service	Access to a distribution service that may or may not include content	Google Stadia, Microsoft xCloud, NVIDIA GeForce Now	$10–20

Source: Author's compilation.

their counterparts in Asia, where free-to-play is the most common model. Different business models—product, service, and media—will simultaneously exist alongside each other, each imposing a distinct configuration of affordances and constraints on global game companies and small independent creative firms alike.

Conclusion

Johannes Vermeer was a seventeenth-century Dutch painter. A master at depicting people in everyday scenes while in deep thought, his best-known works include *Girl with a Pearl Earring* and *The Milkmaid*. For a long time, art historians considered him to be a lone genius. During his life, Vermeer had remained in relative obscurity. It was mostly local patrons who commissioned his portraits rather than foreign buyers, and his work never circulated far beyond the borders of his hometown. After he died, his wife sold several of his works to pay off debts and care for their eleven children. His legacy as one of the greatest painters from the Dutch Golden Age was not secured until two art historians, Gustav Friedrich Waagen and Théophile Thoré-Bürger, rediscovered Vermeer's paintings and published an article in 1866 in which they crowned him the "Sphinx of Delft."[1] Almost a century after his death, Vermeer rose to the highest echelons of Dutch art royalty and became known as a master of light and an artist of singular brilliance.

An exhibition on Vermeer's work in 2017 offers a different reading.[2] Instead of positioning the artist as a solitary figure who labored in obscurity only to achieve success posthumously, the curators argue, Vermeer was, in fact, a well-known figure in the thriving Dutch art business during his life-time. In the mid-1600s, the growing affluence in the Netherlands resulted in increased demand for fine art. In this economic context, Vermeer competed over patronage with many other artists. Consequently, painters often looked to each other's work to get a sense of what images and scenes sold well. According to the museum's curators, "Through comparisons with the works of other artists of the Golden Age, the exhibition brings to light Vermeer's membership to a network of painters specializing in the depiction of everyday life while admiring, inspiring, and vying with each other."[3]

Quite the opposite from the mythology of a lone genius, a broader understanding of the creative business of which Vermeer was part indicates how the painter's work related to a broader economic context. Vermeer is but one of many artists throughout history who was thought to have pursued a creative vision in isolation and outside of competitive pressures. His legacy exemplifies how we erroneously attribute artistic innovation to a single talented person. A growing body of literature refutes this. A study of the difference in critical success between U.S. and French artists found that "the study of market conditions is central to an understanding of the history of modern art."[4] It reads:

> Painters who seek critical and financial success must take account of prevailing exhibition practices in producing their work. In nineteenth-century Paris, the central role of large group exhibitions meant that artists had to devote considerable effort to producing important individual pieces. In twentieth-century New York, the dominance of one-man gallery shows shifted the job of the artist from making striking individual works to producing large numbers of paintings that would make up significant shows.[5]

Similarly, a sociologist at the London School of Economics, Fabien, Accominotti, has concluded that individual creativity is a weak indicator of critical success. In a study on the broader social and economic context, Accominotti dispels the myth of the lone creative genius: "Common membership in an artistic movement (a proxy for interactions such as collaboration or emulation), as well as competition and borrowings between movements, can drive the unfolding of creativity over individual careers and historical time."[6] Artistic innovation depends on interactions between artists, both in a collaborative and competitive sense.

Placing creative industries within the appropriate financial context and understanding how organizations manage, or fail, to overcome strategic challenges adds a critical component to establishing a more comprehensive picture of how the business of interactive entertainment functions. As I've tried to show, economic forces profoundly affect the games we play, the devices we play them on, the genres the industry produces, the type of live events fans attend, the kind of content we stream across devices, or what boxed special editions we buy. The business behind the games is both a critical component in facilitating and limiting creative processes, and a source of immense strategic advantage when companies develop innovative business models.

Game companies compete on strategy as much as they do on creating unique interactive experiences. After the industry's collapse in the 1980s, it was the combination of ingenious design and innovation in how companies operated that revived the industry and established a new economic foundation. Developers claimed their independence and publishers specialized in specific categories and genres. Platform holders became more acutely aware of the need to offer a content portfolio that delivered quality experiences and to distinguish themselves from competitors. More became less important. Then, as digitization transformed the entire entertainment business, the industry shifted again. Moving away from a product-based model, a generation of newcomers introduced new experiences and new distribution and pricing strategies. In this games-as-a-service model, incumbents initially struggled to adapt to the new structural conditions of a global and mainstream market.

Many of the firms covered in this book found their strategic solution and ultimate success in equally emphasizing content creation and business model innovation. We discussed how companies across the value chain managed to formulate, or not, a unique approach to the development, publishing, marketing, and distribution of interactive entertainment. It was their ability to adapt to changing market conditions with the same effort used to overcome technical issues and creative limitations that prepared game makers for the massive shifts in underlying economics that followed the introduction of broadband internet and the popularization of the smartphone. This approach offered an initial foundation for a different "form of knowledge" on how decision-makers tackle the strategic challenges that come with making games: to think creatively both about content and commerce.[7]

Several aspects of this industry benefit all. Many of the successes we reviewed depended on an immediate, positive consumer response. We observed, for instance, that when Valve sought to resolve distribution inefficiencies by launching Steam in 2003, consumers embraced the new platform. This move resulted in a thirteen-million-strong user base by 2007 and revitalized the PC games category. Similarly, Nexon managed to carve out market share in the United States by implementing a strategy tailored to younger audiences who, in response, flocked to *MapleStory* in droves. And when live-streaming and online video reached critical mass, audiences showed a clear preference for gaming content. Gamer audiences proved to be early adopters, and in all of these cases, they readily adopted new distribution models, payment methods, or marketing channels.

Digitization similarly provided several affordances. Transferring information to a digital format made it easier to manipulate and expand the addressable consumer base. Entertainment companies gained the ability to publish their content to a global audience. Not too long ago media firms were limited by natural, physical boundaries, but soon digitization facilitated the worldwide distribution of content. As new markets opened, a broad range of both old and new competitors released an unprecedented array of games to play. Another related benefit was the convergence of technology: as we learned from the discussion around the alleged death of the console, incumbent platform holders managed to successfully compete with emergent rivals and newcomers in mobile by expanding their range of services. Instead of exclusively playing games, consoles aspired to become devices used to watch movies and television. More recently, content creators have expanded adjoining markets (mobile, console, and PC) and facilitated interoperability between platforms for their titles, allowing players from different devices to play together.

Certainly, digitization also presents new challenges. Growth in demand has attracted new competitors. Publishers now have access to markets that previously were inaccessible. So, too, does an entire generation of recently established firms. Operating globally means having to deal with rules and regulations locally. Countries like Brazil and China have tax-related and regulatory obstacles that make it difficult for foreign organizations to compete on equal footing with local incumbents. In addition, in highly competitive economies, price competition with low marginal costs means price deflation. Content is "free" because it is difficult to charge anything for it. Solving distribution issues is meaningless if your audience is unaccustomed or is simply unable to pay for content and related services. Compared with a decade ago, a massive inventory of free games is now available, which, especially in a crowded marketplace, threatens long-term viability.

Digital markets must consider several important economic drivers. For one, traditional value chain participants like console manufacturers and publishers confront high and growing fixed costs in their conventional business practices and look for ways to change this to the low and declining marginal costs of digitalization. Pursuing recurrent revenue models by way of services and content expansions means repositioning external messaging and reconfiguring internal operations. Turning a tanker is an inevitably arduous process.

Network effects of online amusement closely resemble the risk profile of the hit-driven, product-based business. Making games available for free has allowed several notable companies to succeed. Epic Games' free release of *Fortnite* against its competitor's *PlayerUnknown's Battlegrounds*, which required a $30 purchase, allowed the former to skyrocket to success. Despite launching much later, it was the coalescence of its broad appeal and accessibility that powered the game's underlying network effects and propelled it into the mainstream.

Moreover, creative organizations confront the inevitable glut in supply. The process of discovery, which connects consumers with content, continues to be a challenge especially for firms that put out titles that are easily replicable or lack marketing muscle. On platforms like mobile, in particular, it has become difficult to capture share as several powerful incumbents create artificial entry barriers by outspending everyone else on marketing. It forces developers to answer the question whether to create and cultivate their own franchise or try to obtain someone else's. The notion of a digital marketplace that is equally accessible by all its participants may have existed at one point in history, but it no longer does. Marketing budgets in digital gaming today closely resemble those associated with the traditional business.

Finally, advertising is slowly emerging as a new income model, but nevertheless the bulk of the industry continues to rely on direct consumer payment for their livelihood. And even as the possibility of charging advertisers for access to the growing audience for gaming video content and the gradual success in selling media rights around esports events becomes feasible, most creatives remain deeply resistant to the idea of working with brands. Until this third model is successfully established and accepted by consumers, traditional revenue models will remain an important factor in game design and management.

The quadrupling of consumer spending and widespread digitalization of interactive entertainment has resulted in the emergence of new economic complexities and the development of novel properties. More, after all, means different. We can distinguish several recurring themes in innovation as game companies formulate strategies to navigate a new economic environment. A first one centers on pricing strategy. Despite existing in entirely different realms, organizations like GameStop and Nexon have both managed to gain a competitive edge in their respective categories by deploying novel pricing models. GameStop's secondhand sales strategy thus far has proven to be impossible to replicate by its competitors. The promise of finding quality titles at a lower price has been key in driving foot traffic to its stores. As a result, it has continued to provide an important financial resource as the brick-and-mortar retailer wrestles with the momentum behind online commerce and digitalization of entertainment in general. Nexon, in contrast, successfully penetrated the U.S. market by offering its games for free. By entering a mature economy like the United States where consumers were accustomed to paying up to $60 for a newly released blockbuster title, the South Korean publisher managed to quickly claim share. By providing easy access to *MapleStory* and enabling players to spend real-world currency in a digital environment, it successfully captured an audience of predominantly younger players.

Marketing, too, has undergone several clever iterations. Different firms across the value chain have managed to formulate distinct strategies that both elevated their business and established new ways to cater to players. Nintendo combined a focus on quality control with consumer loyalty as the key to reviving the industry following its collapse in 1984. The Japanese giant has continued to do so and remains among the most successful firms in the industry, despite taking a much slower approach to adopt new technologies and platforms. The blockbuster approach, which positioned designers as rock stars and placed them on equal footing with musicians, movie makers, and authors, resulted in Electronic Arts becoming a top publisher even as competition increased. By incorporating more accessible gameplay mechanics and broadly appealing aesthetics, firms like Activision Blizzard and Zynga successfully marketed to general audiences. In their own way, these two organizations each pushed games into the mainstream.

We also observed the audacious strategy of freely giving others access to your intellectual property. Examples include firms like id Software, which opened up its shooter *Doom* and allowed amateur programmers to develop levels for it, and Wizards of the Coast, which streamlined the *D&D* rule system (d20) and allowed others to use it with few restrictions. Both cases resulted in the effective harnessing of the productive and innovative power of a broad group of people and, in the process, they successfully established themselves as category incumbents.

In cases in which pricing, messaging, and marketing are all front-facing strategies, we also discover notable innovation behind the scenes. A developer like Naughty Dog successfully attracts top talent by institutionalizing a flat organizational structure that facilitates input from across its workforce. Giving people ownership and creative input is a strong motivator. Similarly, Supercell produced several of the biggest mobile titles to date by simply focusing its efforts around top talent and keeping its organization small and lean. Valve's approach to enabling creative talent for both its own titles and through its Steam platform has allowed the firm to prosper and develop several of the industry's most influential titles. Often overlooked, organizational innovation is key to creative and commercial success.

Others formulate innovate approaches to content development and distribution. Following the success of *Grand Theft Auto V* (*GTA V*), Take-Two managed to overhaul its dependency on brick-and-mortar distribution by successfully aligning its creative output with a digital distribution model, and in so doing, captured billions in recurrent revenue. When Microsoft and Sony faced the rising popularity of the smartphone and PC, the two manufacturers managed to disprove the ubiquitous expectation that the console was on its way out. Instead, distribution over the internet on dedicated devices managed to add both a greater variety of revenue streams and additional income by adopting microtransactions, free-to-play titles, and streaming content.

Finally, as the games business started to move away from its product-based roots, organizations have come up with new ways to deal with the inevitable clutter typical of a digital marketplace. As game magazines lost share to gaming video content as the primary place for consumers to learn about new titles, publishers like Riot Games, Activision Blizzard, Epic Games, and Electronic Arts learned how to keep the momentum behind their titles by launching ongoing campaigns to engage audiences. Esports has played a critical role in the success of *League of Legends* and *Overwatch*; each of their respective publishers has proven adept at driving viewership and ad sales.

Despite the obvious differences among these organizations, they share an ability to apply creativity in equal measure to strategy as they do to content. To them, business model innovation serves as an important competitive advantage.

We have seen plenty of failures, too. We observed the mistakes made by Atari's executives who misjudged the market's appetite for licensed content and, similarly, the Zeebo fatally overestimated demand for interactive content to Latin America. During periods of growth, the full scale of what audiences want, how much they will pay for it, or what they are accustomed to can be deceiving. Another example of a business decision that misread the market was Microsoft's acquisition of Massive. Spending a bunch of money without establishing the viability of its revenue model, the software giant quickly found out that developers were far from ready to embrace in-game advertising. Instead, the acquisition ran into heavy resistance from creatives and a lack of support before Microsoft eventually disbanded the effort.

Taking a more measured approach and keeping tighter control on inventory or content rollout can prevent firms from exposing themselves to risk. Understanding the differences among audiences and how to cater to them is often overlooked in the frenzy to build for scale. In a global market, country-level traits also must be considered. Both Microsoft Xbox and Tencent wrestled with the Chinese government's regulatory policies. A seemingly innocuous change in policy can upset an entire supply chain and cause the loss of billions. And Electronic Arts did not do itself any favors by implementing an aggressive monetization strategy. Although this approach has worked well for some of its most dedicated fans for the *FIFA* franchise, its loot boxes turned consumers, policy makers, and partners against it when the mechanic showed up in titles that catered to broader, less homogeneous audiences.

The net result of all this innovation and growth is the evolution of video games into a mainstream form of entertainment. Beyond simply releasing superior content, as I've shown, both critical acclaim and financial success in this industry depend on an organization's ability to develop new ways of conducting business. Interactive entertainment has remained relatively obscure for a long time. Today, however, video games sit at the center of the broader media, entertainment, and technology markets. Large conglomerates have integrated it into their business model: Amazon, Apple, Facebook, Google, and Tencent all inextricably have connected their fate to their success in gaming.

Amazon, for example, has made several acquisitions over the years to gain more control over the value chain. As its presence in traditional games retail and e-commerce grew, it acquired Twitch, spent a fortune on establishing its own publishing division (i.e., Amazon Games Studios), and even attempted to develop a proprietary software engine. It is expected to enter the market for cloud gaming in 2021 and compete with Microsoft, Sony, and Google.

So, too, Apple invested in its Arcade, a subscription service, to cater to its global user base. After the explosive success of freemium titles on its platform, Apple now seeks to appeal to more mainstream customers, like parents, and offer them premium-only content without microtransactions. Unlike its efforts in other media categories, Apple made an investment by acquiring mobile-exclusive rights to one hundred titles to stock its offering.

And Google, after arriving late to mobile gaming, spent years trying to catch up. It managed to do so by positioning itself as a lower-end, higher-volume smartphone manufacturer and provider of a mobile operating system, Android. Cloud gaming, too, presents an opportunity for Google. With Stadia, the firm is establishing itself as a more dominant player and claiming a larger share of the desirable gamer market. Google's strategy is ambitious and undoubtedly expensive. It is also a clear admission that the tech giant, like its peers, has come to regard gaming as an important component to future success.

Despite the many challenges and high risk of failure in this industry, the number of multinational firms that invests in gaming continues to grow. As we enter the next generation of console hardware with the PlayStation 5 and Xbox Series X released alongside emergent consumer technologies, such as cloud gaming and augmented reality, the industry resets once again. The popularity of this art form has persuaded an even broader group of large multinationals to stake their claim in this growing entertainment market. Undoubtedly this will impact the industry's landscape and rearrange the array of technological affordances and constraints of newly emerging devices and services. It asks video game companies to answer the one question that historically has determined their fate and has been a true test of their creative abilities: what will the next wave of innovation look like, and how do we design for it?

Appendix
Empirical Procedure

Few myths survive an encounter with data. To illustrate the economic underpinnings of the business of video games and how the industry has changed over the years, I have relied on a primary data set that compiles revenue information for 208 companies over the course of the period 1998 to 2018. That group consists of 77 publicly traded and 131 privately held firms. I collected data for the former from the earnings reports that they are obligated to provide to investors. This is a fairly common way to establish relative market share among industry participants. Where available, the most recently reported figures were used to account for accounting adjustments.

For data on the latter firms, I relied on SuperData Research, a market research firm which I co-founded and where I served as CEO until its acquisition by Nielsen in 2018. Private firms do not have an obligation to report on their performance. Because the industry is largely hit-driven, the vast majority of firms depend on the income from one disproportionally lucrative title. For example, Russian game maker Wargaming, which publishes *World of Tanks*, holds a variety of development assets and is involved in a dozen creative projects at any one time. But upward of 80 percent of its annual revenue comes from its marque title. Using this logic, I established total annual income for privately held firms by aggregating the combined earnings of their various titles. In addition, to ensure accuracy, I made every attempt to match this total against public statements, conference comments, and other available information. I acknowledge that although this may be an imperfect way of doing things, it was the most accurate method available. Most important, by taking this approach, I was able to compare a relatively robust set of companies against each other on key variables and operational aspects.

Two additional comments are necessary. First, in collecting the data for each of these firm types, I emphasized income generated from publishing activities. For organizations like Activision Blizzard, that demarcation is obvious enough. But for platform holders like Sony and Nintendo, I included only revenue derived from the sale of content in this analysis; revenue from hardware and accessory sales was left out to allow for greater transparency and ease of comparison. To that end, I also omitted consumer electronic companies and firms that produce devices and components for interactive entertainment like Apple, Dell, and Nvidia, among others.

Second, considering the time frame of the data set, several firms, especially digital publishers, started off as privately held only to change ownership structure by going public (e.g., Rovio), getting acquired (e.g., Supercell, Riot Games), experiencing both (e.g., King Digital), or going private (e.g., Perfect World). In some instances, this obfuscated the available information and forced me to rely on a combination of data sets.

For all industry participants, the following information was collected: country of origin, ownership structure (public, private), total reported revenue, company type (publisher, platform), origin (legacy, digital), share of revenues generated from interactive entertainment activities, share of revenue by platform (mobile, console, and PC), and share of revenue by geography (North America, Europe, Asia, and Rest of World). Table A.1 lists the companies for which I collected data.

Explanation of Statistical Measures

Throughout this book, I relied on two common statistical measures to provide an intuitive assessment of the industry's structure and its subsegments. First is the C4, which stands for the aggregate total of market share percentage for the four largest participants in a given industry or segment. This measure indicates how concentrated a specific market is. It does not account for the number of active participants. Depending on the relevant

Table A.1

Publicly traded and privately held companies included in this study, 1986–2018

37 Interactive Entertainment	CyberAgent
Acclaim Entertainment	Cygames
Activision Blizzard	D3PA
Activision Publishing	Daybreak Game Company
Aniplex	Deep Silver
Aristocrat Leisure	DeNA
AT&T	DianDian Interactive
Atari	Digital Extremes
Atlus	Dire Wolf Digital
Backflip Studios	Disney (The Walt Disney Company)
Bally Technologies	Double Down Interactive
Bandai Namco Entertainment	DoubleU Games
Bash Games	Dragonplay
Bethesda Softworks	Edge of Reality
Bigben Interactive	Eidos Interactive
Big Fish Games	Electronic Arts
Bigpoint Games	Elex Wireless
Bitsbox	En Masse Entertainment
Blue Mammoth Games	Epic Games
Bluehole (Krafton)	Epic War
Bohemia Interactive	Episode Interactive
Caesars Entertainment	Etermax
Camel Games	Facepunch Studios
Campo Santo	Fat Shark
Capcom	Firefly Studios
CCP Games	Four Thirty Three
CD Projekt	FoxNext
Cervo Media	Freejam
Changyou.com	Fremantle Media
Chucklefish	FromSoftware
Codemasters Software	Frontier Developments
COLOPL	Frostburn Studios
Com2uS	Fun Games For Free
Comcast	Funcom Oslo
CrowdStar	FunPlus

(Continued)

Gaijin Entertainment	LONG TECH NETWORK
Game Show Network	Loong Entertainment
Gameforge 4D	Ludia
GameGuru	Machine Zone
Gamigo	Mail.Ru
Garena	Majesco Entertainment
Giant Interactive	Meteor Entertainment
Glu Mobile	Microsoft
Goodgame Studios	Midway Games
GREE	miHoYo Technology
Grinding Gear Games	Miniclip
GungHo Online Entertainment	Mixi
Happy Elements	Mojang
Harmonix Music Systems	Moon Active
Hasbro	Muifwego
Hi-Rez Studios	My.com
High 5 Games	NCSoft
Huuuge Games	Neowiz Games
Iceberg Interactive	NetEase
IGG	Netmarble
International Game Technology	Nexon
Introversion Software	NHN
Jagex	Niantic
Kabam	Nintendo
Kadokawa Future Publishing	Nordcurrent
Kakao	Nordeus
KamaGames	Octro
KILOO	OpenWager
King Digital Entertainment	Pacific Interactive
King Kong Games Technology	Paradox Interactive
Kingsoft	Peak Games
Koei Tecmo Holdings	Pearl Abyss
Konami Holdings	PerBlue
Krafton (Bluehole)	Perfect World Entertainment
Larian Studios	Piranha Games
Leyou	Pixelberry Studios
LINE Corporation	Pixonic

Plarium

Playdemic

Playrix

Playtika

Pocket Gems

Product Madness

Psyonix

RealNetworks

Realtime Worlds

Red 5 Studios

Riot Games

Roblox

Rovio Entertainment

S2 Games

Scientific Games

Scopely

Sega Sammy

SGN (Social Gaming Network)

Shanda Interactive Entertainment

Slightly Mad Studios

Smilegate

Social Quantum

Softstar Entertainment

Sohu

Sony

Squad

Square Enix

Starbreeze Studios

Stillfront Group

Studio Wildcard

Sumzap

Supercell

Suzhou Stack Paper Network

Take-Two Interactive Software

Tap4Fun

Team17

Team18

Team19

Telltale Games

The 3DO Company

The9

THQ

THQ Nordic

Tiancity

Top Free Games

Trion Worlds

Turbine

Ubisoft Entertainment

Ultimate Games

Unknown Worlds Entertainment

Valve

Vivendi

Warchest

Wargaming Group

Warhorse Studios

Warner Bros. Interactive Entertainment

WarnerMedia

Webzen

Williams Interactive

Wizards of the Coast

YottaGames

ZlongGames

Zloong Entertainment

Zynga

Note: List does not account for mergers or divestitures, and it is possible that some company names appear more than once.

dimensions of a specific market, I used variations of this measure (e.g., C1 or C10). These use the same calculation method but for a different number of firms (e.g., the single largest company or top ten).

The second measure is the Herfindahl-Hirschmann Index (HHI).[1] It is a popular measurement in U.S. antitrust enforcement and is expressed in the sum of the squares of the market shares of all market participants. The HHI can range from 0—where the share of each firm is infinitely small—to 10,000, where a single firm accounts for 100 percent of the market. This index naturally exaggerates when a single organization controls a disproportionate part of the market compared with, say, five equally sized firms: the HHI would be 10,000 and 2,000, respectively. The U.S. Department of Justice uses the HHI to establish whether a particular market is unconcentrated (with an HHI less than 1,000), moderately concentrated (requiring an HHI between 1,500 and 2,500), or highly concentrated (HHI greater than 2,500). The point of using these two statistical measures in this book is to provide an intuitive interpretation on the relative market power of different game companies and to illustrate the impact on the market landscape as a result of the industry's economic foundation and its disruptions.

Limitations

The current data set on the games industry is not exhaustive. For one, it is based on just over two hundred companies, and it is possible that some key firms have been left out unintentionally. In that case, I take full responsibility. The current study should be regarded as the first results of what likely will become an iterative effort. Moreover, revenue distribution is highly skewed. A total of twenty-five companies in the data set had earnings of more than $1 billion in 2018, and combined, the entire analyzed consortium of industry participants generated around $114 billion in aggregate, which, compared with varying market sizing figures available, represents around 85 percent of the total consumer spend, depending on which estimate you use.

Another important limitation to the data is the omission of a slew of smaller firms. Thousands of companies make up the global industry. Many of them, however, do not generate a lot of revenue, and their ability to reach audiences remains limited. Small studios are akin to local radio stations or news publications with a low circulation. It does not make small companies any less important: they play a critical role in the industry's innovation and competition. It does mean that their market power and influence on the overall structure and economics of the industry overall are limited. Conceivably, the HHI in certain markets would be lower if we were to account for them, and market concentration would be lower. Considering these limitations to the data set, I believe the current analysis will serve as a reliable indicator of the structural makeup of the games industry.

Additional Information Sources

As the former founder and chief executive of a market research firm and advisor to several startups in the games industry, combined with a teaching position at New York University's Stern School for Business, I enjoy the great fortune of getting to talk to people about the games business every day. This provides me with access to senior decision-makers in famous and lesser-known organizations, investors, creatives, marketing executives, producers, business intelligence analysts, data scientists, financial analysts, fund managers, students, and journalists who all, in one way or another, have attached the fate of their careers to this industry. In this book, I rely on the conversations about the games business I have had with all of these people over the course of the last twenty years. Throughout the different chapters various quotes can be found from hundreds of formal interviews and casual in-person conversations I've had. In order for my contacts to speak freely, I have granted their requests to remain anonymous. Over time, I have found that true insight into this industry exists in the collective minds of dedicated people and, contrary to my initial beliefs, no single source of information is capable of describing the complexity of the entire interactive entertainment industry. Often, I observed at busy conferences and industry events how the people that truly guide and shape the games industry go unnoticed in a crowd of professionals. For them, there is no red carpet, no international broadcast of an award show, and none of the self-congratulatory practices we find in film, music, print publishing, news reporting, and television. Getting to speak to many of these individuals, or hearing them speak, has been a central source of information—and inspiration—for this book.

In terms of professional sources of information, I have made no distinctions between available sources, with the exception that any figure or alleged fact about the industry would need to be clearly explained in the footnotes and, obviously, be based on a rigorous effort. This excludes infographics, press releases, comments on Twitter, or similar information. Although abundant, I have found this "free" industry data generally poorly researched and regularly incorrect. As a general word of advice, in my experience, well-organized information that is offered up freely generally serves an agenda and always should be approached with a degree of skepticism. Even publicly traded firms, who are legally obligated to report their earnings in addition to other indicators of the health of their operations have an interest in obfuscating the numbers just enough to make them appear a bit more positive. The shift to digital also meant that firms faced new reporting practices: when a player purchases virtual currency, does one recognize the revenue at the moment of purchase, or when that player spends currency in a game? Publishers like Electronic Arts and Activision Blizzard, for instance, only first reconciled their earnings reporting to standard generally accepted accounting principles in the summer of 2016. I have exercised my judgment in accepting or rejecting these sources to the best of my abilities.

Over the years, I have come to trust the writing from financial analysts who follow the market closely for their investor clients and who are barred from investing in any of the organizations they cover. They write notes, provide forecasts, and have access to detailed and sensitive information. Here, a well-known and often controversial industry figure like Michael Pachter from Wedbush Securities was generous enough to answer my questions over the course of countless phone calls, meetings, and dinners. Similarly, I have discussed the underlying drivers of this industry in a myriad of exchanges with Drew Crum from Stifel Financial and Yung Kim from Piper Jaffray.

Finally, the concept of this book first emerged because I was frustrated with the lack of available materials for my students. Existing readings were both subpar and prohibitively expensive. From my experience in this industry, I knew I would be able to cobble together enough data and insights from case studies and projects to make for a sufficient base of reading materials. In this context, I should mention the hundreds of students who have taken my classes over the years, have read and heard me speak on much of the content of the book, and more often than not have managed to surprise me with additional facts and questions. It is in this same academic vein that I publish this writing beyond the confines of my classroom: to engage in a dialogue about an industry that deserves serious inquiry rather than to proselytize based on current work. I welcome and look forward to anyone willing to comment on and improve this work as it stands today.

NOTES

Preface

1. Jason Schreier, *Blood, Sweat, and Pixels: The Triumphant, Turbulent Stories Behind How Video Games Are Made* (New York: Harper, 2017), 74.

2. Bro Uttal, "Famous Victories in Personal Software," *Fortune*, May 2, 1983, 164.

3. Raph Koster, "Practical Creativity" (GDC Next, Los Angeles, November 3, 2014).

4. John Dewey, *Art as Experience* (New York: TarcherPerigee, 2005), 31.

5. "New Super Mario Bros. Wii: The Reason Mario Wears Overalls," Iwata Asks, Nintendo, accessed September 21, 2019, http://iwataasks.nintendo.com/interviews/#/wii/nsmb/0/1.

6. John Sedgwick and Michael Pokorny, "The Characteristics of Film as a Commodity," in *An Economic History of Film*, ed. John Sedgwick and Michael Pokorny (Abingdon, UK: Routledge, 2004), 13.

7. Alan Krueger, *Rockonomics: A Backstage Tour of What the Music Industry Can Teach Us about Economics and Life* (New York: Currency, 2019), 5.

8. David Sheff, *Game Over: How Nintendo Conquered the World* (New York: Vintage, 1994); Jeff Ryan, *Super Mario: How Nintendo Conquered America* (London: Portfolio, 2012); Blake J. Harris, *Console Wars: Sega, Nintendo, and the Battle That Defined a Generation* (New York: It Books, 2014); Dustin Hansen, *Game On! Video Game History from Pong and Pac-Man to Mario, Minecraft, and More* (2016; repr., New York: Square Fish, 2019).

9. Dean Takahashi's *Opening the Xbox: Inside Microsoft's Plan to Unleash an Entertainment Revolution* (Roseville, CA: Prima, 2002), and *The Xbox 360 Uncloaked: The Real Story Behind Microsoft's Next-Generation Video Game Console* (Raleigh, NC: SpiderWorks, 2006).

10. Nick Montfort and Ian Bogost, *Racing the Beam: The Atari Video Computer System*, 2nd ed. (Cambridge, MA: MIT Press, 2009).

11. David Kushner, *Masters of Doom: How Two Guys Created an Empire and Transformed Pop Culture* (2003; repr., New York: Random House, 2004).

12. Casey O'Donnell, *Developer's Dilemma: The Secret World of Videogame Creators* (Cambridge, MA: MIT Press, 2014), 147.

13. Harold L. Vogel, *Entertainment Industry Economics: A Guide for Financial Analysis*, 9th ed. (New York: Cambridge University Press, 2014), 401–21.

14. Mark J. P. Wolf and Bernard Perron, *The Routledge Companion to Video Game Studies* (Routledge Handbooks Online, 2013), https://doi.org/10.4324/9780203114261.

15. Michael Z. Newman, *Atari Age: The Emergence of Video Games in America* (Cambridge, MA: MIT Press, 2017).

16. Carly A. Kocurek, *Coin-Operated Americans* (Minneapolis: University of Minnesota Press, 2015).

17. Nick Dyer-Witheford and Greig de Peuter, *Games of Empire: Global Capitalism and Video Games* (Minneapolis: University of Minnesota Press, 2013); Aphra Kerr, *Global Games: Production, Circulation and Policy in the Networked Era* (New York: Taylor & Francis, 2017); Randy Nichols, *The Video Game Business* (International Screen Industries, British Film Institute, 2014).

18. Kerr, *Global Games*, 37.

19. Kerr, *Global Games*, 37; O'Donnell, *Developer's Dilemma*, 147.

20. Norita B. Ahmad, Salahudin Abdul Rahman Barakji, Tarak Mohamed Abou Shahada, and Zeid Ayman Anabtawi, "How to Launch a Successful Video Game: A Framework," *Entertainment Computing* 23 (November 1, 2017): 10, https://doi.org/10.1016/j.entcom.2017.08.001.

Introduction

1. Keith Stuart, "Activision CEO Bobby Kotick on the King Deal: 'We Have an Audience of 500 Million,' " Games, *Guardian*, November 4, 2015, https://www.theguardian.com/technology/2015/nov/04/bobby-kotick-king-deal-activision-blizzard.

2. For brevity's sake, the company names in this book are intentionally kept short. When discussing a firm like Take-Two Interactive Software, I use Take-Two. Similarly, other names have been reduced to serve the reader.

3. "Ericsson Mobility Report 2018," Ericsson.com, November 20, 2018, https://www.ericsson.com/en/mobility-report/reports/november-2018/mobile-subscriptions-worldwide-q3-2018.

4. Steve Jobs (stevejobsays), "Steve Jobs on Portable Gaming," October 9, 2010, video, 1:01, https://www.youtube.com/watch?v=klXGAyqVTWA.

1. Digitalization of Interactive Entertainment

1. Alex Sherman, "Netflix Says It's More Scared of *Fortnite* and YouTube Than Disney and Amazon," CNBC, January 17, 2019, https://www.cnbc.com/2019/01/17/netflix-more -scared-of-fortnite-and-youtube-than-disney-and-amazon.html.

2. See Charles Baden-Fuller and Stefan Haefliger, "Business Models and Technological Innovation," *Long Range Planning* 46, no. 6 (December 1, 2013): 419–26, https:// doi.org/10.1016/j.lrp.2013.08.023, and Joseph F. Porac, Howard Thomas, and Charles Baden-Fuller, "Competitive Groups as Cognitive Communities: The Case of Scottish Knitwear Manufacturers," *Journal of Management Studies* 26, no. 4 (1989): 397–416, https://doi.org/10.1111/j.1467-6486.1989.tb00736.x.

3. Thomas Porac, and Baden-Fuller, "Competitive Groups as Cognitive Communities."

4. "The Making of Fez, the Breaking of Phil Fish," *Indie Games Plus* (blog), December 13, 2011, https://indiegamesplus.com/2011/12/the_making_of_fez_the_breaking.

5. Jonathan Knee, Bruce Greenwald, and Ava Seave, *The Curse of the Mogul: What's Wrong with the World's Leading Media Companies* (New York: Portfolio, 2009), 261.

6. Ben Parfitt, "Take-Two Not Convinced by Triple-A Free-to-Play," *MCV*, December 4, 2013, https://www.mcvuk.com/take-two-not-convinced-by-triple-a-free-to-play/.

7. Eddie Makuch, "Most Free-to-Play Games Are Not Very Good, GTA Boss Says," *GameSpot*, December 3, 2014, https://www.gamespot.com/articles/most-free-to-play -games-are-not-very-good-gta-boss/1100-6423960/.

8. Richard Garfield, "A game player's manifesto," Facebook, September 20, 2016, https:// www.facebook.com/notes/richard-garfield/a-game-players-manifesto/1049168888532667.

2. Games Industry Basics

1. "Take-Two CEO: We've Sold 5M of Our Basketball Video Games," Bloomberg, February 13, 2015, video, 6:23, https://www.bloomberg.com/news/videos/2015-02-13/we -ve-sold-5m-of-our-basketball-video-games-take-two-ceo.

2. Figures based on 2018 digital revenue on console (all platforms); SuperData Research.

3. Publicly released monthly entertainment software sales data by NPD for the U.S. market, for the period 2006 to 2018.

4. Harold L. Vogel, *Entertainment Industry Economics: A Guide for Financial Analysis*, 9th ed. (New York: Cambridge University Press, 2010), 251.

5. Jeffrey Fleming, "The History of Activision," Gamasutra, July 30, 2007, http:// www.gamasutra.com/view/feature/129961/the_history_of_activision.php.

6. Blake J. Harris, *Console Wars: Sega, Nintendo, and the Battle That Defined a Generation* (New York: Dey Street Books, 2015), 53.

7. "Trip Hawkins Interview," *Upside*, August/September 1990, 56, cited in Adam M. Brandenburger, "Power Play (A): Nintendo in 8-bit Video Games," Harvard Business cast 9-795-102, July 12, 1995.

8. David Sheff, *Game Over: How Nintendo Conquered the World* (New York: Vintage, 1994), 75.

9. Ken Horowitz, "Interview: Trip Hawkins (Founder of Electronic Arts)," Sega-16, August 18, 2006, http://www.sega-16.com/2006/08/interview-trip-hawkins/.

10. Startup Grind Local, "Trip Hawkins (Electronic Arts)—Leaving Apple to Start EA," June 28, 2014, video, 2:53, https://www.youtube.com/watch?v=D4Fo9cPT_DE.

11. Katie McCort, "Analyzing the American Video Game Industry 2016: Statistics on Geographic Volume, Employment, and Growth" (Entertainment Software Association, February 2017).

12. Mathijs de Vaan, Balazs Vedres, and David Stark, "Game Changer: The Topology of Creativity," *American Journal of Sociology* 120, no. 4 (January 2015): 1147, https://doi.org/10.1086/681213. This study measured a development team's success based on critical acclaim instead of revenues.

13. Michael Futter and Mike Bithell, *The GameDev Business Handbook* (London: Bithell, 2018), and Judd Ruggill, Ken McAllister, Randy Nichols, and Ryan Kaufman, *Inside the Video Game Industry* (New York: Routledge, 2016).

14. Jason Schreier, *Blood, Sweat, and Pixels: The Triumphant, Turbulent Stories Behind How Video Games Are Made* (New York: Harper, 2017).

15. Dmitri Williams, "Structure and Competition in the U.S. Home Video Game Industry," *International Journal on Media Management* 4, no. 1 (January 1, 2002): 42, https://doi.org/10.1080/14241270209389979.

16. Michael Pachter, Nick McKay, and Nick Citrin, "Post Hoc Ergo Propter Hoc: Why the Next Generation Will Be as Big as Ever" (Equity Research, Wedbush Securities, February 12, 2014).

17. Paul Morris Hirsch, *The Structure of the Popular Music Industry: The Filtering Process by Which Records Are Preselected for Public Consumption* (Ann Arbor: Institute for Social Research, University of Michigan, 1969).

18. According to Elberse, "in book publishing, distributing a large number of physical books remains a classic tactic." Anita Elberse and Renée Raudman, *Blockbusters: Hit-Making, Risk-Taking, and the Big Business of Entertainment*, unabridged (Grand Haven, MI: Brilliance Audio, 2014).

19. Activision Publishing, Inc., "*Call of Duty: Black Ops II* Delivers More Than $500 Million in Worldwide Retail Sales in First 24 Hours," press release, November 16, 2012, https://investor.activision.com/news-releases/news-release-details/call-dutyr-black-ops-ii-delivers-more-500-million-worldwide.

20. Startup Grind Local, *Trip Hawkins (Electronic Arts)—Leaving Apple to Start EA*, June 28, 2014, video, 2:53, https://www.youtube.com/watch?v=D4Fo9cPT_DE.

21. Startup Grind Local, *Trip Hawkins (Electronic Arts)—Leaving Apple to Start EA*.

22. Bro Uttal, "Famous Victories in Personal Software," *Fortune*, May 2, 1983, 164.

23. Harold Seneker, and Jayne A. Pearl, "Software to Go," *Forbes* 131, no. 13 (June 20, 1983): 93–102.

3. Empire on the Edge of the Volcano

1. Barnes & Noble spun off GameStop in 2004, when it reported $2 billion in revenues across 1,514 retail outlets. In 2012, it reached its peak average on a per-store revenue basis of $1.4 million, based on $10 billion in revenues and 6,683 stores, or up 37 percent compared with 2004.

2. Michael Pachter, Nick McKay, and Nick Citrin, "Post Hoc Ergo Propter Hoc: Why the Next Generation Will Be as Big as Ever" (Equity Research, Wedbush Securities, February 12, 2014).

3. Of course, to maximize its revenue per store, the average GameStop storefront has become noticeably more cluttered over the years.

4. Specialty retailers are highly dependent on driving foot traffic and often offer steep discounts to lure people. According to one executive, "retailers are their own worst enemies" as they regularly forego on their margin just to bring people into the store.

5. Joshua Brustein, "Walmart's Used Video Game Business Won't Kill GameStop," Bloomberg, October 28, 2014, https://www.bloomberg.com/news/articles/2014-10-28/walmarts-used-game-business-wont-kill-gamestop.

6. Koster's data set did not include development costs for any mobile games. Raph Koster, "Industry Lifecycles," February 5, 2018, video, 30:00, https://www.youtube.com/watch?time_continue=271&v=LRSakzs-d-I.

7. Brendan Sinclair, *Resident Evil 6 Sells 4.9 Million, Disappoints*," GamesIndustry.biz, May 8, 2013, https://www.gamesindustry.biz/articles/2013-05-08-resident-evil-6-sells-4-9-million-disappoints.

8. SuperData Research, "Market Brief—2018 Digital Games & Interactive Entertainment Industry Year In Review," January 2019.

9. Richard Fontaine, "Letter to Shareholders," February 3, 2007, http://news.gamestop.com/static-files/9cb07c84-79d4-4fb8-9753-17fb061fd56c.

10. GameStop Corporation, "GameStop Acquires 507 AT&T Mobility Stores," GlobeNewswire News Room, August 2, 2016, http://www.globenewswire.com/news-release/2016/08/02/960824/0/en/GameStop-Acquires-507-AT-T-Mobility-Stores.html.

11. Giovanni Bruno, "Gamestop CEO Raines Talks Pokémon and Virtual Reality on CNBC," TheStreet, July 18, 2016, https://www.thestreet.com/story/13642777/1/gamestop-gme-ceo-raines-talks-pok-eacute-mon-and-virtual-reality-on-cnbc.html.

4. Everyone Is a Gamer Now

1. Ryan Kim and Chronicle Staff Writer, "Game Designers Focus on Girls," SFGate, October 6, 2008, https://www.sfgate.com/technology/article/Game-designers-focus-on-girls-3266775.php.

2. According to Juul: "The casual revolution in the title of this book is a break-through moment in the history of video games. This is the moment in which the simplicity of early video games is being rediscovered, while new flexible designs are letting video games fit into the lives of players. Video games are being reinvented, and so is our image of those who play the games. This is the moment when we realize that everybody can be a video game player." Jesper Juul, *A Casual Revolution: Reinventing Video Games and Their Players* (Cambridge, MA; MIT Press, 2012), 2.

3. Juul, *A Casual Revolution*, 22.

4. Andy Bossom and Ben Dunning, *Video Games: An Introduction to the Industry* (London: Fairchild, 2016), 11.

5. Juul, *A Casual Revolution*, 7.

6. Yuko Aoyama and Hiro Izushi, "Hardware Gimmick or Cultural Innovation? Technological, Cultural, and Social Foundations of the Japanese Video Game Industry," *Research Policy* 32, no. 3 (March 1, 2003): 442, https://doi.org/10.1016/S0048-7333(02)00016-1; see also Hiro Izushi and Yuko Aoyama, "Industry Evolution and Cross-Sectoral Skill Transfers: A Comparative Analysis of the Video Game Industry in Japan, the United States, and the United Kingdom," *Environment and Planning* A 38 (October 1, 2006): 1843–61, https://doi.org/10.1068/a37205.

7. Bjarke Liboriussen and Paul Martin, "Special Issue: Games and Gaming in China," *Games and Culture* 11, no. 3 (May 1, 2016): 227–32, https://doi.org/10.1177/1555412015615296.

8. Dal Yong Jin and Florence Chee, "Age of New Media Empires: A Critical Interpretation of the Korean Online Game Industry," *Games and Culture* 3, no. 1 (January 1, 2008): 38–58, https://doi.org/10.1177/1555412007309528.

9. Michal Bobrowski, Patrycja Rodzin´ska-Szary, and Socha Mariusz, *The State of the Polish Video Games Sector* (Krakow, Poland: Krakow Technology Park, Ministry of Culture and National Heritage of the Republic of Poland, Creative Europe Desk Poland and the Małopolska Province, 2015).

10. Hiro Izushi and Yuko Aoyama, "Industry Evolution and Cross-Sectoral Skill Transfers: A Comparative Analysis of the Video Game Industry in Japan, the United States, and the United Kingdom," *Environment and Planning* A 38 (October 1, 2006): 1843–61, https://doi.org/10.1068/a37205.

11. Ignazio Cabras, Nikolaos D. Goumagias, Kiran Fernandes, Peter Cowling, Feng Li, Daniel Kudenko, Sam Devlin, and Alberto Nucciarelli, "Exploring Survival Rates of Companies in the UK Video-Games Industry: An Empirical Study," *Technological Forecasting and Social Change* 117 (April 1, 2017): 305–14, https://doi.org/10.1016/j.techfore.2016.10.073.

12. Information about where in the world game companies make money was available for about two-thirds of the data set.

13. See, for instance, Michele Willson and Tama Leaver, eds., *Social, Casual and Mobile Games: The Changing Gaming Landscape* (New York: Bloomsbury Academic, 2017).

14. Peyton Maynard-Koran, "Fixing the Internet for Real Time Applications: Part II," Riot Games, February 11, 2016, https://engineering.riotgames.com/news/fixing-internet-real-time-applications-part-ii.

15. Johanna Weststar, Marie-Josée Legault, Chandell Gosse, and Vicki O'Meara, *Developer Satisfaction Survey 2014 & 2015: Diversity in the Game Industry Report* (International Game Developer Association, June 12, 2016), 38, https://cdn.ymaws.com/www .igda.org/resource/collection/cb31ce86-f8ee-4ae3-b46a-148490336605/igda_dss14-15 _diversityreport_aug2016_final.pdf.

16. Carly A. Kocurek, *Coin-Operated Americans* (Minneapolis: University of Minnesota Press, 2015); Casey O'Donnell, *Developer's Dilemma: The Secret World of Videogame Creators* (Cambridge, MA: MIT Press, 2014).

17. T. L. Taylor, *Raising the Stakes: E-Sports and the Professionalization of Computer Gaming* (Cambridge, MA: MIT Press, 2015), 34.

18. Leigh Alexander, " 'Gamers' Don't Have to Be Your Audience. 'Gamers' Are Over," Gamasutra, August 28, 2014, https://www.gamasutra.com/view/news/224400/Gamer.

19. Dmitri Williams, "Structure and Competition in the U.S. Home Video Game Industry," *International Journal on Media Management* 4, no. 1 (2002): 41–54, https://doi .org/10.1080/14241270209389979.

20. GameSpot Staff, "Star Wars Battlefront 2's Loot Box Controversy Explained," *GameSpot* (blog), 20:37:53 UTC, https://www.gamespot.com/articles/star-wars-battlefront -2s-loot-box-controversy-expl/1100-6455155/.

21. Stefanie Fogel, "China Introduces New Game Approval Process This Month," *Variety*, April 22, 2019, https://variety.com/2019/gaming/news/china-game-approvals -1203194653/.

5. Myth of the Mobile Millionaire

1. Maseena Ziegler, "The Accident That Created an App Millionaire," *Forbes*, September 13, 2013, https://www.forbes.com/sites/crossingborders/2013/09/13/the-accident-that -created-an-app-millionaire/.

2. Jay Yarow, "Another App Store Millionaire: 'Doodle Jump' Close to 2 Million Downloads, Over $1 Million in Sales," Business Insider, January 20, 2010, https://www .businessinsider.com/iphone-app-doodle-jump-closing-in-on-2-million-downloads -over-1-million-in-sales-2010-1.

3. "Monument Valley in Numbers," *ustwo games* (blog), September 18, 2015, https:// medium.com/@ustwogames/monument-valley-in-numbers-c945b8658261.

4. Once a platform has proven its worth by reaching a critical mass of consumers, incumbents artificially will drive up the cost of marketing to create new entry barriers. This is also known as endogenous sunk costs.

5. Dean Takahashi, "Supercell's Chief Wants Every Game to Be as Good as Clash of Clans (Interview Part One)," *VentureBeat* (blog), November 25, 2013, https://venturebeat .com/2013/11/25/supercells-ilkka-paananen-wants-every-game-to-be-as-good-as-clash -of-clans-interview-part-one/.

6. Ilkka Paananen, "BAFTA Games Lecture," BAFTA, September 6, 2016, http:// www.bafta.org/media-centre/transcripts/ilkka-paananen-bafta-games-lecture.

7. Rebecca Burn-Callander, "Supercell Boss Vows Clash of Clans Maker Will Never Consider IPO," *Telegraph* (UK), June 13, 2016, https://www.telegraph.co.uk/business /2016/06/13/supercell-boss-vows-clash-of-clans-maker-will-never-consider-ipo/.

8. Paananen, "BAFTA Games Lecture."

9. Tencent, *2010 Annual Report*, 8.

10. Masashi Isawa, "Nintendo Chases More Than Profit with 'Super Mario Run,'" *Nikkei Asian Review*, March 24, 2017, https://asia.nikkei.com/Business/Companies/ Nintendo-chases-more-than-profit-with-Super-Mario-Run.

11. Mike Schramm, "Kotick: App Store and Facebook Games Not a 'big Opportunity' for Activision," Engadget, December 2, 2010, https://www.engadget.com/2010-12-02 -kotick-says-app-store-and-facebook-games-not-a-big-opportunity.html.

6. Greatly Exaggerated Death of the Console

1. Chris Kohler, "Consolation Prize: The Game Console Is Dead. What Will Replace It?" *Wired*, October 26, 2012, https://www.wired.com/2012/10/consolation-prize/.

2. Blake Snow, "Why Console Gaming Is Dying," CNN Business, updated November 9, 2012, accessed November 8, 2019, https://www.cnn.com/2012/11/09/tech /gaming-gadgets/console-gaming-dead/index.html.

3. Collin Campbell, "Are Consoles Dead?" IGN, March 15, 2012, https://www.ign.com /articles/2012/03/15/are-consoles-dead.

4. Benjamin Cousins, "When the Consoles Die—What Comes Next?" GDCVault, accessed April 25, 2019, https://www.gdcvault.com/play/1015679/When-the-Consoles -Die-What.

5. William Usher, "Epic Games' President: What's the Point of Next-Gen Consoles?" CINEMABLEND, August 5, 2011, https://www.cinemablend.com/games/Epic-Games -President-What-Point-Next-Gen-Consoles-34080.html.

6. Brier Dudley, "TechNW: Best and Worst of Times for Games, Valve vs. Apple," *Seattle Times*, October 11, 2011, http://old.seattletimes.com/html/technologybrierdudleys blog/2016469749_technw_best_and_worst_of_times.html.

7. Michael French, "Consoles Set for Extinction Claims Square Enix's Wada," *MCV*, November 27, 2009, 3.

8. Clayton Christensen, *The Innovator's Dilemma: The Revolutionary Book That Will Change the Way You Do Business* (New York: HarperBusiness, 2010).

9. Ben Aslinger, "Video Games for the 'Next Billion': The Launch of the Zeebo Console," *Velvet Light Trap* 66, no. 1 (September 1, 2010), 16, https://doi.org/10.5555/vlt.2010.66.15.

10. See also Joost Rietveld and J. P. Eggers, "Demand Heterogeneity and the Adoption of Platform Complements" (ERIM Report Series Research, Management Erasmus Research Institute of Management, Rotterdam, Netherlands, January 12, 2016), https:// repub.eur.nl/pub/79494/. In their study of 2,921 sixth-generation console video games, the researchers conclude, among other things, that "platform maturity has a negative relationship on video games' unit sales" (2).

11. Chris Morris, "Wargaming: The Biggest Game Publisher You've Never Heard Of," CNBC, June 12, 2013, https://www.cnbc.com/id/100807652.

7. Glorious Return of PC Gaming

1. Timothy Lenoir, "All But War Is Simulation: The Military-Entertainment Complex," *Configurations* 8, no. 3 (2000): 289–335, https://doi.org/10.1353/con.2000.0022.

2. Claire Suddath, "Why There Are No Bosses at Valve," Bloomberg, April 27, 2012, https://www.bloomberg.com/news/articles/2012-04-27/why-there-are-no-bosses-at-valve.

3. TheLBJSchool, "Gabe Newell: Reflections of a Video Game Maker," January 31, 2013, video, 1:02:52 https://www.youtube.com/watch?v=t8QEOBgLBQU.

4. TheLBJSchool, "Gabe Newell: Reflections."

5. Sharon Baker, "A Charmed Half-Life," *Puget Sound Business Journal* (Seattle), February 19, 2003, https://web.archive.org/web/20030219095208/https://www.bizjournals.com/seattle/stories/1999/03/01/smallb1.html.

6. TheLBJSchool, "Gabe Newell: Reflections."

7. Dejoblue, "Rob Pardo Blizzard Game Design Lecture MIT 2014," August 15, 2015, video, 26:22, https://www.youtube.com/watch?v=jVzgWmNJIY4.

8. Dan Gallagher, "Activision Bets Big on PC Game," Business, *Wall Street Journal*, July 16, 2010, https://www.wsj.com/articles/SB10001424052748704682604575369093457494042.

9. Note that the cadence of iterations can vary widely and are expensive to produce. A creative firm needs to adapt to the pace of consumption among its user base and ensure that it produces new content at a rate that is in line with consumption by its player base. For a broader discussion on free-to-play economics, please see, for instance, Will Luton, *Free-to-Play: Making Money from Games You Give Away* (San Francisco, CA: New Riders, 2013).

10. Suzie Ford, "Budget Set at $50 Million Plus," MMORPG.com, August 31, 2010, https://www.mmorpg.com/rift/news/budget-set-at-50-million-plus-1000017950.

11. National Public Radio, "Sony Explains Why Its PlayStation 4 Costs $1,845 in Brazil," NPR.org, accessed July 23, 2019, https://www.npr.org/sections/thetwo-way/2013/10/22/239860325/sony-explains-why-its-playstation-4-costs-1-845-in-brazil.

12. Ryan Flemming, "Wargaming's CEO Explains Free-to-Play, and Discusses the Death of the Retail Model," Digital Trends, June 9, 2013, https://www.digitaltrends.com/gaming/wargamings-ceo-free-to-play-and-discusses-the-death-of-the-retail-model/.

13. Oh Gyuhwan and Ryu Taiyoung, "Game Design on Item-Selling Based Payment Model in Korean Online Games," vol. 4, *Proceedings of the 2007 DiGRA International Conference: Situated Play* (Tokyo, Japan: Digital Games Research Association, University of Tokyo, September 2007).

14. Min Kim, "Going from Free to Pay in Free-to-Play," presented at the GDC Austin/Online 2008, GDCVault, accessed September 27, 2019, https://www.gdcvault.com/play/1011914/Going-from-Free-to-Pay.

244 8. EPIC QUEST FOR INTELLECTUAL PROPERTY

8. Epic Quest for Intellectual Property

1. Nicole LaPorte, *The Men Who Would Be King: An Almost Epic Tale of Moguls, Movies, and a Company Called DreamWorks* (Boston: Houghton Mifflin Harcourt, 2010).

2. Certainly, other types of IP in the games industry play a role in the risk mitigation and strategic decision-making among creatives. For instance, the different technologies and software that companies develop enable creatives to make games. Examples include physics engines as developed by Unity and Epic Games. Similarly, unique game mechanics or other components related to playing that go beyond mere art style or narrative are a third category. Examples are *Fortnite*, for example, which features a building mechanic in a third-person shooter game. This existed previously, of course, but *Fortnite* offers a unique mix of trying to outmaneuver opponents while building structures to gain an advantage. Similarly, *Max Payne* features "bullet time" that allows the player to slow down time during key moments in the game and more accurately shoot antagonists.

3. John Gaudiosi, "Madden: The $4 Billion Video Game Franchise," CNNMoney, September 5, 2013, https://money.cnn.com/2013/09/05/technology/innovation/madden-25/index.html.

4. Chris Trimble, "Hasbro Interactive" (Case Study, Tuck School of Business at Dartmouth, Hanover, NH, March 22, 2004), http://mba.tuck.dartmouth.edu/pages/faculty/chris.trimble/research/Case_Downloads/Hasbro.pdf.

5. Xavier Lecocq and Benoît Demil, "Strategizing Industry Structure: The Case of Open Systems in a Low-Tech Industry," *Strategic Management Journal* 27, no. 9 (2006): 891–98, https://doi.org/10.1002/smj.544.

6. Natalie Robehmed, "Kim Kardashian West, Mobile Mogul: The Forbes Cover Story," *Forbes*, July 11, 2016, https://www.forbes.com/sites/natalierobehmed/2016/07/11/kim-kardashian-mobile-mogul-the-forbes-cover-story/#6f99d2627e4f.

7. SuperData Research. Between its launch in June 2015 and May 2019, *Kim Kardashian: Hollywood* generated $264 million in total revenue across PC and mobile. Approximately $240 million came from mobile players.

8. Perhaps the most prominent scholar investigating how games can incorporate particular ideas is Ian Bogost, an associate professor at Georgia Institute for Technology and experimental game designer. In "Playing Politics: Videogames for Politics, Activism, and Advocacy," Bogost argues that games are effective at representing complex systems and games and simulation can help understand the potential long-term implications of certain political decisions. One example by Bogost, *September 12th* (2002), positions the player overlooking a Middle Eastern cityscape where among a group of civilians there also are a few terrorists. Shooting and killing the terrorists, however, destroys buildings directly surrounding them as well as killing innocent bystanders. After the dust settles, surviving civilians first mourn and subsequently morph into terrorists, and so on. The point of this type of game is its "procedural logic," which Bogost defines as "the way that a videogame embodies ideology in its computational structure. . . . Games become rhetorical opinion texts that players can explore rather than merely read or view." Ian Bogost, *Persuasive Games: The Expressive Power of Videogames* (Cambridge, MA: MIT

Press, 2010), 12; "Playing Politics: Videogames for Politics, Activism, and Advocacy," *First Monday*, 2006, https://doi.org/10.5210/fm.v0i0.1617.

9. Eli M. Noam, *Media Ownership and Concentration in America* (Oxford: Oxford University Press, 2009).

9. Watching Other People Play Video Games, and Why

1. "Gaming Video Content and the New Essential Audience" (market research report, SuperData Research, 2017), https://www.superdataresearch.com/market-data/gaming-video-content/.

2. "Gaming Video Content and the New Essential Audience."

3. "Gaming Video Content and the New Essential Audience."

4. For centuries, games have served a vital role in socialization and education. A technologically mediated manifestation like video games is no different. Consider, for example, the classic work by anthropologist Clifford Geertz, "Deep Play: Notes on the Balinese Cockfight," *Daedalus* 101, no. 1 (1972): 1–37.

5. Jon Robinson, " 'League of Legends,' ESports Growing," ESPN.com, August 8, 2012, http://www.espn.com/blog/playbook/tech/post/_/id/1541.

6. You will recall that one of Nintendo's key strategic components in reviving the industry in the late 1980s was to provide consumers with a review magazine to make purchases more transparent. Also see chapter 6 on GameStop's dominance in this category with its *Game Informer* magazine.

7. David B. Nieborg and Tanja Sihvonen, "The New Gatekeepers: The Occupational Ideology of Game Journalism," in *Breaking New Ground: Innovation in Games, Play, Practice and Theory* (Tokyo, Japan: Digital Games Research Association, 2009), 9; also see David B. Nieborg, Chris J. Young, and Daniel J. Joseph, "Lost in the App Store: The State of the Canadian Game App Economy," *Canadian Journal of Communication* 44, no. 2 (2019), https://doi.org/10.22230/cjc.2019v44n2a3505.

8. "Gaming Video Content and the New Essential Audience."

9. Arjun Panchadar, "Top Gamer 'Ninja' Made $1 Million to Promote EA's 'Apex Legends' . . . ," Reuters, March 14, 2019, https://www.reuters.com/article/us-electronic-arts-apexlegends-idUSKBN1QU2AC.

10. "How Has the Rise of YouTubers Affected How You Make Games?," Gamasutra, June 20, 2014, https://www.gamasutra.com/view/news/219367/How_has_the_rise_of_YouTubers_affected_how_you_make_games.php.

11. Ryan Rigney, "Want to Sell Your Game? Don't Tick Off YouTubers," *Wired*, October 21, 2013, https://www.wired.com/2013/10/stanley-parable-sales/.

12. Julia Alexander, "YouTubers Are Calling out Nintendo for Its Policy on Streaming, Uploads," Polygon, November 6, 2017, https://www.polygon.com/2017/11/6/16612080/youtube-nintendo-super-mario-odyssey-demonetization.

13. "A Note on Persona 5 and Streaming," *Atlus USA* (blog), April 4, 2017, https://atlus.com/note-persona-5-streaming/.

14. Tamoor Hussain, "How Much Money Did PewDiePie Earn in 2014?," *GameSpot* (blog), July 6, 2015, https://www.gamespot.com/articles/how-much-money-did-pewdiepie -earn-in-2014/1100-6428640/.

15. "Gaming Video Content and the New Essential Audience."

16. In their reliance on ad revenue, live-streaming and digital video-on-demand have adopted metrics from the terrestrial television business that values channels and stations based on the cost per thousand (CPM).

17. U.S. Federal Trade Commission, "Warner Bros. Settles FTC Charges It Failed to Adequately Disclose It Paid Online Influencers to Post Gameplay Videos," press release, July 11, 2016, https://www.ftc.gov/news-events/press-releases/2016/07/warner-bros -settles-ftc-charges-it-failed-adequately-disclose-it.

18. Nathan Grayson, "The Messy Story Behind YouTubers Taking Money for Game Coverage," Kotaku, October 8, 2014, https://kotaku.com/the-messy-story-behind -youtubers-taking-money-for-game-1644092214.

19. Dom Sacco, "Germany Labels Twitch a 'Radio Service', Tells Streamers They Now Require a Broadcasting License," Esports News UK, March 27, 2017, https:// esports-news.co.uk/2017/03/27/german-streamers-require-license/.

20. Tess Townsend, "YouTube Creators Have Complained about Declines in Ad Revenue," Recode, March 30, 2017, https://www.recode.net/2017/3/30/15128654 /youtube-creators-revenue-drop-brand-safety-controversy.

21. Paul Tassi, "The U.S. Now Recognizes ESports Players As Professional Athletes," *Forbes*, July 14, 2013, accessed August 14, 2019, https://www.forbes.com/sites/insertcoin /2013/07/14/the-u-s-now-recognizes-esports-players-as-professional-athletes/.

22. Dawn Chmielewski, "Sorry, Twitch: ESPN's Skipper Says ESports 'Not a Sport,'" Vox, September 4, 2014, https://www.vox.com/2014/9/4/11630572/sorry-twitch-espns -skipper-says-esports-not-a-sport.

23. Jin Dal Yong, *Korea's Online Gaming Empire* (Cambridge, MA: MIT Press, 2010), https://mitpress.mit.edu/books/koreas-online-gaming-empire.

24. Mark Rosewater, "Need I Say Morph," *Magic: The Gathering* (blog), accessed August 14, 2019, https://magic.wizards.com/en/articles/archive/making-magic/need-i-say -morph-2019-08-05.

25. Juho Hamari, and Max Sjöblom, "What Is ESports and Why Do People Watch It?," Internet Research, April 3, 2017, 1, https://doi.org/10.1108/IntR-04-2016-0085.

26. According to Hamari and Sjöblom, "What Is Esports and Why Do People Watch It?," "In the context of gymnastics it has been shown that an appreciation of the aesthetic aspects of the sport positively impact viewing" (Sargent et al. 1998).

27. Blizzard Entertainment, "Player Signings, Salaries, and More in the Over-watch League™," Overwatch League, July 28, 2017, accessed May 11, 2019, https:// overwatchleague.com/en-us/news/20937016/player-signings-salaries-and-more-in -the-overwatch-league.

28. Despite its popularity, a title like *League of Legends* has long ignored the need for professional players to rest during an off-season period.

29. "Rick Fox Says He'd Stay with Echo Fox if Racist Investor Leaves," TMZ, accessed June 18, 2019, https://www.tmz.com/2019/05/03/rick-fox-eacho-fox-esports-racist-investor/.

30. Dave Thier, "Tfue Is Suing Faze Clan in an Explosive Lawsuit That's Rocking the Esports World," *Forbes*, May 21, 2019, accessed June 18, 2019, https://www.forbes.com/sites/davidthier/2019/05/21/tfue-is-suing-faze-clan-in-an-explosive-lawsuit-thats-rocking-the-esports-world/.

31. ESPN.com, "Overwatch League Commissioner Nanzer to Join Epic Games," ESPN, May 24, 2019, https://www.espn.com/esports/story/_/id/26815521.

32. Cecilia D'Anastasio, "Shady Numbers and Bad Business: Inside the Esports Bubble," Kotaku, accessed June 18, 2019, https://kotaku.com/as-esports-grows-experts-fear-its-a-bubble-ready-to-po-1834982843.

33. Thomas Wilde, "Live-Streaming Traffic Spikes amid Social Distancing as Streamers Offer Community and Conversation," GeekWire, March 19, 2020, https://www.geekwire.com/2020/live-streaming-traffic-spikes-amid-social-distancing-streamers-offer-community-conversation/.

10. Next-Gen Revenue Models

1. Jonathan Knee, Bruce Greenwald, and Ava Seave, *The Curse of the Mogul: What's Wrong with the World's Leading Media Companies* (New York: Portfolio, 2009), 196.

2. Curt Feldman, "Q&A: Massive Inc. CEO Mitch Davis," *GameSpot* (blog), April 11, 2005, https://www.gamespot.com/articles/qanda-massive-inc-ceo-mitch-davis/1100-6122049/.

3. Between the sixth and seventh hardware generations, the average selling price of a physical video game in the United States jumped from $31 to $39 (weighted average).

4. Randy Nichols, *The Video Game Business*, International Screen Industries series (British Film Institute, 2014).

5. "Microsoft Acquires Massive, Inc.," Stanford University, Case Wiki 2007-353-1, updated May 29, 2007, 8, https://web.stanford.edu/class/ee204/Publications/Massive-Microsoft%20EE353%20CasePublisher%202007-registered.pdf.

6. Ryan Mac, " 'Pokémon GO's Creator Answers All Your Burning Questions (Except That One About Finding Pokémon)," *Forbes*, July 28, 2016, https://www.forbes.com/sites/ryanmac/2016/07/28/pokemon-go-creator-john-hanke-answers-all-your-burning-questions/.

7. Brandy Shaul, "King.Com Dumps Advertising on Its Games," AdWeek, June 11, 2013, https://www.adweek.com/digital/king-com-dumps-advertising-on-its-games/.

8. Jon Russell, "Tencent Shakeup Puts the Focus on Enterprise," *TechCrunch* (blog), October 2, 2018, https://social.techcrunch.com/2018/10/02/tencent-reorg-enterprise/.

9. Tom Hancock, "China 5G Rollout to Boost Cloud Gaming," *Financial Times*, November 4, 2019, https://www.ft.com/content/4a4cd344-fa2f-11e9-a354-36acbbb0d9b6.

10. "Activision Puts In-Game Ads On 'Easy Mode,' Stringer Says—Beet.TV," Beet.TV, October 8, 2019, https://www.beet.tv/2019/10/activision-puts-in-game-ads-on-easy-mode-stringfield-says.html.

11. Active Xbox Live users here are defined as "people who have used the service over the last month." Rebecca Smith, "Xbox Live Has 57 Million Active Users, Gaming Business Is Growing," TrueAchievements, accessed August 23, 2019, https://www

.trueachievements.com/n33654/xbox-live-has-57-million-active-users-gaming
-business-is-growing.

12. In the wake of a scandal around loot boxes, several governments investigated and announced policy changes. One of the main concerns regarding loot boxes centers on this monetization strategy serving as a steppingstone to problem gambling. Consequently, several content creators and platform holders changed their strategy to avoid legal issues. See Wen Li, Devin Mills, and Lia Nower, "The Relationship of Loot Box Purchases to Problem Video Gaming and Problem Gambling," *Addictive Behaviors* 97 (October 2019): 27–34, https://doi.org/10.1016/j.addbeh.2019.05.016.

13. Alyson Shontell and Ben Gilbert, "Microsoft CEO Satya Nadella Just Laid out the Company's Vision for Its 'Netflix for Games,'" Business Insider, January 16, 2019, https://www.businessinsider.com/microsoft-ceo-satya-nadella-xbox-netflix-for-games-2019-1.

Conclusion

1. Willem Burger, "Van Der Meer de Delft," *Gazette Des Beaux Arts, Courier Europeen de l'Art et de La Curiosité* 21, no. 121 (October 1, 1866): 297–330. "Later—after 1848, having become, by force, a foreigner, and, by instinct, a cosmopolitan, living in turn in Angelerre, Germany, Belgium, Holland, I was able to study the museums of Europe, collect the traditions, read, in any language, the books on art, and seek to unravel a little the still confused history of the schools of the North, especially of the Dutch school, of Rembrandt and his entourage—and my sphinx van der Meer" (299). Translation by author.

2. "Vermeer Was Brilliant, but He Was Not without Influences," *The Economist*, October 12, 2017, https://www.economist.com/books-and-arts/2017/10/12/vermeer-was-brilliant-but-he-was-not-without-influences.

3. Cecilia Rodriguez, "The Art Show of the Year: Vermeer Masterpieces Together for the First Time at Paris Louvre," *Forbes*, February 24, 2017, accessed July 9, 2019, https://www.forbes.com/sites/ceciliarodriguez/2017/02/24/why-vermeer-masterpieces-at-paris-louvre-are-already-the-show-of-the-year/.

4. David W. Galenson, "Masterpieces and Markets: Why the Most Famous Modern Paintings Are Not by American Artists" (working paper, National Bureau of Economic Research, Cambridge, MA, October 2001), 25, https://doi.org/10.3386/w8549.

5. Galenson, "Masterpieces and Markets," 25.

6. Fabien Accominotti, "Creativity from Interaction: Artistic Movements and the Creativity Careers of Modern Painters," *Poetics* 37, no. 3 (June 1, 2009), 286, https://doi.org/10.1016/j.poetic.2009.03.005.

7. Aphra Kerr, *Global Games: Production, Circulation and Policy in the Networked Era* (London: Routledge, 2017).

Appendix: Empirical Procedure

1. For more information see "Herfindahl–Hirschman Index," U.S. Department of Justice, updated July 31, 2018, https://www.justice.gov/atr/herfindahl-hirschman-index.

BIBLIOGRAPHY

Accominotti, Fabien. "Creativity from Interaction: Artistic Movements and the Creativity Careers of Modern Painters." *Poetics* 37, no. 3 (June 1, 2009): 267–94. https://doi.org/10.1016/j.poetic.2009.03.005.

Activision Publishing, Inc. "*Call of Duty: Black Ops II* Delivers More Than $500 Million in Worldwide Retail Sales in First 24 Hours." Press release, November 16, 2012. https://investor.activision.com/news-releases/news-release-details/call-dutyr-black-ops-ii-delivers-more-500-million-worldwide.

"Activision Puts In-Game Ads On 'Easy Mode,' Stringer Says—Beet.TV." Beet.TV, October 8, 2019. https://www.beet.tv/2019/10/activision-puts-in-game-ads-on-easy-mode-stringfield-says.html.

Ahmad, Norita B., Salahudin Abdul Rahman Barakji, Tarak Mohamed Abou Shahada, and Zeid Ayman Anabtawi. "How to Launch a Successful Video Game: A Framework." *Entertainment Computing* 23 (November 1, 2017): 1–11. https://doi.org/10.1016/j.entcom.2017.08.001.

Alexander, Julia. "YouTubers Are Calling out Nintendo for Its Policy on Streaming, Uploads." Polygon, November 6, 2017. https://www.polygon.com/2017/11/6/16612080/youtube-nintendo-super-mario-odyssey-demonetization.

Alexander, Leigh. " 'Gamers' Don't Have to Be Your Audience. 'Gamers' Are Over." Gamasutra, August 28, 2014. https://www.gamasutra.com/view/news/224400/Gamer.

Alvisi, Alberto, Alessandro Narduzzo, and Marco Zamarian. "Playstation and the Power of Unexpected Consequences." *Information, Communication and Society* 6, no. 4 (December 1, 2003): 608–27. https://doi.org/10.1080/1369118032000163286.

Anand, Bharat. *The Content Trap: A Strategist's Guide to Digital Change*. New York: Random House, 2016.

Anthony, Wen, Devin Mills, and Lia Nower. "The Relationship of Loot Box Purchases to Problem Video Gaming and Problem Gambling." *Addictive Behaviors* 97 (October 2019): 27–34. https://doi.org/10.1016/j.addbeh.2019.05.016.

Aoyama, Yuko, and Hiro Izushi. "Hardware Gimmick or Cultural Innovation? Technological, Cultural, and Social Foundations of the Japanese Video Game Industry." *Research Policy* 32, no. 3 (March 1, 2003): 423–44. https://doi.org/10.1016/S0048-7333(02)00016-1.

Aslinger, Ben. "Video Games for the 'Next Billion': The Launch of the Zeebo Console." *Velvet Light Trap* 66, no. 1 (September 1, 2010): 15–25. https://doi.org/10.5555/vlt.2010.66.15.

Baden-Fuller, Charles, and Stefan Haefliger. "Business Models and Technological Innovation." *Long Range Planning, Managing Business Models for Innovation, Strategic Change and Value Creation* 46, no. 6 (December 1, 2013): 419–26. https://doi.org/10.1016/j.lrp.2013.08.023.

Baker, Sharon. "A Charmed Half-Life." *Puget Sound Business Journal* (Seattle), February 19, 2003. https://web.archive.org/web/20030219095208/https://www.bizjournals.com/seattle/stories/1999/03/01/smallb1.html.

Balland, Pierre-Alexandre, Mathijs De Vaan, and Ron Boschma. "The Dynamics of Interfirm Networks along the Industry Life Cycle: The Case of the Global Video Game Industry, 1987–2007." *Journal of Economic Geography* 13, no. 5 (September 1, 2013): 741–65. https://doi.org/10.1093/jeg/lbs023.

Banerjee, Scott. "EA to Buy Jamdat Mobile for $680M." MarketWatch, December 8, 2005. https://www.marketwatch.com/story/electronic-arts-to-buy-jamdat-mobile-for-680-million.

Blizzard Entertainment. "Player Signings, Salaries, and More in the Overwatch League™." Overwatch League, July 28, 2017. Accessed May 11, 2019. https://overwatchleague.com/en-us/news/20937016/player-signings-salaries-and-more-in-the-overwatch-league.

Bobrowski, Michal, Patrycja Rodzin´ska-Szary, and Socha Mariusz. "The State of the Polish Video Games Sector." Krakow, Poland: Krakow Technology Park, Ministry of Culture and National Heritage of the Republic of Poland, Creative Europe Desk Poland and the Małopolska Province, 2015.

Bogost, Ian. *Persuasive Games: The Expressive Power of Videogames*. Cambridge, MA: MIT Press, 2010.

——. "Playing Politics: Videogames for Politics, Activism, and Advocacy." *First Monday*, 2006. https://doi.org/10.5210/fm.v0i0.1617.

Bossom, Andy, and Ben Dunning. *Video Games: An Introduction to the Industry*. London: Fairchild, 2016.

Browne, Ryan. "Apple 'One of the Biggest Gaming Companies in the World,' Analyst Says," CNBC, June 5, 2018. https://www.cnbc.com/2018/06/05/apple-one-of-the-biggest-gaming-companies-in-the-world-analyst-says.html.

Bruno, Giovanni. "GameStop CEO Raines Talks Pokémon and Virtual Reality on CNBC." TheStreet, July 18, 2016. https://www.thestreet.com/story/13642777/1/gamestop-gme-ceo-raines-talks-pok-eacute-mon-and-virtual-reality-on-cnbc.html.

Brustein, Joshua. "Walmart's Used Video Game Business Won't Kill GameStop." Bloomberg, October 28, 2014. https://www.bloomberg.com/news/articles/2014-10-28/walmarts-used-game-business-wont-kill-gamestop.

Burn-Callander, Rebecca. "Supercell Boss Vows Clash of Clans Maker Will Never Consider IPO." Telegraph (UK), June 13, 2016. https://www.telegraph.co.uk/business/2016/06/13/supercell-boss-vows-clash-of-clans-maker-will-never-consider-ipo/.

Cabras, Ignazio, Nikolaos D. Goumagias, Kiran Fernandes, Peter Cowling, Feng Li, Daniel Kudenko, Sam Devlin, and Alberto Nucciarelli. "Exploring Survival Rates of Companies in the UK Video-Games Industry: An Empirical Study." Technological Forecasting and Social Change 117 (April 1, 2017): 305–14. https://doi.org/10.1016/j.techfore.2016.10.073.

Campbell, Collin. "Are Consoles Dead?" IGN, March 15, 2012. https://www.ign.com/articles/2012/03/15/are-consoles-dead.

Cheshire, Tom. "In Depth: How Rovio Made Angry Birds a Winner (and What's Next)." Wired (UK), March 7, 2011. https://www.wired.co.uk/article/how-rovio-made-angry-birds-a-winner.

Chmielewski, Dawn. "Sorry, Twitch: ESPN's Skipper Says ESports 'Not a Sport.' " Vox, September 4, 2014. https://www.vox.com/2014/9/4/11630572/sorry-twitch-espns-skipper-says-esports-not-a-sport.

Christensen, Clayton. The Innovator's Dilemma: The Revolutionary Book That Will Change the Way You Do Business. New York: HarperBusiness, 2010.

Cohendet, Patrick, David Grandadam, Chahira Mehouachi, and Laurent Simon. "The Local, the Global and the Industry Common: The Case of the Video Game Industry." Journal of Economic Geography 18, no. 5 (September 1, 2018): 1045–68. https://doi.org/10.1093/jeg/lby040.

Cousins, Benjamin. "When the Consoles Die—What Comes Next?" GDCVault. Accessed April 25, 2019. https://www.gdcvault.com/play/1015679/When-the-Consoles-Die-What.

Dal Yong, Jin. Korea's Online Gaming Empire. Cambridge, MA: MIT Press, 2010. https://mitpress.mit.edu/books/koreas-online-gaming-empire.

D'Anastasio, Cecilia. "Shady Numbers and Bad Business: Inside the Esports Bubble." Kotaku. Accessed June 18, 2019. https://kotaku.com/as-esports-grows-experts-fear-its-a-bubble-ready-to-po-1834982843.

Dejoblue. "Rob Pardo Blizzard Game Design Lecture MIT 2014." August 15, 2015. Video, 26:22. https://www.youtube.com/watch?v=jVzgWmNJIY4.

De Vaan, Mathijs, Ron Boschma, and Koen Frenken. "Clustering and Firm Performance in Project-Based Industries: The Case of the Global Video Game Industry, 1972–2007." Journal of Economic Geography 13, no. 6 (November 1, 2013): 965–91. https://doi.org/10.1093/jeg/lbs038.

Dewey, John. Art as Experience. New York: TarcherPerigee, 2005.

Donovan, Tristan. *Replay: The History of Video Games*. East Sussex, UK: Yellow Ant, 2010.

"DOOM's Development: A Year of Madness." Accessed September 10, 2019. Video, 44:12. https://www.youtube.com/watch?v=eBU34NZhW7I&t=610s.

Dredge, Stuart. "EA Financials: 76 percent of Revenues Digital, and Apple Its Biggest Retail Partner." Technology, *Guardian*, July 25, 2013. https://www.theguardian.com/technology/appsblog/2013/jul/25/ea-digital-revenues-mobile-apple.

Dudley, Brier. "TechNW: Best and Worst of Times for Games, Valve vs. Apple." *Seattle Times*, October 11, 2011. http://old.seattletimes.com/html/technologybrierdudleysblog/2016469749_technw_best_and_worst_of_times.html.

Dyer-Witheford, Nick, and Greig de Peuter. *Games of Empire: Global Capitalism and Video Games*. Minneapolis: University of Minnesota Press, 2013.

Elberse, Anita, and Renée Raudman. *Blockbusters: Hit-Making, Risk-Taking, and the Big Business of Entertainment*. Unabridged. Grand Haven, MI: Brilliance Audio, 2014.

"Ericsson Mobility Report 2018." Ericsson.com, November 20, 2018.

Feldman, Curt. "Q&A: Massive Inc. CEO Mitch Davis." *GameSpot* (blog). April 11, 2005. https://www.gamespot.com/articles/qanda-massive-inc-ceo-mitch-davis/1100-6122049/.

Fleming, Jeffrey. "The History of Activision." Gamasutra, July 30, 2007. http://www.gamasutra.com/view/feature/129961/the_history_of_activision.php.

Flemming, Ryan. "Wargaming's CEO Explains Free-to-Play, and Discusses the Death of the Retail Model." Digital Trends, June 9, 2013. https://www.digitaltrends.com/gaming/wargamings-ceo-free-to-play-and-discusses-the-death-of-the-retail-model/.

Fogel, Stefanie. "China Introduces New Game Approval Process This Month." *Variety*, April 22, 2019. https://variety.com/2019/gaming/news/china-game-approvals-1203194653/.

Ford, Suzie. "Budget Set at $50 Million Plus." MMORPG.com, August 31, 2010. https://www.mmorpg.com/rift/news/budget-set-at-50-million-plus-1000017950.

Forster, Winnie. "Game Machines 1972–2012." In *The Encyclopedia of Consoles, Handhelds and Home Computers*, edited by Heinrich Lenhardt and Nadine Caplette. 2nd edition. Utting, Germany: Enati Media, 2011.

Futter, Michael, and Mike Bithell. *The GameDev Business Handbook*. London: Bithell, 2018.

Galenson, David W. "A Portrait of the Artist as a Very Young or Very Old Innovator: Creativity at the Extremes of the Life Cycle." Working Paper, National Bureau of Economic Research, Cambridge, MA, May 2004. https://doi.org/10.3386/w10515.

——. "Analyzing Artistic Innovation: The Greatest Breakthroughs of the Twentieth Century." Working Paper, National Bureau of Economic Research, Cambridge, MA, May 2006. https://doi.org/10.3386/w12185.

——. "Masterpieces and Markets: Why the Most Famous Modern Paintings Are Not by American Artists." Working Paper, National Bureau of Economic Research, Cambridge, MA, October 2001. https://doi.org/10.3386/w8549.

Gallagher, Dan. "Activision Bets Big on PC Game." Business, *Wall Street Journal*, July 16, 2010. https://www.wsj.com/articles/SB10001424052748704682604575369093457494042.

GameStop Corporation. "GameStop Acquires 507 AT&T Mobility Stores." GlobeNewswire News Room, August 2, 2016. http://www.globenewswire.com/news-release
/2016/08/02/960824/0/en/GameStop-Acquires-507-AT-T-Mobility-Stores.html.

GameStop Staff. "Star Wars Battlefront 2's Loot Box Controversy Explained." *GameSpot*
(blog), 20:37:53 UTC. https://www.gamespot.com/articles/star-wars-battlefront-2s
-loot-box-controversy-expl/1100-6455155/.

"Gaming Video Content and the New Essential Audience." Market research report. Super-
Data Research, 2017. https://www.superdataresearch.com/market-data/gaming
-video-content/.

Garfield, Richard. "A game player's manifesto." Facebook, September 20, 2016. https://www
.facebook.com/notes/richard-garfield/a-game-players-manifesto/1049168888532667.

Gaudiosi, John. "Cloud Gaming Prospects for 2012." Cloud Gaming USA Conference &
Exhibition, San Francisco. FC Business Intelligence, September 11, 2011.

———. "Madden: The $4 Billion Video Game Franchise." CNNMoney, September 5, 2013.
https://money.cnn.com/2013/09/05/technology/innovation/madden-25/index.html.

Geertz, Clifford. "Deep Play: Notes on the Balinese Cockfight." *Daedalus* 101, no. 1
(1972): 1–37.

Grayson, Nathan. "The Messy Story Behind YouTubers Taking Money for Game Coverage."
Kotaku, October 8, 2014. https://kotaku.com/the-messy-story-behind-youtubers
-taking-money-for-game-1644092214.

Gyuhwan, Oh, and Ryu Taiyoung. "Game Design on Item-Selling Based Payment Model
in Korean Online Games." Vol. 4. *Proceedings of the 2007 DiGRA Conference*,
Tokyo, Japan: Digital Games Research Association, University of Tokyo, September 2007: 650–57

Hamari, Juho, and Max Sjöblom. "What Is ESports and Why Do People Watch It?"
Internet Research, April 3, 2017. https://doi.org/10.1108/IntR-04-2016–0085.

Hancock, Tom. "China 5G Rollout to Boost Cloud Gaming." *Financial Times*, November
4, 2019. https://www.ft.com/content/4a4cd344-fa2f-11e9-a354-36acbbb0d9b6.

Hansen, Dustin. *Game On! Video Game History from Pong and Pac-Man to Mario,
Minecraft, and More.* Reprint edition. 2016; New York: Square Fish, 2019.

Harris, Blake J. *Console Wars: Sega, Nintendo, and the Battle That Defined a Generation.*
New York: It Books, 2014.

Hirsch, Paul Morris. *The Structure of the Popular Music Industry: The Filtering Process
by Which Records Are Preselected for Public Consumption.* Ann Arbor: Institute for
Social Research, University of Michigan, 1969.

Horowitz, Ken. "Interview: Trip Hawkins (Founder of Electronic Arts)." Sega-16, August
18, 2006. http://www.sega-16.com/2006/08/interview-trip-hawkins/.

"How Has the Rise of YouTubers Affected How You Make Games?" Gamasutra,
June 20, 2014. https://www.gamasutra.com/view/news/219367/How_has_the_rise
_of_YouTubers_affected_how_you_make_games.php.

Hussain, Tamoor. "How Much Money Did PewDiePie Earn in 2014?" *GameSpot* (blog),
July 6, 2015. https://www.gamespot.com/articles/how-much-money-did-pewdiepie
-earn-in-2014/1100-6428640/.

Isawa, Masashi. "Nintendo Chases More Than Profit with 'Super Mario Run.' " *Nikkei Asian Review*, March 24, 2017. https://asia.nikkei.com/Business/Companies /Nintendo-chases-more-than-profit-with-Super-Mario-Run.

Izushi, Hiro, and Yuko Aoyama. "Industry Evolution and Cross-Sectoral Skill Transfers: A Comparative Analysis of the Video Game Industry in Japan, the United States, and the United Kingdom." *Environment and Planning* A 38 (October 1, 2006): 1843–61. https://doi.org/10.1068/a37205.

Jin, Dal Yong, and Florence Chee. "Age of New Media Empires: A Critical Interpretation of the Korean Online Game Industry." *Games and Culture* 3, no. 1 (January 1, 2008): 38–58. https://doi.org/10.1177/1555412007309528.

Jobs, Steve (stevejobsays). "Steve Jobs on Portable Gaming." October 9, 2010. Video, 1:01. https://www.youtube.com/watch?v=klXGAyqVTWA.

Johns, Jennifer. "Video Games Production Networks: Value Capture, Power Relations and Embeddedness." *Journal of Economic Geography* 6, no. 2 (April 1, 2006): 151–80. https://doi.org/10.1093/jeg/lbi001.

Juul, Jesper. *A Casual Revolution: Reinventing Video Games and Their Players*. Cambridge, MA: MIT Press, 2012.

Kerr, Aphra. *Global Games: Production, Circulation and Policy in the Networked Era*. London: Routledge, 2017.

——. "Aphra Kerr Lecture." April 12, 2011. Accessed December 4, 2019. Video, 56:39. https://www.youtube.com/watch?v=11clbjdwy8U.

Kim, Ryan, and Chronicle Staff Writer. "Game Designers Focus on Girls." SFGate, October 6, 2008. https://www.sfgate.com/technology/article/Game-designers-focus-on -girls-3266775.php.

Knee, Jonathan, Bruce Greenwald, and Ava Seave. *The Curse of the Mogul: What's Wrong with the World's Leading Media Companies*. New York: Portfolio, 2009.

Kocurek, Carly A. *Coin-Operated Americans*. Minneapolis: University of Minnesota Press, 2015.

Kohler, Chris. "Consolation Prize: The Game Console Is Dead. What Will Replace It?" *Wired*, October 26, 2012. https://www.wired.com/2012/10/consolation-prize/.

Korlicki, Kevin. "Japan's Video Game Visionary: The Console Is Dying." Reuters, April 7, 2010. https://www.reuters.com/article/us-japan-kojima-idUSTRE6362GF20100407.

Koster, Ralph. "Industry Lifecycles." Presented at the Casual Connect USA 2018, San Francisco, CA, February 5, 2018. Video, 30:00. https://www.youtube.com/watch?time _continue=271&v=LRSakzs-d-I.

Krueger, Alan. *Rockonomics: A Backstage Tour of What the Music Industry Can Teach Us About Economics and Life*. New York: Currency, 2019.

Kushner, David. *Jacked: The Outlaw Story of Grand Theft Auto*. Hoboken, NJ: Turner, 2012.

——. *Masters of Doom: How Two Guys Created an Empire and Transformed Pop Culture*. Reprint edition. 2003. New York: Random House, 2004.

LaPorte, Nicole. *The Men Who Would Be King: An Almost Epic Tale of Moguls, Movies, and a Company Called DreamWorks*. Boston: Houghton Mifflin Harcourt, 2010.

Lecocq, Xavier, and Benoît Demil. "Strategizing Industry Structure: The Case of Open Systems in a Low-Tech Industry." *Strategic Management Journal* 27, no. 9 (2006): 891–98. https://doi.org/10.1002/smj.544.

Lenoir, Timothy. "All But War Is Simulation: The Military-Entertainment Complex." *Configurations* 8, no. 3 (2000): 289–335. https://doi.org/10.1353/con.2000.0022.

Liboriussen, Bjarke, and Paul Martin. "Special Issue: Games and Gaming in China." *Games and Culture* 11, no. 3 (May 1, 2016): 227–32. https://doi.org/10.1177/1555412015615296.

Luton, Will. *Free-to-Play: Making Money from Games You Give Away.* San Francisco, CA: New Riders, 2013.

Mac, Ryan. " 'Pokémon GO's' Creator Answers All Your Burning Questions (Except That One About Finding Pokémon)." *Forbes*, July 28, 2016. https://www.forbes.com/sites/ryanmac/2016/07/28/pokemon-go-creator-john-hanke-answers-all-your-burning-questions/.

Macey, Joseph, and Juho Hamari. "Investigating Relationships between Video Gaming, Spectating Esports, and Gambling." *Computers in Human Behavior* 80 (March 1, 2018): 344–53. https://doi.org/10.1016/j.chb.2017.11.027.

Mack, Christopher. "Mature Korean Gaming Companies Still Seeing Revenue Growth." AdWeek, September 4, 2009. https://www.adweek.com/digital/mature-korean-gaming-companies-still-seeing-revenue-growth/.

"The Making of Fez, the Breaking of Phil Fish." *Indie Games Plus* (blog), December 13, 2011. https://indiegamesplus.com/2011/12/the_making_of_fez_the_breaking.

Makuch, Eddie. "Here's Why Valve Won't Put Ads on Steam." *GameSpot* (blog), October 15, 2015. https://www.gamespot.com/articles/heres-why-valve-wont-put-ads-on-steam/1100-6431454/.

——. "Most Free-to-Play Games Are Not Very Good, GTA Boss Says." *GameSpot* (blog), December 3, 2014. https://www.gamespot.com/articles/most-free-to-play-games-are-not-very-good-gta-boss/1100-6423960/.

"Market Brief—2018 Digital Games & Interactive Entertainment Industry Year In Review." SuperData Research, January 2019.

Maynard-Koran, Peyton. "Fixing the Internet for Real Time Applications: Part II." Riot Games, February 11, 2016. https://engineering.riotgames.com/news/fixing-internet-real-time-applications-part-ii.

McCort, Katie. "Analyzing the American Video Game Industry 2016: Statistics on Geographic Volume, Employment, and Growth." February 2017. https://docplayer.net/49619853-Analyzing-the-american-video-game-industry-2016.html.

"Microsoft Acquires Massive, Inc." Stanford University. Case Wiki, 2007-353-1. Updated May 29, 2007. https://web.stanford.edu/class/ee204/Publications/Massive-Microsoft%20EE353%20CasePublisher%202007-registered.pdf.

Min, Kim. "Going from Free to Pay in Free-to-Play." Presented at the GDC Austin /Online 2008. GDC Vault. Accessed September 27, 2019. https://www.gdcvault.com/play/1011914/Going-from-Free-to-Pay.

Montfort, Nick, and Ian Bogost. *Racing the Beam: The Atari Video Computer System.* 2nd edition. Cambridge, MA: MIT Press, 2009.

"Monument Valley in Numbers." *ustwo games* (blog), September 18, 2015. https://medium
.com/@ustwogames/monument-valley-in-numbers-c945b8658261.

Morris, Chris. "Wargaming: The Biggest Game Publisher You've Never Heard Of."
CNBC, June 12, 2013. https://www.cnbc.com/id/100807652.

National Public Radio. "Sony Explains Why Its PlayStation 4 Costs $1,845 in Brazil."
NPR.org. Accessed July 23, 2019. https://www.npr.org/sections/thetwo-way/2013
/10/22/239860325/sony-explains-why-its-playstation-4-costs-1-845-in-brazil.

Needleman, Sarah E. "The Man Behind 'Fortnite.' " Technology, *Wall Street Journal*,
June 15, 2019. https://www.wsj.com/articles/the-man-behind-fortnite-11560571201.

Newman, Michael Z. *Atari Age: The Emergence of Video Games in America*. Cambridge,
MA: MIT Press, 2017.

"New Super Mario Bros. Wii: The Reason Mario Wears Overalls." Iwata Asks, Nintendo. Accessed September 21, 2019. http://iwataasks.nintendo.com/interviews
/#/wii/nsmb/0/1.

Nichols, Randy. *The Video Game Business*. International Screen Industries Series.
London: British Film Institute, 2014.

Nieborg, David B, and Tanja Sihvonen. "The New Gatekeepers: The Occupational
Ideology of Game Journalism." In *Breaking New Ground: Innovation in Games,
Play, Practice and Theory*, 9. Tokyo, Japan: Digital Games Research Association,
University of Tokyo, 2009. http://www.digra.org/digital-library/publications/the
-new-gatekeepers-the-occupational-ideology-of-game-journalism/.

Nieborg, David B., Chris J. Young, and Daniel J. Joseph. "Lost in the App Store: The
State of the Canadian Game App Economy." *Canadian Journal of Communication*
44, no. 2 (2019). https://doi.org/10.22230/cjc.2019v44n2a3505.

Noam, Eli M. *Media Ownership and Concentration in America*. Oxford: Oxford University Press, 2009.

"A Note on Persona 5 and Streaming." *Atlus USA* (blog), April 4, 2017. https://atlus.com
/note-persona-5-streaming/.

O'Donnell, Casey. *Developer's Dilemma: The Secret World of Videogame Creators*.
Cambridge, MA: MIT Press, 2014.

"Overwatch League Commissioner Nanzer to Join Epic Games." ESPN, May 24, 2019.
https://www.espn.com/esports/story/_/id/26815521.

Paananen, Ilkka. "BAFTA Games Lecture." BAFTA, September 6, 2016. http://www
.bafta.org/media-centre/transcripts/ilkka-paananen-bafta-games-lecture.

Pachter, Michael, Nick McKay, and Nick Citrin. "Post Hoc Ergo Propter Hoc: Why the
Next Generation Will Be as Big as Ever." Equity Research, Wedbush Securities,
February 12, 2014.

Panchadar, Arjun. "Top Gamer 'Ninja' Made $1 Million to Promote EA's 'Apex Leg-
ends' . . ." Reuters, March 14, 2019. https://www.reuters.com/article/us-electronic
-arts-apexlegends-idUSKBN1QU2AC.

Parfitt, Ben. "Take-Two Not Convinced by Triple-A Free-to-Play." MCV, December 4,
2013. https://www.mcvuk.com/take-two-not-convinced-by-triple-a-free-to-play/.

Pearl, Jayne., and Harold Seneker. "Software to Go." *Forbes*, June 20, 1983.

Pew Research Center: Internet, Science & Tech. "Demographics of Internet and Home Broadband Usage in the United States." Pew Research Center, June 12, 2019. https://www.pewresearch.org/internet/fact-sheet/internet-broadband/.

Porac, Joseph F., Howard Thomas, and Charles Baden Fuller. "Competitive Groups as Cognitive Communities: The Case of Scottish Knitwear Manufacturers." *Journal of Management Studies* 26, no. 4 (1989): 397–416. https://doi.org/10.1111/j.1467-6486.1989.tb00736.x.

"Rick Fox Says He'd Stay with Echo Fox if Racist Investor Leaves." TMZ. Accessed June 18, 2019. https://www.tmz.com/2019/05/03/rick-fox-eacho-fox-esports-racist-investor/.

Rietveld, Joost, and J. P. Eggers. "Demand Heterogeneity and the Adoption of Platform Complements." ERIM Report Series Research in Management, Erasmus Research Institute of Management, Rotterdam, Netherlands, January 12, 2016. https://repub.eur.nl/pub/79494/.

Rigney, Ryan. "Want to Sell Your Game? Don't Tick Off YouTubers." *Wired*, October 21, 2013. https://www.wired.com/2013/10/stanley-parable-sales/.

Robehmed, Natalie. "Kim Kardashian West, Mobile Mogul: The Forbes Cover Story." *Forbes*, July 11, 2016. https://www.forbes.com/sites/natalierobehmed/2016/07/11/kim-kardashian-mobile-mogul-the-forbes-cover-story/#6f99d2627e4f.

Robinson, Jon. "'League of Legends,' ESports Growing." ESPN.com, August 8, 2012. http://www.espn.com/blog/playbook/tech/post/_/id/1541.

Rodriguez, Cecilia. "The Art Show of the Year: Vermeer Masterpieces Together for the First Time at Paris Louvre." *Forbes*, February 24, 2017. Accessed July 9, 2019. https://www.forbes.com/sites/ceciliarodriguez/2017/02/24/why-vermeer-masterpieces-at-paris-louvre-are-already-the-show-of-the-year/.

Rosewater, Mark. "Need I Say Morph." *Magic: The Gathering* (blog). Accessed August 14, 2019. https://magic.wizards.com/en/articles/archive/making-magic/need-i-say-morph-2019-08–05.

Ruggill, Judd, Ken McAllister, Randy Nichols, and Ryan Kaufman. *Inside the Video Game Industry.* New York: Routledge, 2016.

Ryan, Jeff. *Super Mario: How Nintendo Conquered America.* London: Portfolio, 2012.

Sacco, Dom. "Germany Labels Twitch a 'Radio Service,' Tells Streamers They Now Require a Broadcasting License." Esports News UK, March 27, 2017. https://esports-news.co.uk/2017/03/27/german-streamers-require-license/.

Saint-Exupéry, Antoine de. *The Little Prince.* Translated by Richard Howard. San Diego: Mariner Books, 2000.

Schreier, Jason. *Blood, Sweat, and Pixels: The Triumphant, Turbulent Stories Behind How Video Games Are Made.* New York: Harper, 2017.

Sedgwick, John, and Michael Pokorny. "The Characteristics of Film as a Commodity." In *An Economic History of Film*, edited by John Sedgwick and Michael Pokorny, 6–23. Abingdon, UK: Routledge, 2004.

Shaul, Brandy. "King.Com Dumps Advertising on Its Games." AdWeek, June 11, 2013. https://www.adweek.com/digital/king-com-dumps-advertising-on-its-games/.

Sheff, David. *Game Over: How Nintendo Conquered the World*. New York: Vintage, 1994.

Sherman, Alex. "Netflix Says It's More Scared of *Fortnite* and YouTube Than Disney and Amazon." CNBC, January 17, 2019. https://www.cnbc.com/2019/01/17/netflix-more-scared-of-fortnite-and-youtube-than-disney-and-amazon.html.

Shontell, Alyson, and Ben Gilbert. "Microsoft CEO Satya Nadella Just Laid out the Company's Vision for Its 'Netflix for Games.'" Business Insider, January 16, 2019. https://www.businessinsider.com/microsoft-ceo-satya-nadella-xbox-netflix-for-games-2019-1.

Sinclair, Brendan. "*Resident Evil 6* Sells 4.9 Million, Disappoints." GamesIndustry.biz, May 8, 2013. https://www.gamesindustry.biz/articles/2013-05-08-resident-evil-6-sells-4-9-million-disappoints.

Smith, Rebecca. "Xbox Live Has 57 Million Active Users, Gaming Business Is Growing." TrueAchievements. Accessed August 23, 2019. https://www.trueachievements.com/n33654/xbox-live-has-57-million-active-users-gaming-business-is-growing.

Snow, Blake. "Why Console Gaming Is Dying." CNN Business. Updated November 9, 2012. Accessed November 8, 2019. https://www.cnn.com/2012/11/09/tech/gaming-gadgets/console-gaming-dead/index.html.

Startup Grind Local. "Trip Hawkins (Electronic Arts)—Leaving Apple To Start EA." June 28, 2014. Video, 2:53. https://www.youtube.com/watch?v=D4Fo9cPT_DE.

Stuart, Keith. "Activision CEO Bobby Kotick on the King Deal: 'We Have an Audience of 500 Million.'" Games, *Guardian*, November 4, 2015. https://www.theguardian.com/technology/2015/nov/04/bobby-kotick-king-deal-activision-blizzard.

Suddath, Claire. "Why There Are No Bosses at Valve." Bloomberg, April 27, 2012. https://www.bloomberg.com/news/articles/2012-04-27/why-there-are-no-bosses-at-valve.

Sugg, Darren. *Fortnite*. PlayStation 4, Nintendo Switch, Android, Xbox One, iOS, Microsoft Windows, Macintosh operating systems. Warsaw, Poland: Epic Games Poland, People Can Fly, 2017.

Takahashi, Dean. *Opening the Xbox: Inside Microsoft's Plan to Unleash an Entertainment Revolution*. Roseville, CA: Prima, 2002.

——. "Supercell's Chief Wants Every Game to Be as Good as Clash of Clans (Interview Part One)." *VentureBeat* (blog), November 25, 2013. https://venturebeat.com/2013/11/25/supercells-ilkka-paananen-wants-every-game-to-be-as-good-as-clash-of-clans-interview-part-one/.

——. *The Xbox 360 Uncloaked: The Real Story Behind Microsoft's Next-Generation Video Game Console*. Raleigh, NC: SpiderWorks, 2006.

"Take-Two CEO: We've Sold 5M of Our Basketball Video Games." Bloomberg, February 13, 2015. Video, 6:23. https://www.bloomberg.com/news/videos/2015-02-13/we-ve-sold-5m-of-our-basketball-video-games-take-two-ceo.

Tassi, Paul. "The U.S. Now Recognizes ESports Players as Professional Athletes." *Forbes*, July 14, 2013. Accessed August 14, 2019. https://www.forbes.com/sites/insertcoin/2013/07/14/the-u-s-now-recognizes-esports-players-as-professional-athletes/.

Taylor, T. L. *Raising the Stakes: E-Sports and the Professionalization of Computer Gaming*. Cambridge, MA: MIT Press, 2015.

TheLBJSchool. "Gabe Newell: Reflections of a Video Game Maker." January 31, 2013. Video, 1:02:52. https://www.youtube.com/watch?v=t8QEOBgLBQU.

Thier, Dave. "Tfue Is Suing Faze Clan in an Explosive Lawsuit That's Rocking the Esports World." *Forbes*, May 21, 2019. Accessed June 18, 2019. https://www.forbes .com/sites/davidthier/2019/05/21/tfue-is-suing-faze-clan-in-an-explosive-lawsuit -thats-rocking-the-esports-world/.

Thomes, Tim Paul. "In-House Publishing and Competition in the Video Game Industry." *Information Economics and Policy, Big Media: Economics and Regulation of Digital Markets* 32 (September 1, 2015): 46–57. https://doi.org/10.1016/j.infoecopol.2015.07.005.

Thoré, Théophile. *Van der Meer de Delft*. Paris: Gazette des Beaux Arts, 1866.

Toor, Amar. "Mark Zuckerberg Says Video Games Can Help Kids Become Programmers." The Verge, May 22, 2015. https://www.theverge.com/2015/5/22/8643065/mark -zuckerberg-video-games-good-for-kids.

Townsend, Tess. "YouTube Creators Have Complained About Declines in Ad Revenue." Recode, March 30, 2017. https://www.recode.net/2017/3/30/15128654/youtube-creators -revenue-drop-brand-safety-controversy.

Trimble, Chris. "Hasbro Interactive." Case Study. Tuck School of Business at Dartmouth, Hanover, NH, March 22, 2004. http://mba.tuck.dartmouth.edu/pages/faculty /chris.trimble/research/Case_Downloads/Hasbro.pdf.

"Trip Hawkins Interview," *Upside*, August/September 1990.

Tschang, F. Ted. "Balancing the Tensions Between Rationalization and Creativity in the Video Games Industry." *Organization Science* 18, no. 6 (December 1, 2007): 989–1005. https://doi.org/10.1287/orsc.1070.0299.

U.S. Federal Trade Commission. "Warner Bros. Settles FTC Charges It Failed to Adequately Disclose It Paid Online Influencers to Post Gameplay Videos." Press release, July 11, 2016. https://www.ftc.gov/news-events/press-releases/2016/07 /warner-bros-settles-ftc-charges-it-failed-adequately-disclose-it.

Usher, William. "Epic Games' President: What's the Point of Next-Gen Consoles?" CINEMABLEND, August 5, 2011. https://www.cinemablend.com/games/Epic-Games -President-What-Point-Next-Gen-Consoles-34080.html.

Uttal, Bro. "Famous Victories in Personal Software." *Fortune*, May 2, 1983.

Vaan, Mathijs de, Balazs Vedres, and David Stark. "Game Changer: The Topology of Creativity." *American Journal of Sociology* 120, no. 4 (January 2015): 1144–94. https://doi.org/10.1086/681213.

"Vermeer Was Brilliant, but He Was Not Without Influences." *The Economist*, October 12, 2017. https://www.economist.com/books-and-arts/2017/10/12/vermeer-was-brilliant -but-he-was-not-without-influences.

Vogel, Harold L. *Entertainment Industry Economics: A Guide for Financial Analysis*. 9th edition. New York: Cambridge University Press, 2014.

Vollmer, Asher, and Greg Wohlwend. "The Rip-Offs & Making Our Original Game." Accessed January 20, 2019. http://asherv.com/threes/threemails/#letter.

Wallis, Alistair. "Q&A: Nexon America Talks Maple Story." Gamasutra, February 28, 2007. www.gamasutra.com/view/news/103880/QA_Nexon_America_Talks_Maple_Story.php.

Wen, Li, Devin Mills, and Lia Nower. "The Relationship of Loot Box Purchases to Problem Video Gaming and Problem Gambling." *Addictive Behaviors* 97 (October 2019): 27–34. https://doi.org/10.1016/j.addbeh.2019.05.016.

Weststar, Johanna, Marie-Josée Legault, Chandell Gosse, and Vicki O'Meara. *Developer Satisfaction Survey 2014 & 2015: Diversity in the Game Industry Report.* International Game Developer Association, June 12, 2016. https://cdn.ymaws.com/www .igda.org/resource/collection/cb31ce86-f8ee-4ae3-b46a-148490336605/igda_dss14 -15_diversityreport_aug2016_final.pdf.

Williams, Dmitri. "Structure and Competition in the U.S. Home Video Game Industry." *International Journal on Media Management* 4, no. 1 (January 1, 2002): 41–54. https://doi.org/10.1080/14241270209389979.

Willson, Michele, and Tama Leaver, eds. *Social, Casual and Mobile Games: The Changing Gaming Landscape.* New York: Bloomsbury Academic, 2017.

Wolf, Mark J. P., and Bernard Perron. *The Routledge Companion to Video Game Studies.* Routledge Handbooks Online, 2013. https://doi.org/10.4324/9780203114261.

Yarow, Jay. "Another App Store Millionaire: 'Doodle Jump' Close to 2 Million Downloads, Over $1 Million in Sales." Business Insider, January 20, 2010. https://www .businessinsider.com/iphone-app-doodle-jump-closing-in-on-2-million-downloads -over-1-million-in-sales-2010-1.

Ziegler, Maseena. "The Accident That Created an App Millionaire." *Forbes*, September 13, 2013. https://www.forbes.com/sites/crossingborders/2013/09/13/the-accident-that -created-an-app-millionaire/.

INDEX

CPSIA information can be obtained
at www.ICGtesting.com
Printed in the USA
LVHW111500111022
730456LV00011B/68/J